Baby Steps

The "Whys" of Your Child's Behavior in the First Two Years

Baby Steps

The "Whys" of Your Child's Behavior in the First Two Years

Claire B. Kopp, Ph.D.

With the assistance of Donna L. Bean

W. H. FREEMAN AND COMPANY
NEW YORK

Footprints courtesy of Loizos Milan Loizou.

Life drawings by Clare Wood; illustrations on pages 249 and 253 by Network Graphics.

Library of Congress Cataloging-in-Publication Data

Kopp, Claire B.
    Baby steps : the "whys" of your child's behavior in the first two years / Claire B. Kopp, with the assistance of Donna L. Bean.
    p.   cm.
    Includes bibliographical references and index.
    ISBN 0-7167-2390-5 — ISBN 0-7167-2499-5 (soft)
    1. Infant psychology.   2. Infants—Development. 3. Child rearing.
I. Bean, Donna L.   II. Title.
BF719.K67 1993
305.23'2—dc20   93-10365
                                          CIP

Printed in the United States of America

1 2 3 4 5 6 7 8 9 0   VB   9 9 8 7 6 5 4 3

For my family

Contents

Examines toys by turning carefully in hand
Interested in social games
Makes social bids to keep interactions going
Wary of strangers

Developmental Close-up
Social Play
Social Bids

NINE MONTHS   123

Stands without assistance
Dramatic cognitive changes
Remembers without cues
Begins to understand cause and effect
Acts with restraint
Frowns

Developmental Close-up
Recall Memory

TEN MONTHS   133

Creeps
Holds objects more securely
Investigates objects carefully, is interested in details
Gestures are clearer; points and nods
Looks at parents for visual cues

Developmental Close-up
Social Referencing

ELEVEN MONTHS   143

Cruises around crib
Can voluntarily release objects
Better able to participate in social games
Gender-based toy preferences
Temperament is more pronounced

Developmental Close-up
Temperament

Developmental Close-up
Joint Attention

TWENTY-ONE MONTHS   205

Wants to be in control, exacting; balance is better
Less restless
Says I, me, and own name
Describes own emotions in shorthand
More interested in peers but interaction still limited
Fewer tantrums but still quick to anger on occasion

Developmental Close-up
Toilet Training

TWENTY-FOUR MONTHS   217

Runs, jumps, and squats
Uses 2-, 3-, or 4-word sentences
More creative problem solver
Engages in pretend play
Likes consistency in family routines
Can be contrary
Has sense of humor

Developmental Close-up
Parenting

DEVELOPMENTAL OVERVIEW: THE SECOND YEAR   232

AFTERIMAGES   237

Looking Back
Looking Forward
Is My Child Okay?

CHARTING THE FIRST TWO YEARS   247

Maturation of Grasp
Visual Perception
Speech Acquisition

Preface

*U*nderstanding the behavior of babies and young toddlers: that's what this book is all about. I talk about the extraordinary changes that occur from the newborn period to the end of the second year. I describe why babies are able to do certain things and not others, how they think, and what they feel. As you read this book, I hope you'll find that your baby's behavior makes more and more sense.

Why do parents want to know about the development of babies and toddlers? First, parents want and need advice every now and then. There are plenty of books that offer prescriptions about how to care for babies and young toddlers, but ultimately parents have to choose which advice to follow. It has been my experience that parents are best able to take advantage of such information when they understand when, how, and why their child's behavior changes. Parents who participate in my research projects confirm this view. In fact, my interest in writing this book came about because many of these parents suggested that I write a parent guide to early child development.

Another reason for helping parents understand what their babies are experiencing is to take some of the hassle out of parenting. At one time or another every parent has wondered, "Why is my baby acting this way?" Although a baby can't talk to us with words, if we know a few things about development, her behavior can tell us much about her needs and wants.

Learning to read behavioral clues takes some of the stress out of dealing with young children. Suppose a 3-month-old cries after watching a mobile for five minutes. "Spoiled," we might be tempted to say. But that's unlikely: she's too young to be "spoiled." Rather, the baby is probably telling us in her own way that she is tired of the mobile. Perhaps she wants something else to stare at or maybe she needs some cuddling.

Or take the 7-month-old who repeatedly throws food from his high chair. We could say he is ornery, but we would be more accurate if we think of him at his age as a miniature rocket scientist experimenting with objects to learn about space and gravity. He needs the throwing experience, so parents have to find the right kinds of objects and places for him to throw. And if they join in his game as a retriever, they can help him learn more quickly—and get some fun out of the activity themselves.

Parents who understand child behavior can be more confident about their ability to handle situations. They know they can figure out how to help their child by accurately interpreting the child's signals for comfort, stimulation, or quiet time alone. With efficient decision-making, parents can have more time to enjoy their young child. Some parents tell me that knowing what to expect and what not to expect at any age has not only reassured them about how to care for their baby but also made them feel better about the whole experience of parenting. They like being informed when making decisions. Parents who take the time to learn when, how, and why behavior changes know what they can do to help their young child grow and when they need to seek assistance.

As I've answered parents' questions over the years, I've often wished that researchers had more opportunities to provide parents with information they can use to make sense out of their child's behavior. Our understanding of the how and why of early development has increased dramatically in the last twenty-five years or so. This does not mean that the people who study early development have all the answers; we still only vaguely understand how some behavior comes about. Researchers also have some disagreements about the meaning of specific behavior. On the whole, researchers do agree about the key themes that characterize growth in the first 24 months, and in this book I discuss behavior in the context of these key themes. Wherever possible, I use conversations with parents and actual child behavior as examples.

Scientific research helps us to know what kinds of behavior to expect when our children are about 1 month, 6 months, and so on. That is not to say that babies follow a rigid timetable for growth, but rather that behavior usually develops in a fairly predictable fashion. Every baby develops at his own pace and in his own way, but most babies experience the same patterns of growth. In this book I describe the sequences of behavior changes that most young children follow.

You won't find everything about baby or toddler development in this book. The first two years is a period of rapid change and incomparable growth. If someone wrote a book describing every change, it would be so long that parents would not have the time to read it. Instead, what I do here is to highlight some of the most important changes.

I am pleased to have this opportunity to help parents understand child behavior. There were times when I thought it might not happen. For years, the demands of preparing papers and presentations, university teaching commitments, editing a research newsletter, and managing my research program never seemed to leave me enough time to work on the book. The birth of my first grandchild a few years ago brought a stream of questions from my daughter-in-law. As I tried to answer them, ideas for the book became clearer, and I began to organize the bits and pieces of information I'd accumulated over the years. Then, not long ago, one of my research assistants expressed interest in helping me compose my notes into a book, and quite unexpectedly, time constraints no longer prevented me from preparing this parent guide.

In putting my notes together I remembered that parents and students often point out that not everyone is familiar with the terms used in the study of child development. I address this issue in the first chapter of the book. I call this chapter the mini guide; it talks about what child development means and discusses some of the ideas researchers use to describe behavior. I then present separate chapters for specific ages. In the first year I talk about behavior for every month, and then in the second year I look at 15, 18, 21, and 24 months.

The last chapter recaps the first two years and suggests behavior to look for in the third year. Next, there are charts that trace key features of development from birth to 24 months. Finally, I provide a brief list of readings for parents who would like to learn more about the when, how, and why of specific behavior and a comprehensive bibliography.

My experiences as a parent and a grandparent helped me gather ideas for this book, and I have also benefitted from more than thirty years of working with young children, first as an occupational therapist and then as a developmental psychologist. As a research psychologist, I have studied infants, toddlers, and preschoolers for more than twenty years.

I have many people to thank for directly and indirectly contributing to this book. I am indebted to the parents and students who have shared ideas with me. Although too numerous to mention individually, I want to acknowledge their thoughtfulness and generosity. In addition, I extend my sincerest thanks to colleagues, graduate students, and research assistants who have been invaluable collaborators in my recent research: J. Heidi Gralinski, Sandra Kaler, Bonnie Klimes-Dougan, Joanne B. Krakow, Cathy Matheson, Irma Röder, and Brian E. Vaughn.

My dear friend Toni Marcy, M.D., University of California, Los Angeles, taught me the ins and outs of infant testing many years ago. Toni provided a careful critique of the book and checked many of my developmental timetables. I deeply appreciate her contribution to my professional growth and to this project.

Celia Brownell, Ph.D., University of Pittsburgh, is a colleague and friend who is truly the developmentalist's developmentalist. Perceptive, knowledgeable, and sensitive, she has a comprehensive understanding of infants and toddlers. Celia read two drafts of the book, and her numerous insightful suggestions have enriched it in many ways.

Lois Bloom, Ph.D., Edward Lee Thorndike Professor of Psychology and Education, Columbia University, is one of the world's most renowned language researchers. I am grateful for her critique, especially the suggestions she made for the language sections.

Risa Silverstein, former student and research assistant and mother of four, provided detailed comments that helped me make important clarifications. I also want to thank Margaret Brennan Narin, Holly O. Ross, Deborah Strauss, and Leslie Carr, who reviewed this book at the request of my publishers. I appreciate their comments.

Susan Brennan, my recent editor, helped me see how to finish this book and expertly guided me through the production process. Jonathan Cobb, my original editor at W. H. Freeman and Company, graciously continued to provide encouragement and advice even after he moved on to other responsibilities. Jodi Creditor and Penny Hull, project editor and copy editor respectively, added clarity and offered good suggestions; they were a joy to work with. I thank them and everyone else at Freeman who helped make this book a reality.

Special thanks go to Lynn Chui Fong who typed endless versions of the manuscript with inordinate patience and good cheer. Donna L. Bean assisted me in preparing this manuscript—her help has been invaluable.

Finally, I thank my husband, Eugene H. Kopp, for being my anchor, and my children, Carolyn, Michael, and Paul, for many rewards, a few challenges, and lots of pleasure. My daughter, Carolyn, has been a supportive friend and confidant to whom I often turned as I labored to tell this story. I deeply value her contribution.

With all this help the book should be free of errors, but such errors that might remain are my sole responsibility. The content reflects my visions of development.

Claire B. Kopp
June 1993

Early Development
A Mini Guide

❧

*T*his miniguide defines development and describes how it comes about. In it, I share some of the ideas I use with parents and students when explaining the behaviors of infants and toddlers. Invariably, my explanations are couched in a developmental framework on the premise that it is easier to understand a particular behavior if you can see how it fits into the overall scheme of things.

Take throwing as an example. Parents of a 15-month-old might interpret throwing toys as a sign of belligerence. Actually, throwing at this age is simply an activity the toddler enjoys. It gives him a sense of accomplishment while also developing muscle strength in his upper arm. "Too bad," you might say, "I don't want my child throwing *anything* in the house!" Fair enough; that's a reasonable everyday rule for toddlers. But if in looking at the broader scheme of things you can see that this is an age when it is developmentally appropriate to encourage behavior that leads to a sense of accomplishment, you can see that as a parent it is just a matter of finding the right toy (a ball) and the right place (a yard, a playground) for throwing.

Development and Change

In everyday conversation, the word *development* has different meanings. We sometimes speak of an *event*, such as a promotion, as a development. Sometimes we mean a *stage of progress*; for instance, a child's development as a pianist advanced faster than her music teacher had anticipated. A third use of the word describes a *process*—how film is changed into snapshots, for example.

Which of these definitions is synonymous with what scientists mean when they talk about child development? All of them! Important events in a child's life are development: the first word and the first step are among the most obvious. Researchers also speak of certain stages of progress, such as the toddler years, as development. The changes that occur during these age periods are dramatic and have significant implications for later development. Scientists also speak about processes as important features of development. For example, paying attention to surroundings is a process that is part of the development of thinking and acquiring knowledge.

The study of children's development is the study of change. It involves observing the behaviors children display, asking why the behaviors occur, and figuring out how the behaviors come about. Sometimes researchers study emerging behaviors, called "nascent" behaviors, and other times they study how a behavior such as baby's play becomes more elaborate and complex. Researchers are particularly interested in understanding change as a key to children's ever-increasing competencies: the ability to talk leads to profound effects on social interactions.

Principles of Early Development

There are so many dimensions of change in the first two years, that making any sense of them might seem difficult. Not so. Scientists have identified a few principles that characterize early child development.

First, biology provides the baby with blueprints for particular abilities such as head control, the social smile, the beginnings of grasp, and some of the basic emotions. How can we be sure there are biological blueprints? Well, babies around the world, in spite of remarkable differences in cultures, show remarkable similarities in many aspects of their early development. Additional evidence for blueprints is that blind babies show a social smile even though they have never seen a smile, while deaf babies coo and babble just like hearing babies even though they do not hear sounds.

A second theme is that key components of early development unfold in orderly, predictable patterns. Babies "say" vowel sounds before they say consonants, and they babble before they talk. Bear in mind though that "orderly" does not mean that steps in development are taken with unwavering, military precision. Most babies crawl before they walk, but some babies do not crawl at all. They just learn to stand and then to walk. There is nothing wrong with this developmental sequence; it is just a variation. Of course, this sudden transition to walking can be disconcerting to parents of a 9-month-old who weren't expecting a toddler for another three months or so!

A third principle of development involves experience. Biology does not work alone; the baby's daily experiences provide the means to successfully move blueprints from drawing board to the real world. The baby's grasp, for example, is immature at first, but it becomes precise and coordinated over time as his parents provide him with opportunities to use his hands every day and in a variety of ways. The baby picks up bits of food, clutches his father's tie or his mother's hair, rubs his body, and takes hold of his bottle.

I use the term experience to mean all kinds of events and influences the baby encounters: the interactions between parents and baby, the availability of playthings, parents' health and well-being, parents' education, family economic conditions, and the presence of neighbors and friends as support systems. Experiences significantly influence the rate of a baby's development and the richness and quality of his behaviors. For example, research shows that babies reared by sensitive, caring parents who talk and play with them make more complicated sounds and play behaviors than babies who receive minimal attention.

Experiences also account for much of children's learning and socialization that occur after early infancy. It is an indisputable fact that parents and other primary caregivers are key shapers of a baby's experiences and thus play an enormously important role in early development. Positive experiences in infancy are a kind of inoculation against vulnerability. The baby is better prepared to face the challenges of childhood.

Developmental Norms and Variability

Biological blueprints produce similarities in behaviors that emerge during the early months of life. Thus, by observing thousands of children, developmentalists have a good idea of what to expect of babies when they are 2, 5, or 15 months old. These expectations are called "norms." In other words, norms describe behaviors, forms of specific behaviors, and characteristic behaviors at different ages. Norms involve ages and age ranges for particular skills. As an example, many babies start to walk on their own at about 12 or 13 months, but it is developmentally normal for the onset of walking to occur any time between the ages of 9 and 17 months. Similarly, most babies sit before they stand, but it is all right if a baby stands first as long as she eventually learns to sit. This pattern of behavior may be uncommon in terms of normative sequences, but it does not indicate that something is developmentally wrong.

Norms are useful guideposts, provided they are not employed too rigidly, because there is a good deal of variability in the way young children develop. I cannot emphasize enough how important it is for parents to keep in mind the ideas of acceptable ranges of behaviors and alternative paces of development. While I describe age-related behaviors in this book using the order, the form, and the pace that research and my own experience indicate they most regularly come about, an individual baby and toddler's development will invariably differ from time to time. Again I emphasize that it is only extreme variations that tend to be cause for concern. For example, a baby who is not walking at 20 months of age is signaling that something is developmentally amiss.

An open mind, informed observation, and thoughtful assessment are the keys to the prudent use of developmental norms. Many a child development specialist has said, "Change is the only constant in early child development." I use this phrase myself from time to time, but I usually go on to say, "And in late infancy and early toddlerhood, variability in the pace of growth is one of the most important child development norms."

Patterns of Development

🍂 *Growth Rates.* Some kinds of development move forward rapidly, others move slowly. The baby's thumb-forefinger grasp usually appears around 9 months, although the first indications of grasp are likely to emerge at about 4 months of age. Contrast this five-month period of growth with the extensive amount of time required to develop a sense of personal identity. At 18 months, most toddlers show genuine signs of selfhood (concern about a dirty face or embarrassment when introduced to an unfamiliar person are specific examples), but the steps to selfhood start over a year earlier (around 3 months) when the baby first begins to realize that his own body is separate from that of another person.

✤ *Growth Patterns.* Development of a specific skill sometimes involves a kind of stair-step path, with periods of consistent improvement alternating with phases of relatively little gain. The growth of language is one of the best examples of this kind of pattern. There can be a spurt with the development of several new words, then weeks or even months when nothing new happens. Sometimes a leveling off in the pace of growth indicates that one or more other developments is commanding a young child's attention and he just doesn't have the energy and attention for two things at once. For example, toddlers who are novice walkers often monitor their posture by focusing on room cues, which requires a lot of attention. Thus, if learning to walk and learning to talk are both occurring, as they often do between the ages of 12 and 18 months, walking often wins out. It just seems to be easier to focus on walking—and perhaps it is more fun.

Development sometimes takes another form: it inches laboriously along in a forward direction and then actually shifts into reverse gear for a while. Growth characterized by these kinds of stops and starts is a common feature of early development. One of my favorite examples concerns young children and everyday family rules. Toddlers and preschoolers often find it difficult to go along with rules, but they gradually make progress and begin to comply. Then for one or another reason, some just stop complying and get a little ornery and assertive besides. Then, to parents' relief, they begin to follow rules again. Of course, parents help get them back on the track by consistently offering reminders and guidance.

✤ *Deletions of Behavior.* Developmental growth may "require" that some behaviors appear for a time and then disappear forever. Creeping is a good example. When the 12-month-old starts to walk, she begins to creep less. Walking is more efficient than creeping and a more enjoyable way to see the world. Eventually creeping is discarded—though, of course, the toddler could creep if she really wanted to; she doesn't forget how to do it.

A developmental disappearance also occurs with newborn reflexes. Many of these reflexes are inhibited (they disappear from the baby's behavior repertoire and are forgotten) because of maturation of the central nervous system. If early reflexes did not disappear, they might limit additional learning and exploration. Let's look at the newborn grasp reflex. This is typically elicited by stretching the tendons of the baby's palm with a gentle pull on the baby's hand. The result is that the baby's hand closes into a fist. The reflex is not very practical for later everyday activities. There is not much one can do with a grasp that comes about only when the tendons of the hand are stretched! The grasp reflex must be inhibited so that voluntary grasp can emerge. Then the baby can use her hands in any number of ways.

❧ *Consolidations of Behavior.* In early development there are some age levels when many new behaviors emerge together. These periods often are preceded or succeeded by months when changes are not very dramatic. These intermittent periods of consolidation perform an extremely important function: they allow the baby to solidify specific skills, to practice combining basic skills into more complex behaviors, and to rest a bit from the stresses of constant change.

Sometimes a period of consolidation seems to encompass all aspects of development and other times only one or two areas of behavior appear to be affected. Regardless of the breadth of consolidation, it is important to realize that these periods are not "dormant states" of little developmental significance. On the contrary, the subtle changes at these ages, in combination with the opportunity to replenish energy stores, are important to the overall process of development.

❧ *Behavior Domains*

We've talked about terms used to describe change; we are also interested in studying the specific behaviors that babies show. To simplify communicating with one another, we group related behaviors together into seven domains: motor, perception, cognition, social, language, emotions, and sense of self.

Motor

Not long ago a four-month-old and her mother visited my infant development class. The baby had good head control when lying on her tummy, as well as when her mother held her upright. She looked around with an alert expression. When I held a colorful rattle in front of her, she wriggled, gasped, grunted, pumped her arms up and down, opened and closed her hands, and reached again. But she was unable to make contact with the rattle. Pleasure gave way to frustration and she fretted.

Despite the baby's inability to take hold of the rattle, she had already mastered some developmentally important motor controls. She moved her head at will and kept her head upright most of the time. Her shoulder muscles were strong enough to let her raise her upper chest when she lay on her tummy. These controlled body movements are called "gross motor skills," skills that also include rolling over, sitting, creeping, standing, and walking. In contrast to her gross motor control, the baby was just beginning to develop her "fine motor skills." These skills are used in grasp and precise hand movements and involve the palm, fingers, and thumb.

The basics of gross and fine motor development are acquired in the first year, although not all at once. It takes months from the time babies first begin to reach and grasp to develop a precise thumb-forefinger pickup. Likewise, it takes months from the time babies first pull themselves up to a standing position until they easily stand on their own and take tentative steps.

Perception

The term perception refers to the ability to distinguish objects, people, and events by using the senses (taste, touch, smell, vision, and hearing). Perception involves paying attention to something and identifying it as being similar to (or not similar to) something else. The ability to perceive that things are different is referred to as discrimination or differentiation.

Even newborns, whose vision is blurry, can make some impressive perceptual discriminations. They can distinguish a small black-and-white bull's eye pattern from black-and-white squares. This ability tells us that some of the newborn's contrast discrimination skills are part of his basic biological endowment. Stated another way, newborns have not had previous experience with contrasts, much less black-and-white shapes! For the most part, perceptions are fine-tuned by the experience of living. Being carried, rolling about in the crib, creeping, and walking all provide the baby with opportunities to develop visual perception skills such as depth, size, and shape. Most perceptual abilities (for example, hearing different sounds, depth perception) mature during the first year.

Cognition

Behaviors that are classified as cognition include memory, attention, problem-solving skills, comprehension, and learning. In effect, cognition is the shorthand word for knowledge and how knowledge is acquired. A subset of the behaviors in the cognition domain is called intelligence. Basically, intelligence is a word that refers to how skillfully we use the knowledge we have.

In the first two years of life important developments in the domain of cognition include the emergence of memory, understanding cause-and-effect relationships, and learning associations between two events (a parent's appearance and being picked up). Although very young babies do display some cognitive skills (for example, cued memory at 3 months), it is not until an explosive period of growth between 9 and 12 months that babies exhibit robust cognitive skills. Another period of rapid cognitive development occurs between 18 and 24 months.

Do babies display intelligent behavior? Yes, toward the end of the first year. At that time it is possible to differentiate intelligence from general cognitive activity by observing a baby's behaviors. At 10 months, Ann recognizes that her bottle contains something to drink (even though she doesn't know the word drink) and knows exactly what to do when the bottle is handed to her. This cognitive activity demonstrates that Ann has already acquired some knowledge, that is, she knows what a bottle is used for.

Now—Ann is sitting on the floor drinking from her bottle when big sister approaches with her new doll. Ann drops her bottle and looks at the doll. Accidentally, her sister kicks the bottle and it rolls behind a large stuffed chair. Ann sees the bottle disappear, and she creeps around the chair to retrieve it. Ann could have cried and done nothing, but she didn't: she came up with a solution and an action. Her behavior demonstrates elementary problem-solving ability, a component of intelligence.

Social

Scientists include many kinds of behaviors under the term social development. They study babies' interactions with parents and other caregivers; how and when babies learn to use other people's cues (social referencing); the development of affection; the social skills of babies who are placed in day care; toddlers' learning of everyday do's and don'ts; and the nature of toddlers' play with other children.

Some aspects of social development are influenced by family and cultural conventions (family rules, for example), but the basic features of "becoming social" are similar across cultures. For 2-month-olds, a social skill involves maintaining eye contact with another person. A social skill at six months might entail grunting to send a signal to someone to "pay attention to me." Toward the end of the first year, social acts often involve a coordinated sequence of behaviors: a baby turns to his father, pulls on his arm, babbles, points to a toy, and then looks back at his father.

Professionals who study social development tend to have strong opinions and many debates. Young children are after all socialized by parents and other caregivers, and debates about "good" social development have been around a long time. Contemporary disagreements involve the meaning of attachment (see Seven Months: Close-up), the implications of early day care, and the meaning of one or another behavior. I'll talk about some of these issues later on.

Language

The development of language is one of the most impressive achievements of the first two years, and it doesn't come easily. In the second year my grandson Andrew began to say his first words. Slowly he discovered that words are labels; he struggled to find the right words after recognizing that he made word mistakes; he gradually learned to associate a picture with a word (he saw a company logo on a truck and exclaimed "cheese"); he discovered the past tense; he realized he could ask for help; he learned to refer to himself as "me." He even realized—and accepted—that he could not always be understood. All of this occurred over the course of a year or so. But Andrew's language development was not remarkable; it was very similar to the language growth of other children his age. What I find remarkable is the extent of language learning that takes place in almost every child within a relatively brief time span.

Young children's primary language challenges are to comprehend speech and to produce speech. Many related behaviors precede the emergence of mature language skills. For comprehension, these include distinguishing one sound from another, discriminating intonations of language, and learning to associate sounds and gestures with objects and people. Most young children comprehend far more than they can say.

For production, the precursors to speech include vocalizations that include all kinds of cries as well as the nonfretful sounds of coos, babbles, and jargon. Vowel sounds are the baby's first "speech," then consonants, and still later the baby is able to mix vowels and consonants to produce the familiar "bababa, mamama," and so on. Babies reared in English-speaking families tend to produce more nouns than verbs at first; and, when they begin to use sentences, they often say the noun first and then the verb ("daddy tired," "baby cry"). But they might also invert verb and noun and correctly say "throw ball."

Around the world vocalization development occurs in a very predictable sequence, with vowels appearing before consonants. In addition, within a linguistic culture language develops in a fairly predictable way (in English-speaking cultures, children master words in the noun, verb, object sequence of English sentences).

Emotions

Scientists are interested in how babies express emotions, how emotions develop, how babies learn to read others' emotions, and how babies come to understand their own emotions. Researchers also study the implications of emotional development on cognitive and social skills.

Emotions are first shown in a baby's facial expressions. In general, over the first two years infants display emotions in a particular sequence: discomfort, pleasure, fear and anger (displeasure), frustration and rage in the first year, then jealousy, shame, and guilt in the second. Still later, the emotions of pride, envy, and contempt emerge. Scientists refer to shame and pride as social emotions because the child's emotional reaction stems from her realization that her behavior has been positively or negatively evaluated by others.

Emotions don't just magically appear—they evolve. Babies basically learn about emotions, their own as well as others', from social interactions. The emotion of shame is a good example. A nascent form of shame is seen toward the latter part of the second year. It is indicated by turning away, crying, and dropping the head to the chest after a parent's request has been ignored. In order to have this emotion the child has to be able to recognize disapproval in a parent's voice/facial expression and to realize that the disapproval is directed at her own actions. Only then can the child experience the sense of having been "caught in the act." Shame is a developmental tool because it helps move along the process of socialization. Combined with the feeling of pride, it helps shape children's behaviors so that they conform to family and societal conventions.

Sense of Self

A child's sense of himself can tell a great deal about his overall developmental status. A long time ago I was asked to try to assess the developmental capabilities of a toddler who had a very severe physical handicap. The boy was not quite two years old; he spoke in two-word sentences. As I slowly approached him with the intention of talking about a toy, he told his mother that I was to stay away. In effect he did not want me to intrude into his personal and psychological space. Frankly, I was in awe of the child's sense of self. I was sure this display of selfhood indicated that his physical disabilities were not restricting his mental development. In time the boy came to trust me, and in the long and slow process of evaluating him I confirmed my initial impressions of his developmental normality.

The sense of self is our identity. It is a source of psychological protection and vulnerability as well as a reflection of our feelings, desires, and beliefs. Selfhood first comes about as babies learn that they have a personal physical identity. They obtain this knowledge by exploring their own bodies, and then experiencing their bodies in interactions with objects and other people. A young child's concept of self develops in an orderly fashion: recognition of the body, awareness of feelings and capabilities, and then self-evaluation. The sense of self is barely present at 3 months but is a powerful force by 24 months. Behaviors that demonstrate the evolution of self include preoccupation with competence and mastery, self-consciousness with strangers, and the word that for awhile says it all: "MINE!"

After the baby's first birthday the development of self is helped along primarily by two factors: parents and the advent of increased language production skills. Parents provide opportunities for interaction, exploration, and play, and these opportunities help the baby develop his skills and thereby increase his independence. When the baby has adequate communication skills he can share his personal thoughts and feelings with others while simultaneously reinforcing and expanding his understanding of himself.

By the time the child is two years old he forcefully asserts his independence and is insistent about exercising his autonomy. These behaviors, though often a trial for parents, are important developmental behaviors because a self-concept is essential for later social and cognitive growth. The formidable challenge for parents is to foster the toddler's growth of self while simultaneously socializing him to follow formal rules and other social conventions.

Integration and Organization of the Domains

Although I have classified behaviors in terms of seven distinct categories, more often than not the baby's behavior reflects the interrelationships of the categories. A 12-month-old who plays with her toys, toddles over to her mother to show her a doll, says "da" (doll) to her mother, and then resumes play on her own provides examples of gross and fine motor skills, cognitive activity, language abilities, and social interaction competencies. All of these skills are inextricably intertwined, and this interdependency of the various domains of behavior is a key feature of development. The codependency of behaviors in different domains increases as the child ages. This is one reason why it is important for the foundation behaviors in each domain to develop adequately during the baby's first two years. In this context, adequately means not only that a behavior has emerged around the time it is expected but also that the quality of the behavior is sufficient to support other developments.

Researchers often specialize in the study of a particular domain of behaviors such as cognitive or social development, but their projects generally incorporate ideas drawn from more than one behavior domain. In this book I discuss many instances where developments in one domain are prerequisites for advancements in another. As an example, a child must have knowledge of an object as a discrete and permanent item (that is, the object does not "disappear" even though it is out of sight) before he can begin to ascribe a word to the object: cognitive developments must precede the emergence of language abilities. As another example in the social domain, babies become wary of strangers and actively move toward their familiar caregivers only after they have learned to perceptually discriminate the facial features of their parents, siblings, and other family members through growth in memory skills.

❧ *Using This Book*

I think of this book as a "field guide" to early child development. The book guides parents to an understanding of development by describing behaviors, much like the books used by naturalists watching birds or botanists trying to identify a particular plant. But as a botany field guide does not describe every variation of every plant, so this field guide does not describe every variation of normal behavior. Furthermore, not every baby will display every behavior described in this book. Like most field guides, this book is organized so that a parent may sample it from time to time or read it from cover to cover. It can be used by parents who prefer to read about behaviors at individual ages or to review selected features of development at different ages.

The book is divided into four age groups: birth to 3 months, 4 to 7 months, 8 to 12 months, and the second year. The Previews broadly describe developments during each of these age periods. At the end of each age group is a chart summarizing major developments and listing some hints for promoting development. Following the chart is a list of behaviors that suggest development might not be on the right track. Parents may want to seek advice from their pediatrician.

The developments at a particular age are organized under three headings: Snapshot, Images of Development, and Developmental Close-ups. Snapshots is a collection of brief highlights of developmentally significant behaviors at each age. Images of Development describe behavioral features at each age in the seven key domains in child development: motor, perception, cognition, language, social, emotions, and sense of self. Developmental Close-ups are detailed discussions of interesting topics in early development that are particularly relevant for the age period. In the last chapter of the book, I summarize many of the major behavioral changes we've already talked about. I also provide a preview of changes you can expect in the next year. Finally, I offer some hints to parents who may be concerned about their baby's development.

In terms of each chapter's content, I do not spend much time on behavior changes in social conventions. These include a family's preferences for the way children learn the use of household implements, eating styles, and participation in dressing and bathing routines. Cultural backgrounds and family customs play a big part in shaping the specific form and the pace of development of these behaviors, so it's fruitless to make generalizations about them. I do devote a good bit of attention to cognitive development and, in particular, to what play behaviors can tell about a child's developing mental abilities. In addition, I have made a special effort to identify how cognitive skills affect a young child's social interactions, emotional displays, and sense of self. Understanding cognitive growth can enrich parents' time with their child, so I encourage parents to read more about this topic.

To deal with the issue of gender, I use two conventions in describing the behaviors of babies and toddlers. First, I sometimes refer to the baby as he and sometimes as she. Second, in many of the chapters I refer to Ann and Michael, two fictional babies, to provide an example or to illustrate a point.

However you use this guide, this book will be most helpful if you don't lose sight of three basic ideas.

1. *Every child is unique.* The normative behaviors described in this book are illustrative; individual variability is a fact of life.

2. *Guidelines should not be taken too literally.* Your child is not necessarily the normative child described in these pages, and that is all right. Indeed, there are some disagreements among scientists about what constitutes developmental trends in some abilities and just what form they take.
3. *No matter how much we learn about child development, we can never fully explain a baby or toddler's growth.* But the information in this book will help you participate more fully in your young child's development.

Birth to Three Months

PREVIEW

🌿

*M*any new parents are surprised by the relative unsociability of the very young baby. Babies are unsocial for a good reason. Most of a baby's energy is absorbed in coordinating her efforts to breathe, eat, and sleep. While babies are working on these challenges, reflexes and spontaneous movements exercise the body so that muscle tone is maintained. It almost seems as if human genetic material includes programs that restrict movements until vital functions are secure. Gradually these reflexes become inhibited.

Once their vital systems are working smoothly, babies have more total energy, and some of it can be freed for other enterprises. As sleeping and eating become more routine, the baby gains increasing control of her motor movements: she holds her head up and turns it from side to side.

As physical abilities improve—head control, reach, and grasp—babies begin to explore their surroundings. As they explore, they learn about their environment. At 2 months of age, babies have the ability to retreat from too much visual stimulation (they can turn their heads), and their visual perception skills become more capable of making discriminations. In turn, improved vision combines with better hearing skills to broaden their arena of exploration.

Facial muscle tone—strengthened by the sucking by which a baby gets nourishment—enables her to form facial expressions. At two months a little smile appears, and suddenly everybody wants to be her friend. This little smile grows broader, occurs more frequently, and propels her into an array of social interactions.

Social interaction provides the baby with more learning opportunities. She learns that some events seem to happen together, that touching her fingers together is pleasurable, and that if she watches her hand she can actually make it move. By 3 months, the tissues in her larynx are flexible enough to make sounds. As soon as she emits these sounds, at first accidentally by her body, she sets about learning how to reproduce them.

Overall, in just three short months, vital systems function smoothly, the senses (except for vision) are relatively mature, and the baby can make some controlled movements with her head, arms, and hands. She has vocal mechanisms to begin to develop speech, she can form her first ideas, such as understanding that some events are associated with one another, and she has learned there is an emotion that we call pleasure. Instead of fretful, intermittent sleeping she has acquired the habit of a lengthy nighttime sleep and longer daytime periods of wakefulness. Not bad for only three months' work!

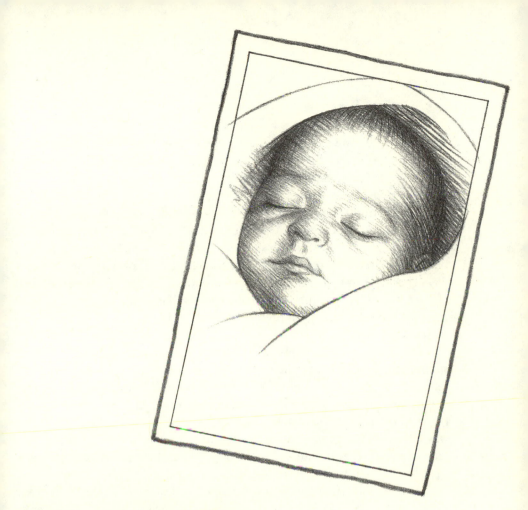

The Just Born

all senses are intact and working

can move head from side to side, and can
briefly lift head

curled-up body position (fetal posture)

❧ Snapshot

Birth launches the newborn into a whole new world. He has to make accommodations to simply survive, much less flourish, outside the womb. Suddenly, he has to breathe on his own, swallow food to get nourishment, lie on a solid surface rather than floating in a fluid space, and regulate his own body temperature. A newborn's physiological disorientation is akin to what we would experience if we were suddenly propelled to outer space.

When the umbilical cord is cut the newborn begins his solo flight. The baby has to keep his plane aloft even though not all of his vital processes were checked out before lift-off and even though he has not been schooled about what to do if something malfunctions. Fortunately, human genetic material includes biological predispositions that help babies sustain life in their new environment.

The newborn's biologically endowed survival kit includes reflexes, spontaneous movements, and the senses. A reflex is a fairly predictable and relatively unchanging movement of a part of the body in response to a particular stimulus; an adult example is the knee-jerk response. Reflexes perform many functions for babies. The sucking reflex provides him with a way to take in food now that nourishment is no longer automatically supplied through the umbilical cord. Coughing and sneezing keep passages clear for ingestion and respiration.

Spontaneous movements are uncontrolled actions of the body; they are generally grand, jerky motions rather than precise, smooth movements. Scientists aren't sure what causes these movements, but some liken these actions to tropisms. A tropism is like a reflex but it involves movement of the entire body rather than just one body part.

Tropisms may look like purposeful movement, but they don't involve intelligence. For example, even a plant "knows" to grow the roots downward and the stalk upward, regardless of the orientation of the seed in the ground. This looks like goal-directed behavior, but it is only a tropism. Similarly, it may look as if a baby has decided he needs to stretch, but rather than a conscious thought, this is only a spontaneous movement caused by some stimulus. These movements keep muscles toned at a time when a baby cannot voluntarily initiate movements to exercise his trunk or limbs.

A newborn's survival kit also includes his senses (touch, smell, vision, hearing, and taste). These provide him with information about his new surroundings. The baby's senses of touch, smell, and taste are all intact, but he needs more exposure to different stimuli to learn to detect subtle differences in these inputs. Likewise, the baby hears pretty well. He can distinguish some sounds from others, but he has to refine these skills. His vision is far from being fully functional; his visual world is often filled with fuzzy, blurry images, even for objects that are nearby. Overall, newborns differ appreciably from toddlers or adults in the quality and quantity of what they take in through the senses.

The limitations of a baby's perceptual abilities actually help him cope. For example, by seeing less, hearing less distinctly, and feeling less intensely than an older baby the newborn is less likely to become overwhelmed by sensory stimulation. Because the baby cannot move around at will (about the only thing he can reliably move is his head from side to side), he doesn't have ways to get away from bright lights, loud noises, or too many touches.

Overall, the newborn is just a little physical being struggling to exist in a foreign environment. Thanks to biological programs his vital processes can function, and the baby's nascent motor, sensory, and perception skills help him maintain and organize these processes. With parents' assistance, newborns successfully pilot their way through this period of adjustment.

❧ Developmental Close-up

Born Early and Small

About 7 percent of all babies born in the United States are born early and are small. The criterion for early birth is a gestation period of 37 weeks or less, and low birth weight is defined as 5 pounds or less. Early births can be roughly divided into two groups—babies weighing 3 to 5 pounds and babies weighing less than 3 pounds. In general, the smaller the baby the greater the medical and developmental (cognitive, emotional, social, and language) vulnerability.

Early babies, variously called preemies, prematures, preterms, and low-birth-weight infants look and act differently than the typical 7 pounder. Their reddish coloring, wrinkled skin texture, poor muscle tone, weak cries, and tremulous movements all set them apart from full-term babies, at least for now. Their arrival is also often difficult. The birth itself comes at an unexpected time, and the early interruption of development in the womb causes concerns about survival as well as longer-term prospects for health and functional ability.

From a developmental perspective, the long-term outlook for preemies has improved dramatically during the last two decades. Much of this change has come about because of a greater understanding of the special needs of early babies. Modifications in newborn intensive care and the training of the physicians (neonatalogists) who treat these babies have advanced significantly. Treatment today is exquisitely sophisticated.

Developmental outcomes are also a function of sensitive and responsive rearing. Studies repeatedly show that as a group preemies raised in social circumstances with plenty of caregiver sensitivity do better than those reared in poverty or by neglectful parents. Taking care of a tiny preemie demands a lot of time and energy. There is no doubt that early in life, many preemies do not sleep as well, take longer to feed, are more irritable, and are less sociable than full-term babies. During infancy their development sometimes shows a few more irregularities than full-term babies. These factors can place considerable strains on parents. But when parents adapt, attentive caregiving can often prevent these disruptions from influencing long-term outcomes.

Given that parents ably meet the challenges presented by early birth, what does the longer-term developmental picture look like? Over 92 percent of preemies weighing more than 3 pounds have no significant mental dysfunction and no major sensory or motor disorders. The picture is less optimistic for babies weighing less than 3 pounds; research data suggest that up to 30 to 40 percent may have some developmental problems. The reason for such a wide range in outcomes depends on the number and severity of early complications as well as the adequacy and appropriateness of the treatment that tiny preemies receive.

Can one predict developmental outcomes from the newborn period? The relationship between developmental status at birth and longer-term growth is tenuous, especially for babies who weigh less than 3 pounds. Even the tiniest preemie who is sick and sluggish may eventually be indistinguishable from the infant who went full term.

Parents of preemies should be especially aware of the fact that development timetables for infancy, particularly the first year, are calculated from the time of conception, not the date of birth. This means that a 4-month-old born six weeks early is more developmentally similar to a $2\frac{1}{2}$-month-old than another 4-month-old born at full term. This method of measurement reflects the strong biological basis for early infant development. Early birth may upset the timetable somewhat but it does not change its overall form and sequence. When preemies are evaluated by measuring from the date of birth, they may appear to be developmentally delayed when in fact they are not. That is why a correction should be made for the shorter length of their prenatal period.

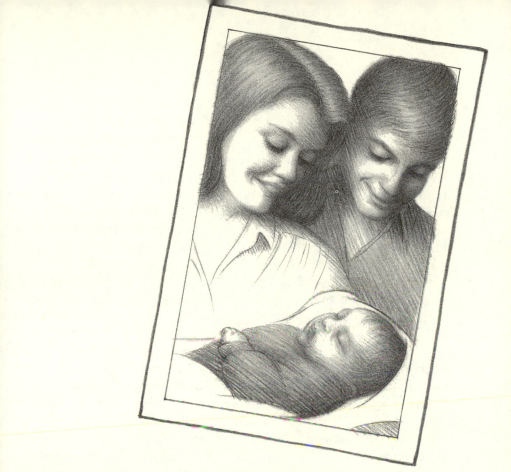

The Early Weeks

most responsive to touch and gentle rocking

will look around when awake and alert but
vision is blurry

can soothe self if mildly upset by sucking on
fist or fingers

❧ *Snapshot*

A few hours after birth the baby's heart and blood system begins to work effectively, but not all vital processes stabilize this quickly. Even at three weeks of age, respiration, sleep, ingestion and digestion, and modulation of body temperature have still not completely settled into smooth and steady functioning. Nor are all these systems synchronized with one another. Hiccups, slight quivers, fussing, jumpiness, spitting up and restlessness are body upsets that signify temporary disruptions in the baby's journey toward physiological stability.

Maintaining physical functioning is hard work for the 3-week-old. Ann's parents sometimes coax her into looking at them, but on these occasions she soon tires. The baby just doesn't have the strength for sustained social interaction.

Sleep gives body processes a chance to function without external distractions and lets the baby recharge her energy. She has only a small amount of energy to store and consumes large amounts in just a short period of wakefulness. Young babies require a great deal of rest, and they sleep as much as 20 hours in each 24-hour period.

All the baby's senses are functioning, but some work better than others. Touch, taste, and smell develop early in the fetal period. In the womb the fetus was constantly swathed by the light pressure of surrounding fluids over body surfaces, and now the baby is comforted by caresses and light touches. Light stroking reduces her fretfulness and promotes sleep. Though the young baby's sense of touch is not fully activated, she does seem to feel marked discomfort to significant pressure. However, the pain associated with pressure is a subjective experience, and a baby may be more or less finicky than other newborns about being accidentally pinched or tightly held.

A 2- to 3-week-old already prefers sweet formula over all others and easily tells the difference between sour and bitter solutions. Scientists don't know for sure if she can tell when something is salty. Ann is also able to distinguish differences in the smells of things around her. Babies even show by respiration and body movements that they dislike the smell of foul substances as much as adults do. Research also shows that a baby quickly learns the scents associated with her mother and possibly her father. At this age, the baby can distinguish different kinds of sounds. She responds to speech by becoming still or sometimes with startle movements. Her vision is still blurry.

Despite the overall immaturity of babies of this age, they are not totally at the mercy of their surroundings. They have two highly effective means of coping with the world: they can cry and they can soothe themselves. A cry indicates that something is not right and summons parents to provide care and comfort. Reflexes enable the baby to execute a series of coordinated actions that help her soothe herself when she is mildly fretful.

Self-soothing goes like this. As 3-week-old Ann is lying on her tummy, her arms are bent at the elbows, and her fisted hand is close to her face. Her fist happens to rub her right cheek, and her head turns to the right because of the rooting reflex (see the Motor Reflexes Close-up in this chapter). When her head turns, her mouth brushes against her hand. When her lips are touched, Ann's mouth opens to suck because of the sucking reflex. Sucking her fist decreases her fretfulness; she calms down. Now that she's calm, she lies quietly in a drowsy state that soon leads to sleep.

❧ *Images Of Development*

Motor

Most movements in the first few weeks of life are not controlled. The baby doesn't even know he has a hand, much less know how to move one. He won't be able to reach out until more connections develop between his brain, nerves, and muscles.

During the prenatal period the fetus's arms and legs moved, and sometimes these movements were pronounced. Now the baby's limbs move vigorously, but these movements are still mostly a result of reflexes and spontaneous movements rather than controlled actions. The baby does have a couple of maneuvers he can initiate. He is able to move his head from side to side (when lying on his tummy). He can also raise his head an inch or two off the pillow when he's lying on his back.

A big impediment to a baby's ability to move his body is that he's still naturally constrained by the vestiges of the fetal position. Until his neck and shoulder muscles are stronger, he won't be able to control his head movements effectively. Right now even holding his head up briefly is not something he does easily or for any length of time.

Sensation and Perception

❧ *Vision.* Young babies' visual acuity, sensitivity to contrasts, and accommodation (focusing on objects that are at different distances) are not equivalent to an adult's perceptual abilities. Newborns are near-sighted and cannot see objects clearly even if they are close, as can near-sighted adults. People and objects are blurry even when they are within the baby's best range of vision (7 to 9 inches). Blurry vision is one reason why the baby's face often shows a blank look.

At this age babies see objects best when they have sharp contrast. Baby Ann's vision is pulled toward her father's mouth: his white teeth stand out against his otherwise blurry-looking facial features. Research shows that when the baby looks at an object she doesn't see all of the object. She sees only a portion of what she is looking at, most typically a section of the edge of the item because of its high contrast, so Ann probably sees only a corner of her dad's mouth. That's fine for now.

Babies can't easily coordinate turning their heads to visually track objects that are slowly moved in front of them. However they can visually follow objects that are moved within a 90-degree arc, their visual range without head movement. A baby peers at these moving stimuli with jerky, short, eye movements that scientists call saccades.

Overall, the baby does a lot better at making visual discriminations when a parent holds her upright and supports her neck so that her head doesn't wobble. Humans have a mechanism (called vestibular sensitivity) that negates the influence of head movement on vision, but at this age the mechanism hasn't quite finished developing. A wobbly head interferes with looking, so that's why a baby's visual discrimination is a bit better when a parent helps her hold her head still.

Hearing. Hearing abilities are more mature than visual abilities. The baby can not only hear sounds but also differentiate one sound from another. Although very young babies hear many kinds of sounds, they can't hear all of the variations in sound that might appear in a melody nor capture sounds that are very soft. They cannot distinguish whispers from silence. However, they are very responsive to pitch and respond more to sounds that have a high pitch rather than a low pitch.

Very young babies sometimes exhibit a skill that lets them use sound to identify location. In adults, the process is called sound localization. I cannot see a key turn a lock, but the sound of the bolt moving tells me that the door is being opened. When baby Michael's mother shakes a rattle next to his left ear, he sometimes turns his head to the left. This indicates that Michael has a nascent ability to respond to an object by the location of its sound. For Michael, sound localization is actually a reflex response rather than the sign of coordinated, mature perception. In a few months' time he will regularly use his spatial perception and hearing skills to locate the sources of sounds, just as adults do.

The reason that hearing at this age is relatively well developed is that the auditory system becomes functional before birth. Sounds, or at least vibrations, pass through the mother's abdominal wall and bathe the fetus in communications from the world outside the womb. Toward the end of the prenatal period, around the middle of the seventh month, fetuses actually begin to hear speech intonations (a form of sound vibration) and to differentiate what they hear. Because the fetus hears the speech of one person—the biological mother—more than any other, studies have shown that babies in the first few weeks of life outside the womb not only differentiate their mother's speech but actually prefer it. A reasonable explanation for this preference is that familiarity attracts the young baby, and the speech of his biological mother is the most familiar speech sound in his new world.

❧ *Developmental Close-up*

Sleep and Wakefulness

During the first few weeks of the baby's life the topic of sleep—the parents' as well as the baby's—dominates the parents' consciousness. On a minimum six-times-a-day feeding schedule, parents don't sleep much, and like the dieting person who craves food and fantasizes about eating luscious desserts, parents hunger for sleep. They never get enough.

Like so much of newborn activity, the baby's ability to sleep soundly and consistently has to become synchronized with the patterns of the outside world. Fortunately for parents, this is one process that does not take too long to establish. For most babies sleep evolves into predictable time patterns within a month or two. Some babies take longer and others take only a few weeks.

At first the baby has no awake and sleep routine. Upsets in his physiological processes contribute to early sleeping irregularities. As physiological processes stabilize at around six weeks, many babies begin to establish a rhythm of four hours of sleep, a short time of wakefulness, and then four hours of sleep, and so on. This pattern is determined in great part by the baby's need to have food at relatively frequent intervals.

In addition to the number of hours slept, the characteristics of the baby's sleep change over the first few months. A few weeks after birth a baby has periods of sleep and alertness and an interim transition state where he is neither awake or asleep. When the baby is actually sleeping, he experiences periods of quiet sleep and active sleep (this is also called REM, for "rapid eye movement," sleep; rapid eye movements occur only in this sleep stage). During quiet sleep the baby's heart rate and respiration are even, his face is relaxed and eyes motionless, and his muscles have tone. In active sleep, the baby's respiration and heart rate are irregular. Muscle tone is also markedly reduced, and this accounts for body twitches, facial grimaces, and rapid movement of the eyes under his closed eyelids. Facial grimaces are sometimes mistakenly interpreted for frowns and smiles in a sleeping baby. No, the baby is not having a pleasant dream or a nightmare. As the baby's sleep patterns stabilize, the proportion of REM sleep decreases and quiet sleep increases.

Around the third or fourth month babies begin to sleep in patterns that replicate adult sleep. At that time they tend to have a long period of wakefulness during the daytime and as long as a five- or six-hour sleep period at night. The length of nighttime sleep is often determined by how well the baby stores food. When storage gets efficient, intake of food during the day can compensate for the loss of a nighttime feeding period.

All these developments in sleeping hours and sleep states are largely a function of neurophysiological mechanisms, but environmental influences play a role. Studies show that even the sleep of babies can be influenced by variations in room temperature, sounds, and the style of caregiving, including breast versus bottle feeding. Scientists who study sleep suggest that sensitive caregiving can help very young babies establish orderly, restful sleep routines.

Motor Reflexes

Human genetic heritage endows the baby with many motor reflexes. Long ago, all these reflexes had survival value, but today only a few are important to adaptation to living outside of the womb. While no longer serving the purpose of survival, some of these reflexes are useful in other ways. Some help babies and their parents get to know each other. A few are used by physicians to evaluate the baby's nervous system.

The motor reflexes that disappear over the baby's first six months are called developmental reflexes. Some, such as the grasp reflex, are ultimately replaced by voluntary actions that enable a baby to respond to more various and more complex demands. Other reflexes such as the palmomental reflex (mouth opens when pressure is applied to the palms), are not replaced; they go away, never be seen again.

Six developmental reflexes are especially interesting. Two developmental reflexes that continue to serve survival functions are the head-turning response and the sucking reflex. The former is "insurance" providing the baby with the ability to breathe by evoking a turn of her head whenever her nostrils are accidentally covered. The second reflex allows the baby to take nourishment because it fosters automatic sucking when a nipple—or blanket or fist—is placed in her mouth.

Among the reflexes that don't seem to serve a survival function, the Moro reflex somewhat resembles an adult's startle reaction to a surprising or fearful event. A physician invokes this reflex by holding the baby up in both of his hands. One hand supports the head and shoulders while the other supports the back and bottom. The legs dangle. Using a controlled but sudden movement, the doctor lets the head "drop" an inch or two. The drop elicits the Moro. When this reflex is invoked, the baby looks as if she is about to hug someone. If this reflex is hardly noticeable or very pronounced, the physician will conduct tests to ensure that the atypical response is not signaling an underlying neurological or physiological impairment.

When the baby lies on her back, the tonic neck reflex makes her assume the posture of a miniature fencer in the en garde position. Her head turns to one side and one arm moves in front of her face and bends at the elbow. The other arm lies straight alongside her body. This position is fairly pronounced in the early weeks and gradually becomes inhibited (disappears) by the time babies are 6 months old. If a baby regularly assumes this position after 6 months, a thorough neurological examination is warranted.

Two reflexes promote an emotional bond between the baby and her parents. The rooting reflex makes the baby's head turn toward her mother when she touches a corner of her mouth. Ann's mother interprets this head turn as a sign of Ann's interest in her. Being "welcomed" like this invites her parent's reciprocal interest and spurs more interaction.

The grasp reflex occurs when a baby's parent opens her hand and touches her palm with a finger. The baby's hand closes protectively around the parent's finger. This act of physical bonding promotes the development of mutual affection and fosters interest in continuing interaction.

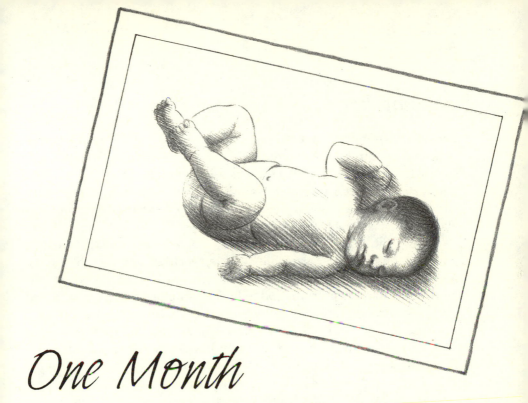

One Month

body movements constrained by reflexes

alert when talked to

differentiates speech from other sounds

late-day irritability

Average Boy: Length is 21.5 inches, with most between
20 and 22.5+ inches. Weight is 9+ pounds, with most
between 7.5 and 11 pounds.
Average Girl: Length is 20.5 inches, with most between
19.5+ and 21.5+ inches. Weight is 8.5+ pounds, with
most between 7 and 10 pounds.

❧ Snapshot

Behaviors that most obviously set 1-month-olds apart from newborns are better head control, longer periods of visual attentiveness, and greater sensitivity to human voices. Babies are also beginning to have more regular sleep patterns. Overall, however, 1-month-olds are still struggling to satisfy basic biological needs and are most content when fed, talked to, and then allowed to fall asleep in a quiet spot.

One of the most pleasing changes in the baby's behavior is his growing power of observation. When fully awake, Michael now and then gazes intently at nearby shadows on the wall in his room. He sometimes turns his head and tentatively peers around to look at his mother when he is picked up. Lying in his crib, the baby raises his head to study brightly-colored toys. These periods of looking are often accompanied with a wide-eyed expression of alertness. It seems as if Michael has discovered that he can find things to look at. Michael also strains to listen closely to sounds. His muscles tighten a little and he barely moves while listening.

Michael's new-found attentiveness is a delight for his parents. However, attentiveness at this age often goes along with an increase in irritability, particularly late in the afternoon. This is a temporary annoyance that Michael's parents grudgingly accept because the underlying reason for his increase in irritability is a natural unevenness in developmental maturity. As Michael's ability to look around improves, some attractive and forceful visual stimuli capture his attention for seconds or minutes at a time, and he finds it difficult to turn away at will. The energy expended in staring, along with feedback responsiveness to input coming from the other senses, causes fatigue.

It is difficult to predict which visual stimulus might capture a baby's attention. For six-week-old Ann it was one of the toys that hung on the side of her crib. Totally mesmerized by it, she studied it repeatedly. In a matter of days, she was overaroused and worn out by early evening. She was difficult to soothe, and instead of falling asleep easily she fretted even when held and rocked.

Fortunately, for most babies late-day irritability tends to last only a few weeks. It declines as babies learn to control their attention, i.e., they look at something of interest, they turn away, then look again. They also get better at doing other things, such as beginning to reach for an attractive toy, and these activities help keep them entertained.

Sleep is very important for 1-month-old babies, and they still sleep a large part of every 24 hours. Babies' sleep periods can be unpredictable, but this inconsistency is gradually going away. By five or six weeks of age, some begin to show a day-night sleep cycle in which a longer sleep period is part of the nighttime routine along with added wakefulness during the day. Day wakefulness gradually settles into a pattern with three or four hours of sleep, a wakeful period, and then three to four hours of sleep again.

Images of Development

Motor

At one month the baby's head is usually turned to one side when she lies on her back. One arm is usually stretched out straight while her other arm is bent at the elbow. Her arm movements are jerky; when she is excited, both of her arms straighten out and she thrusts them out in front of her face and chest.

When Ann is on her tummy, she lifts her head momentarily an inch or two off the mattress. When her head drops, she turns it to one side. While lying in this position her legs spontaneously move and she looks as if she's trying to crawl. Ann really has little control over these movements, and the repeated bending and straightening of her legs is not forceful enough to propel her body forward.

Babies of this age cannot roll over or crawl on their own, but they can roll over as part of a spontaneously induced, reflexive movement. For this reason it's best not to leave them alone on a bed.

When Ann's father props her into a sitting position (supporting her with his hands), her back is rounded like a big C. Her trunk muscles are weak. Most of the time her head droops forward when she is held in a sitting or standing position

Hint

When you are holding your baby, cup your hand behind her head for support.

and her head sags forward more when she is tired. In fact, when Ann's father holds her with both hands below her tummy, everything droops—head, shoulders, back, hips, and legs. The hands of 1-month-olds are usually closed into fists because of the grasp reflex. But this reflex is not as strong as it was in the newborn period, and if the baby's hands are opened by someone else, she can hold onto a rattle momentarily.

Sensation and Perception

✤ *Vision.* The 1-month-old shows a variety of looking behaviors. Michael gazes with interest at his mother's face or a bright toy. Sometimes he looks at an object for minutes at a time; sometimes he looks around with eyes that have a vacant, vague expression as if he were daydreaming; and he switches back and forth between attentiveness and vacant staring like a light bulb going on and off. He tends to switch off when he's tired or trying to look at something that he isn't able to see clearly. Michael's mother has learned that he sees best when she holds him snugly and upright in her arms. But even when Michael is held in this position and is fully attentive, his face is expressionless.

On his back with his head turned to one side, Michael visually follows a bright object when it is moved slowly from his side up towards the middle of his chest. When his head is not turned, he will keep his eyes on a bright object that is rotated in a small circle. Already he has learned how to coordinate head movements with the direction of his gaze.

One of the distinguishing features of 1-month-olds' vision is the difficultly they have in seeing all parts of a toy or a mobile that hangs over the crib. They can take in only a portion at a glance; most of the time they look at part of the outline or edge of the toy. A baby will look toward the center of a toy if it has high contrast and also moves. A mobile that has a red ring with a bright ball suspended in the middle is a perfect target for visual attention.

Faces appeal to babies of this age because faces have high-contrast features: lips are darker than teeth, foreheads lighter than hairlines and hair. The mouth region, because of the contrast and movement of skin, lips, teeth, and tongue, draws the baby's attention like a magnet. The eyes also have big appeal.

> ## Hint
>
> When your baby is awake and alert, talk to him with your head about 12 inches away from his face. Smile and sing to him, and move your head from side to side.
>
>

✤ *Hearing.* Babies must learn to recognize different components of speech. With this ability, they eventually learn to put sounds together to form recognizable words. As early as 1 month of age, babies begin to respond to human sounds (speech) as distinct from noises in general. Ann becomes still and turns her head when speech is directed to her. She appears to like to listen to the sounds humans make as much as she likes to stare at their faces. This attraction to human speech is a convenient, biologically prepared tendency that prompts the baby to listen to the sounds that will allow her to develop her own communication skills.

Research shows that babies of this age also begin to differentiate the specific sounds of speech. Under controlled laboratory conditions, scientists have found that 1-month-olds can discriminate a sound such as "pa" from a sound such as "ba" when each is presented as a single stimulus. It has also been shown that in only a few more weeks babies begin to detect the difference between two-syllable contrasts such as "dada" and "baba."

Vocalizations

This month the baby takes his first steps toward becoming a vocal partner. Initially, the sounds he makes are like the soft noises we produce when clearing our throats. Then at about six weeks, one or two of his vocalizations become distinguishable. These sounds are soft and pleasing and are like the vowels of "ah," "eh," or "uh."

One reason that babies can begin to make varied sounds is the changes that are occurring in the parts of the throat associated with speech. The larynx, for example, is becoming more flexible and mobile so that it is physically possible to produce discrete and distinguishable sounds apart from cries. At first, the baby doesn't plan to make vowel sounds; these noises are accidentally emitted. Soon the baby learns how to reproduce the sounds he has generated, and by 2 to 3 months he repeatedly utters these soft vowels.

Cognition

Taste and touch senses are fairly mature at birth, and signs of early learning are often observed with these senses. During the first month, for example, many babies quickly learn to differentiate nipples, their own fingers, and pacifiers. Now when hungry they will turn away from pacifiers and seek the nipple associated with food.

Social

The 1-month-old is more socially responsive than a newborn. There are more times during the day when Ann looks alert when spoken to, and she looks longer at faces. There are still times when she has to be coaxed into looking at a person; in other words, she is still not in the "right state" to be receptive to vocal or visual stimulation. Sometimes she shows the faintest beginning of a smile or vocalizes a little. But at this age, she cannot simultaneously smile and make sounds because that takes a degree of visual and vocal coordination that she does not yet have.

Hint

Talk gently and sing to the baby when you change her diaper, feed her, and carry her.

At about six weeks or so, Ann's behavior signals that she's learning about social interactions. She begins to change her behavior—by being very quiet or looking more alert or even breathing rapidly—when she is picked up, changed, or fed. This type of behavior tells us that she is aware of a difference between social and nonsocial events, a first step toward sociability. Ann's behavior also signifies cognitive activity: she demonstrates an ability to learn about the external social world.

❧ Developmental Close-up

Muscle Development

Most babies become bigger in the first month; they gain a little weight and grow taller than when they were born. Parents are often concerned with the baby's diet because of the connection between food and weight gain.

As babies grow, all of their muscles also grow and get stronger. However, some muscles get stronger earlier and are used more effectively than other muscles. The progression of effective use of muscles is largely driven by biological heritage; the sequence is neck, shoulders and upper trunk, and then abdomen, hips, and legs. This means that as long as Michael's neck muscles are too weak to hold his head upright for any length of time, his trunk and back muscles are too weak to support his back for sitting up on his own. While there may be overlap in increasing muscle strength (upper and lower trunk together, for example), in normal development a baby's trunk muscles do not get stronger before his neck muscles.

The practical side of knowing about this sequence is that we can see how Michael's motor development is progressing simply by observing his behaviors. The shoulder muscles are strong when he is able to prop himself up when lying on his tummy. When his upper trunk muscles are sturdy, Michael can roll over regularly. As the lower trunk muscles strengthen, Michael is able to sit by himself. Later, when each part of the trunk and lower limbs are strong, he can support his own weight while standing. Most babies make their way through this sequence of development by the time they are a year old.

Why is head control a first priority in muscle development? Well, human babies (and children) are best able to take in visual information when their bodies are in an upright position and their heads are upright and stable. Thus, from the standpoint of early learning, it makes sense to have a biological program that says, "head first."

Another biologically programmed pattern of muscle development involves a gradual increase in strength that starts at the middle of the chest and works out to the arms and then the hands. The muscles in Michael's shoulders and arms become stronger before the muscles in his hands.

One explanation for this developmental sequence is that controlled hand movements are a distinctly human capacity. It seems entirely possible then that in the evolution of the species the programming that provides for manual dexterity comes at the end of a biological sequence. Meanwhile, as a practical matter, without the strength in the shoulders to hold up the arms, strength in the hands would be of limited value.

While all physically normal babies show these sequences of development, babies differ in the rate at which these changes occur. Most babies develop all of the motor abilities within the age ranges described in this book, but some babies develop abilities earlier than these norms and a few babies' abilities are late to blossom. Minor variations in the pace of motor developments tend to be inconsequential. However, when the sequences of motor development do not occur until months after they are reasonably expected or the quality of some skills is suspect, parents should seek the advice of a child development specialist.

Crying

Most cries in the first month or two relate to physiology. That is, the baby is having difficulty digesting food, she's hungry, or hiccups are disturbing her sleep. Even cries that communicate discomfort have a plus side; crying helps babies increase their lung capacity.

Crying is a fact of life. Hearing the baby cry is enough to make the parent of the baby, especially a young baby, anxious. Most of us associate crying with distress, sorrow, and pain, so we tend to interpret the baby's cry as a negative event. Although persistent and unremitting crying may suggest that the baby has an underlying problem, most crying is not all bad.

Learning to understand the baby's cries is a little like learning a new language; it's terribly confusing at first. Even so, many mothers are able to distinguish their own infant's cry from those of other babies just a few days after the baby's birth. By the age of 1 month, a mother (or the baby's most regular caregiver) usually recognizes a pain cry, a cry associated with hunger, and cries signaling general discomfort. The hunger cry is most easily identified. Cries associated with fatigue and boredom are often short and are more like frets than real cries.

During the third and fourth months crying becomes less tied to physiological upsets and increasingly related to psychological needs. The baby's cry may signal boredom, a desire for company or a change of scene, or just plain frustration. Of course, the baby doesn't know the meaning of boredom or frustration. Parents decipher what a cry means by looking at what's happening and how the baby responds to attempts to soothe her. As the baby's cries become less frequent, parents are better at figuring out what cues and events are the cause of an upset. At 3 or 4 months, parents are often able to distinguish among the various cries that signal psychological forms of discomfort.

Humans differ in a lot of ways physically and emotionally. We know that genetics as well as life experiences plays a role in these differences. One way babies differ is how they cry. Some cry often and others only infrequently. Some cry as if their hearts were breaking, while others barely whimper even when a favored toy disappears. There is no denying that babies who get upset easily or cry intensely are hard to deal with.

There are many points of view about handling the baby's crying. What to do depends on the baby's age, her general well-being, her temperament, and the specific situation. One certainty about crying is that it's the baby's attempt to say that things are not right. In this context, it is hard to sub-

> ## Hint
>
> Baby snugglers (canvas slings that hold the baby to your chest) work well to calm the baby, particularly when she is having a difficult day. Your body warmth and movement act as a soother. Both parents can use snugglers!

scribe to the idea that parents should let a young baby "cry it out." Some effort should be made to find out what is wrong and to ease the discomfort. As a practical matter, letting the baby collapse from the sheer exhaustion of continued crying may only prolong the problem, since sleep that follows fatigue tends not to be restful sleep. Generally, research has shown that tending to babies' cries, even those of older babies, does not spoil them but rather makes them more contented in the long run.

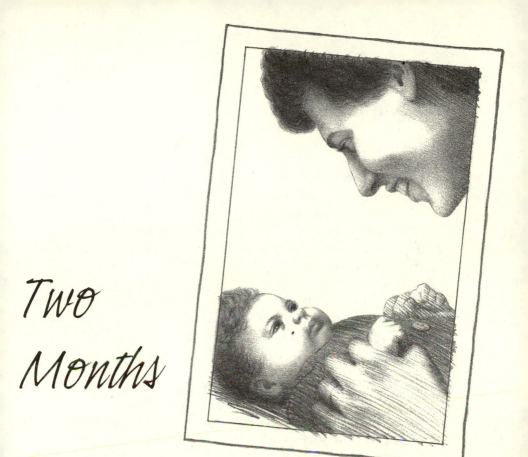

Two Months

lifts head and shoulders above mattress

stays awake longer during day

makes eye contact with parents

responds differentially to vocal intonations

smiles weakly

Average Boy: Length is 22.5+ inches, with most between 21.5+ and 24 inches. Weight is 11.5 pounds, with most between 9 and 13+ pounds.
Average Girl: Length is 22+ inches, with most between 20.5+ and 23+ inches. Weight is 10+ pounds, with most between 8.5 and 12+ pounds.

❧ Snapshot

After two months of living outside the womb the baby's physiology works fairly well. Sucking on the breast or bottle is accomplished without too much dribbling, hiccups are less frequent, digestive upsets are decreasing, and sleep is relatively trouble free. As body discomforts lessen, the baby has more energy and attention for other things, such as being social. She has started to make eye contact with her parents, and when alert she turns to toys that interest her. Occasionally she smiles. She coordinates her head and eye movements without much effort and holds her head up higher and longer than a month ago.

At 2 months Ann now remains awake for longer periods, and this wakefulness occurs more and more during daytime hours. On the average, she is awake two to three hours at a time. At night a long period of sleep now often takes place; she may sleep from around 10:00 P.M. to 3:00 or 4:00 A.M. When Ann is awake, she tends to be visually attentive. Now there is no mistaking when she is awake or when she is asleep, whereas a month ago her states of semiwakefulness were common.

Most babies' surroundings are filled with interesting patterns and colors, and the 2-month-old visually flits from one intriguing stimulus to another. Controlled attention is difficult at this age, and most babies have to work hard to keep their visual attention focused on a particular toy or a person. You can appreciate the magnitude of this challenge if you think of the first time you went to an amusement park. Do you remember the energy it took to decide what to look at, where to go, and what attractions to ride?

Fortunately, parents are there to help babies focus attention. Ann's parents have intuitively created a bag of tricks. If she is awake and her head droops more than usual, her mother holds her in her lap with her hand lightly supporting her head. She talks to her and intensifies variations in her voice intonation. Ann listens to her mother's voice and works to hold up her head. Finally, with animated talking, smiling, and head movement her mother has helped Ann make eye contact. Alert once again, Ann focuses attention on her mother.

❧ Images of Development

Motor

Muscle control is one way to tell the 2-month-old from the younger baby. Head control leads the way. Now when Michael is on his tummy, he lifts his head and shoulders several inches above the mattress and rests on his forearms, sometimes holding this position for a number of seconds. When his energy runs out, his head and shoulders suddenly drop to the mattress. Then after a brief pause, he picks up his head and repeats the routine.

At 2 months the upper trunk has more strength, as shown by the muscles in Michael's upper back: they tense slightly when he is held in a sitting position. Other indications of back muscle development are that his back is less curved and that he briefly supports his own head when braced against a parent's shoulder. When he is on his tummy his legs are bent, but he actively straightens them out again and again and makes crawlinglike movements. His body now shifts around because of the motion he generates.

When Michael lies on his back, the position of his arms is very different from that of just a month ago. Now both arms are often raised above the head, making a U shape. This position indicates that the baby is moving toward a symmetrical arm posture. Soon he will be able to move both arms to his sides or in front of his body, and each arm will be able to assume a position that is a mirror image of the other. This postural adjustment will soon be followed by reaching movements.

At 2 months, the grasp reflex is also weakening considerably. When the reflex was strong, Michael's fingers would close tightly around a rattle placed in his hand. Now his fingers generally open as they touch a rattle. If he momentarily manages to hold a toy, he tries to bring it toward his mouth. Eventually, the baby will be capable of holding a toy, moving it into his field of vision, and looking at it—but he's not there yet.

> ## Hint
>
> When the baby is on his tummy and is alert and looking around, place a small, colorful toy about 12 inches or so from his face. He can practice head control and at the same time improve his attention skills.

Sensations and Perceptions

❧ *Vision.* This month there is definite improvement in how effectively a baby surveys his surroundings and in the accuracy of his ability to look directly at a person or object. Now both eyes often work together, and this helps the baby see better. Improved vision makes a 2-month-old look more alert than a younger baby.

Better head/eye coordination makes possible faster and more coordinated visual scan. Michael systematically follows a bright object that is moved back and forth from one side of his head to the other and tracks the object in one movement rather than the series of starts and stops that characterized 1-month-old's scan. He will also follow a toy that is moved up and down in a vertical track.

When 2-month-old Ann looks at a face, her gaze sometimes rests on the hairline area, sometimes on the lips, and sometimes on the eyes. If she's alert, she usually maintains eye contact. Of course, she doesn't know yet that eye contact is important for interpersonal communication; she is merely responding to the movement and the light and dark contrast of the other person's eyes.

Ann's increasing interest in faces and her attraction to motion mean that she prefers to look at talking faces more than any other object. Because she repeatedly directs her visual attention to faces, she also begins to recognize the faces she sees most often. In fact, at this age Ann is very keen to look at any familiar stimuli, that is, almost all the things that regularly appear in her field of vision.

Hint

Hold the baby on your lap facing you. Support her head. Softly sing a song to her, gently and slowly moving your head from side to side.

The improvement in the 2-month-old's ability to look at visual targets has been carefully measured by researchers. If a baby of this age is given a two-dimensional drawing of a triangle, she is more accurate than a 1-month-old in finding the outline of the triangle. She also scans a greater portion of the outline. Finally, if she's presented with the outline of a square that has a dot inside, she is more likely to look beyond the outline and attend to the dot than she was a month ago. Researchers have documented that at 2 months babies have many visual discrimination skills, including being able to distinguish shapes and contours, light and dark contrasts, movement, red or deep blue from white, and some familiar people and toys.

Hearing. Two-month-old Michael can hear a variety of nonhuman and human sounds that differ in pitch, intensity, and intonation. We know this because he stops moving when he hears a ringing bell, a simple melody, or a person speaking. A common feature of all these sounds is some sort of variability. A bell attracts attention because the ringing consists of high-pitched sounds that start and stop. Melodies contain variations in tone. Voices contain rising and falling intonations. In speaking to babies, parents often use exaggerated intonations, as in "HI, baby!" Babies are particularly responsive to the emphasized "hi." For the most part, exaggerated intonation is a behavior that mothers (and others) use intuitively with the aim of eliciting a baby's attention; this kind of speech is therefore sometimes called "motherese." Because of the baby's natural attraction to sounds with variation, motherese usually produces the desired result—it gets the baby's attention.

Vocalizations and Language

There are two significant changes in sound production at 2 months. The first is what scientists call a vocal volley. In a vocal volley the baby imitates a string of sounds that are made by an adult, for example, "AAH, aah, aaah." Because at this age the baby can reproduce only sounds that are already in his vocal production repertoire, and since almost all of his sounds are vowels, he can echo an adult only if the adult's speech just contains vowels. The second change in the baby's vocalization is that his "speech" sounds show some of the distinctive intonations of adult speech: his sounds rise and fall, rise and fall.

Social

Being social demands a lot from 1-month-olds. At 2 months, being social has less competition from bodily functions and takes less available energy. Michael's increased wakefulness means more periods of alertness, and his parents direct some of his rapt attention toward social contact. Interactions are more frequent, but there are limits to Michael's ability to engage in social activity for long periods of time. When he becomes overstimulated by social contact, he turns away, closes his eyes, or frets intermittently.

Periods of social alertness allow parents to bring the baby into a nascent form of conversation. It goes like this: Michael's father makes eye contact with him, smiles, and talks to him in short sentences, speaking with exaggerated intonation. He then stops talking, and Michael starts to make sounds and even produces a faint smile that shows his enjoyment. He stops making sounds, and his father starts talking again. He raises his voice slightly in order to hold Michael's attention. The "dialogue" goes on for several minutes and is suspended when the baby gets tired. This conversational game brings pleasure to parents as well and is an important step in emotionally uniting parents with their baby. As one mother of a 2-month-old said, "Everything was worth it when she started to smile and play with me."

Research shows that toward the middle of the third month (ten weeks), the baby begins to initiate actions when a person moves out of his line of vision. These actions may include visually following the person, becoming quiet, or showing a change from a smiling to a neutral expression. Such behaviors indicate not disappointment over being left alone but rather an awareness of and fascination for the most interesting object that was in the baby's range of vision. It is only coincidental that the object was a person.

One advantage of the 2-month-old's heightened sociability is that he is more sensitive to others' attempts to soothe him by talking or looking at him. Provided the baby is fretting gently or at most crying softly, talking can now be as effective in comforting him as rocking.

> ## Hint
>
> Talk to your baby, pause if you hear him make a sound to you, then when he has stopped, talk again. Repeat a few times.

Cognition

Controlled attention is a prerequisite for learning about events, objects, and people. From time to time Ann works really hard to focus her attention; and as a consequence, at 2 months she begins to develop some rudimentary cognitive skills.

Ann and her age mates show forms of elementary learning particularly at feeding time. Ann is bottle fed. When hungry and fretting, she occasionally stops crying just at the sight of her bottle. Her friend Michael is breast fed, and he stops crying when positioned on his mother's lap for nursing. Because of these kinds of responses, we know that at 2 months babies are already beginning to associate two events that occur close in time. These associations are basic building blocks in cognitive development.

Emotions

With the onset of the smile, the baby's face now shows something akin to an expression of outright pleasure. She breathes heavily and squirms when a familiar toy is shown to her, demonstrating that she is pleasurably excited by this event. At this age her facial expressions also reveal discomfort. However, most of the time her face shows little at all in the way of emotion. Her still somewhat vacant stare reflects her incompletely formed vision as well as yet underdeveloped facial muscles.

❧ Developmental Close-up

The Baby's Emotions

Adults tend to assume that a baby's facial expression indicates a particular emotion. But do babies' facial expressions tell us what they are actually feeling? Do very young babies even know anger or fear or joy?

At least as far back as Charles Darwin, scientists have been debating the answers to these questions, and developmentalists are still divided on these issues. One group of scholars follows in the tradition of Darwin and emphasizes that emotions have a strong biological basis. They believe that as a result of evolutionary forces some emotions are part of humans' natural endowment—every human is born with certain emotions. The contemporary scientists from this school of thought say that babies experience distinct emotions very early in life and that these emotions are reflected in facial expressions and other physiological features such as pulse and respiration rate. They propose that the basic emotions include disgust, anger, fear, and happiness; other emotions, such as jealousy and pride, emerge over time as the result of the fine-tuning of six core emotions during various life experiences.

Another group of psychologists believes that feelings of anger, fear, and pleasure all develop over time as the result of learning experiences. They assert that the young baby's facial expressions reflect any number of things, some linked to emotions and some not. Finally, they believe that it is only through experience that facial expressions and feelings are eventually linked. These views are in sharp contrast to the idea that emotions and their accompanying facial expressions come prepackaged in the newborn and simply await the right circumstances to spring into evidence.

How does the second group of scientists explain why the baby's facial expressions look like expressions of emotions? They allow that humans' evolutionary heritage includes certain biological programs for facial expressions. Some expressions, a frown for example, may be linked to the discomfort a baby feels when he is hungry. But there are other expressions such as surprise or sadness that are unlikely to be linked to the actual feelings of surprise or sadness. We know these feelings on the basis of many experiences which very young babies have not had—and could not understand.

Both groups of scientists agree that, by two to three months, the baby's facial expressions include one that seems to indicate pleasure or happiness. The behaviors and events surrounding the facial expression and the baby's facial expression itself, provide us with clues for determining the emotional state.

What perspective should parents adopt in trying to "read" the emotions of their babies? Whatever makes them comfortable. In the early months of the baby's life, it is sometimes difficult to tell one form of crying from another, much less to specifically determine the emotion the cry is expressing. But if it is easier for parents to deal with the crying by attributing it to a particular emotion, then by all means they should do so. Later on babies' emotions become clearer, and there is less guesswork in figuring out the baby's emotional state.

This discussion should convey two important messages for parents of 2-month-olds. First, almost everyone agrees that the baby experiences something akin to the emotion of pleasure about this age. Second, remember that learning about a baby's feelings is not something that can be rigidly prescribed. We can say that the baby's emotions can be best ascertained by knowing the specific context in which a behavior occurs and that those who are most familiar with the nuances of a particular baby's behavior are in the best position to accurately assess his emotional state.

Three Months

when alert, follows movement, gazes at others, smiles and coos

brings arms to midline of body and plays with hands

head is bobblingly erect when held upright

anticipates everyday routine, such as opening mouth at appearance of nipple

Average Boy: Length is 24 inches, with most between 22.5 and 25 inches. Weight is 13+ pounds, with most between 10+ and 15+ pounds.
Average Girl: Length is 23 inches, with most between 22 and 24.5 inches. Weight is 12 pounds, with most between 9.5+ and 14 pounds.

❧ Snapshot

At this age babies' behaviors suddenly seem wonderfully coordinated. When fully awake, fourteen-week-old Ann regularly holds her head up and focuses her eyes. She looks intently at toys, pictures on the wall, and anybody that approaches. Last month Ann had a little smile that she directed to anything, to anybody, and sometimes to nothing at all. This month, her smile is big, and she specifically directs it to people and to toys.

Ann's microworld is endlessly intriguing to her. She looks at a suspended mobile for minutes at a time and sometimes explores the entire surface of an object. She visually follows moving objects whether they are moved across a table top or held at the level of her eyes and moved slowly from side to side. Sometimes her eyes and arms operate in tandem—she begins to tentatively extend her arms as if to reach for objects she sees. There is no mistaking her genuine pleasure in these experiences.

In addition to pleasure, Ann shows the emotions of interest, boredom, and frustration. A new toy elicits attention, cooing, smiling, and pleasurable wriggling, but old toys may be greeted with yawns, averted gazes, and fretting. Ann's smiles tell us now she likes to be entertained. Toys and mobiles are fun, but now people are Ann's favorite entertainment.

In an impressive display of early independence, Ann begins to create her own amusements by playing with her fingers. Raising both arms and hands in front of her eyes, she touches her fingers, moves them apart, and touches them again. Seeing and feeling her hands move is so compelling that she prolongs the game. This diversion staves off boredom and tiredness when there's no one else around.

At 3 months babies have a primitive memory. Michael remembers some of his most familiar experiences surely for minutes, probably for hours, and maybe for days if he has sufficient visual cues and reminders. He moves with pleasurable excitement when he sees his bottle and may open his mouth in anticipation of a soon-to-happen feeding. Michael remembers now—a bottle signals food! He also recognizes simple, sequential associations; for example, a door opening is usually followed by the sounds of footsteps. If a delay occurs in a routine that he has come to recognize (like feeding), he cries to let us know that he's not happy that something is amiss.

Overall, so many distinctly human mental and social behaviors emerge at this age that 3 months is a major transition point in early infant development. The baby is no longer just a physical being; she is also a psychological being with likes, dislikes, and pleasures. She has some memory capability.

Moreover, many of her reflexive, biologically mandated survival behaviors have already been replaced by more functional, albeit nascent, motor skills. From now on, motor skills change rapidly. It is amazing how quickly she continues to shift from an almost helpless being to a relatively adept little girl.

❧ *Images Of Development*

Motor

This month unmistakable changes occur in the baby's head position and control, her arm movements, and her body control. Her head is held higher and for a longer period of time. Her arm movements are directed at things in a purposeful though largely uncoordinated manner. Her shoulder muscles are stronger and her shoulders straighter.

The baby gives all kinds of signals that her body is getting prepared for rolling over, crawling, creeping, and eventually standing. When she's on her tummy, she holds her head up for minutes at a time at an angle between 45 and 90 degrees above the mattress surface. She kicks actively and purposefully when on her tummy or back. When she's held upright, her legs support a fraction of her weight.

Remember the tonic neck reflex (The Just Born: Developmental Close-up)? It's less and less noticeable. The baby's head is mostly held in the midline when she's lying on her back. When she's alert and quiet, her arms are mirror images of each other; if one arm is lying at her side then the other is also in this position. When she's resting, both arms usually lie on the mattress at shoulder level with elbows bent and hands near her head. The baby looks as if she has been surprised and thrown her arms up in exclamation.

Now that she can keep her head in midline and arms in symmetry, the baby can visually attend to things that are straight in front of her. Her new skills also include bringing her hands into eye range for visual inspection and play. This begins a wonderful collaboration of eyes and hands and new opportunities for learning.

At 3 months the effectiveness of reaching movements still leaves a bit to be desired; reaches are weak and unsteady. But the baby keeps on trying and does her best at reaching when lying on her back. In this position, babies do not have to strain to keep head upright and shoulders stable while simultaneously trying to reach for a toy.

Grasp continues to mature into a more useful tool. In a propped position, 3-month-old Michael opens one hand if a small toy is presented to

Hint

Try to find a crib mobile that has a brightly colored ring 3 to 4 inches in diameter. Suspend the mobile so that the baby can see the ring clearly and can reach for it. She may be able to lightly brush the ring with her hand.

him. But he can hold onto the toy only briefly. His grasp does not yet involve his thumb, and at this point he primarily uses his palms and fingers. Importantly, fewer spontaneous body movements occur when he attempts to hold onto something, so his grasp is less disrupted by unwanted activity.

Michael seems to have an instinctual awareness of the unique value of his fingers. When a small toy is held in front of him, he briefly and unskillfully moves his fingers over it like miniature space probes. Occasionally he can manage to use his hands to carry a toy to his mouth. This hand behavior is not guided by his vision; it is simply an elaboration of earlier reflexive hand-to-mouth activity. Still, it marks another important step because Michael is beginning to learn how useful his hands can be.

Sensation and Perception

Vision. Acuity, the ability to see objects clearly, is better now, and 3-month-olds can attend to details that they missed in earlier explorations. In the laboratory, researchers have learned about a process that helps babies of this age clearly see objects that are nearby or at a short distance. The process is called accommodation, the rapid adjustment of the curvature of the lens; it assures that a baby's visual focus is good regardless of distance. Just how well does a 3-month-old see? Well, he can now differentiate faces that have smiles from those that have frowns. In fact, he smiles to a smiling face and rarely smiles at someone who is frowning.

Babies of 3 months also discriminate different shapes; that is, they can tell a bottle from a stick or a ball from a person's head. This ability is called form perception. A baby even briefly remembers the configuration of simple forms or shapes, an ability called shape constancy. Michael recognizes that his bottle retains the same basic shape, the bottle shape, whether it's upside down or sideways and whether the light is dim or bright.

Spatial perception is clearly improving. Michael seems to understand that reaching for a nearby bottle may mean success, whereas reaching for a bottle that is on a table across the room means no contact. Also, this month he can distinguish red from green and blue/green from white. It is possible that different colors may influence his psychological state.

✿ *Hearing.* Measuring how well a baby hears different speech sounds and how well she hears loud and soft noises is far more difficult than measuring different responses to facial smiles and frowns. Research and common experience show that hearing is getting better; it is difficult to say how much better. At three months babies turn their heads when they hear a localized sound, such as a nearby telephone) or a rattle, demonstrating that they can discriminate particular sounds.

Cognition

More and more the baby's mind takes on human qualities. Ann quiets when something interesting comes into view, and she remains still so that she can give the object of interest her undivided visual attention. She listens with the same concerted effort.

Research shows that the 3-month-old remembers better than before (see Close-up). Sometimes Ann learns from activities she does on her own; this learning can happen quite accidentally.

> ## Hint
>
> Talk to the baby when you are walking toward her or even when you are walking away from her. You want the baby to get used to the sound of your voice and to recognize what your voice sounds like when you are nearby and relatively far away. Your voice helps her learn about near and far space in her mini-world.

One day, while lying in her crib, she moves her hands toward her chest. Her hands happen to meet, and her fingers touch each other. She enjoys the feel of fingering her hands, and she likes to look at what she is doing. This unplanned event happens another day and then another. Then one day when seeing her hands Ann remembers her hand movements, and she voluntarily initiates hand play. She quickly associates the sight of her hands with play. Because the activity is interesting and pleasurable, Ann repeatedly plays with her fingers and hands. All the while this activity helps her exercise nascent memory skills and also teaches Ann that her own activities can be a source of pleasure.

The 3-month-old's own body is not the only source now of her learning experiences. Ann can reach out, and she does so now with avid interest. She touches a cuddly toy and knows that it feels different than her rattle. Reaching and exploring are often repeated because these activities are pleasing to her, and with every one of these repetitions Ann learns a little more about her body and her environment.

Hint

Give the baby time to get to know some of her toys. When you introduce new toys, introduce them one at a time, waiting a few days or even a week to introduce another new one.

Social encounters also are now providing lessons. Ann is beginning to discriminate between the way one person holds her and the hold of another person. She may stiffen somewhat if an unfamiliar person holds her. This is not the expression of concern about strangers that we see later on at about 8 months. Rather, it is simply a reaction to newness. To be able to recognize that something is new means that Ann must have learned the characteristics of something that is familiar.

The notion of recognizing the familiar has ramifications for changes made in the baby's routines. When a 3-month-old is introduced to a new regime of care (for example, a new babysitter), she may show periodic upsets for a few days. This does not mean that she is spoiled; it's just her response to unfamiliar people and/or routines. Holding her, talking to her, and comforting her makes adjustments in routines easier because these familiar sensations are reassuring. As new settings and people become more familiar, she once again shows pleasure with her surroundings.

Vocalizations and Language

Until this month the baby's sounds were mainly squeals, hiccups, and cries. Cries could be used to register distress, but the baby didn't have a sound that indicated he was experiencing pleasure or enjoying something that was interesting. Now the vocal system has developed to the point that different vowel sounds can be regularly and voluntarily produced. These sounds are called coos and sound like *ooh, aah, uuh.* When Michael discovers that he can make these sounds, they soon become one of his favorite pastimes and he coos repeatedly. He is particularly fond of cooing when he is content, amused by a toy, or captivated by his mother's voice. Michael even begins to initiate coos when he sees his mother come into view.

Hearing coos is itself exhilarating for most parents, but there's an added benefit. Babies begin to engage in reciprocal imitation: they respond to coo sounds, their parents make similar coos. This is called vocal tennis, and it is a sign that the baby is tuning in to his parents. At 3 months the overriding limitation to vocal tennis is that the baby can only echo sounds that are already part of his repertoire. If a baby can produce *ooh* but not *uh*, then he'll imitate *ooh* but not *uh*.

Social

For the past few weeks Michael has smiled every so often; and when he was attentive, his mother could occasionally elicit a smile from him. However, no matter how hard his parents tried, Michael did not smile consistently. Now when he sees his mother or father, he breaks into a smile. Neither parent has to coax Michael to be blessed with a grin. This spontaneous smile is called the social smile.

With the social smile, barriers to social exchanges melt away. The baby is besieged by people competing to be the recipient of his warm smile. They tickle, they babble, they laugh, and they cajole. This competition provides the baby with a first-class schoolroom for exercising social skills.

Emotions

The social smile shows that the baby feels a pleasurable emotion when she is with people. At first, she smiles indiscriminately, beaming at almost anyone who comes nearby. She hasn't yet formed feelings about familiar people as opposed to less familiar ones. Later, when she begins to make these distinctions, her smiles will be directed to the people who are most often around her. But for now, she smiles, coos, and moves her body excitedly with enjoyment and pleasure when anyone talks or smiles to her.

At about 3 months emerge behaviors indicating that the baby experiences displeasure as well as pleasure. Ann cries when she is seemingly bored or frustrated. These cries of displeasure sound different from cries that have a distinctly physiological origin, such as digestive upsets. However, it can be difficult for parents to figure out what is disturbing the baby. As time passes the reasons for negative emotions will become more obvious, and parents will find it easier to respond to the baby's distress. For now, the important point from a developmental standpoint is that a repertoire of emotions is developing. Ann's primitive vocalizations communicate that she has wants, needs, pleasures, and displeasures.

❧ Developmental Close-up

Becoming Aware of Others

The psychological growth of babies is most evident in interactions with others. Michael's behaviors show that he clearly enjoys being part of social activity. In turn, his responsiveness acts like a magnet to his parents, who actively try to get him to respond again and again. His engaging social smile entices others to talk and play.

The more these pleasant interactions occur, the more babies seem to enjoy them. The plus side is that both parents and the baby get an emotional lift from being with each other. The negative side is that the baby will object to being left alone and will cry. This crying is not a sign of being "spoiled"; it's an indication that the baby is a person who likes social contact.

Although babies don't have to be taught to enjoy social interactions, they do need help in learning how to modulate their pleasures and displeasures. A 3-month-old easily becomes overexcited. Then he frets. Parents often intuitively know how to handle this. If the baby starts to fret, parents assume a more subdued air and soothe by talking softly and caressing. When the baby is quiet, parents make attempts to reinstate smiling by raising their voices, making more animated facial expressions, and exaggerating their body movements. Parents' distinct sequences of arouse, soothe, arouse, soothe are one way babies get practice in how to control their emotions so that they can maintain social interaction.

Parents also have a profound influence on the baby's continued interest in social interactions. As early as 3 months babies are bothered when parents' smiles are replaced by frowns or other unhappy expressions. An example is a mother who now looks worried because of family troubles when previously she often smiled at her baby.

A researcher who was studying mother-and-baby interactions asked mothers of 3-month-olds to be unreactive and still-faced instead of animated. Typically, the babies initially cooed to their mothers but gave up and turned away when they saw that their mothers were not responding. In another study, mothers were asked to briefly simulate a depressed state by not touching their babies, speaking in a monotone, and otherwise being inactive. Babies of 3 months responded to these behaviors by crying and looking away.

Does all this mean that a 3-month-old knows a person's habitual mood or even the sequence of a daily routine? Unlikely. What seems to be happening is that a 3-month-old is simply building some elementary associations between behaviors emitted by himself and behaviors of another, and vice versa. A smile should beget a smile, and a cry should bring a parent. Smiles now greeted with frowns or being ignored are unexpected events and unpleasant to the baby. He reacts the only way he can—by turning away or crying. Don't worry if the baby frets once in a while if you are having a bad day!

Infant Memory

What would our lives be like if we could never remember an event, a favored memento, a loved one? It's difficult even to imagine such a state. Our memories are incredibly detailed and complex and tied to a multitude of experiences. Much of what we remember is linked to our thoughts and words, although we also hold some vivid memories of feelings, scents, or tastes.

Very young babies probably have memories of odors (for example, the mother's body scent on a pillow), their caregivers, the ways they are touched and soothed, and the taste of milk and juice. However, it's likely that these remembrances are quickly lost, because babies can't use words or ideas as a way to hold on to them. Babies do remember events that repeatedly occur in tandem such as food in a bottle, mother's footsteps, father's touch. Displeasure at disruption of these events is one piece of evidence scientists use to support the idea that very young babies do have some form of memory.

As adults, we retrieve information from our memories in several ways. Sometimes we access information when presented with a specific, though circumstantial, cue: a familiar face prompts retrieving a name. We also use planned cues, such as shopping lists or reminders taped to refrigerator doors. Finally, we actively recall things without cues of any kind. "What did my sister tell me yesterday?" we ask ourselves, and somehow we access this information.

Young babies can use only cued memory. Scientists call this type of recollecting recognition memory. Research suggests that around 3 months of age recognition memory develops fairly rapidly. Babies now have recognition memory for simple visual shapes and uncomplicated sounds.

Simple but ingenious techniques are used to test the baby's recognition memory. One test involves showing the baby a two-dimensional drawing (a black-and-white circle), measuring the amount of time he looks at the circle, and then removing the circle after an established period of time. The drawing is kept out of sight for a set interval and then presented again to the baby. This sequence is repeated many times, and each time the amount of looking time is carefully measured. With an awake and alert baby, the amount of looking time decreases each time the drawing is re-presented. The drawing activates the baby's memory of circle; the baby looks less because he "remembers" the circle from past exposures and no longer finds it a novel stimulus. Scientists call this process habituation, which simply means that as something becomes more familiar we pay less attention to it. The key to inferring that the baby has memory is that something can become familiar only if one can remember it.

Researchers have demonstrated that some memories of 3-month-olds may last a week and that other memories can be reactivated and may last for two weeks or more. In one series of studies, a colorful mobile was hung in the baby's crib. A ribbon was connected from the mobile to one of the baby's legs. The baby was allowed a certain amount of time in which moving his leg jiggled the mobile; and in due course, most babies learned that kicking their legs controlled the movement of the mobile. The researcher recorded the number of kicks when the mobile was present and again when the mobile was absent.

Did the baby remember that his kicking is associated with a moving mobile? Two, five, seven, or ten days later the baby and the mobile were reunited. The baby's memory was measured by comparing the ratio of kicks that occurred after the re-presentation of the memory (the mobile) to those emitted after the initial training period. If the baby remembered, he should have begun to kick at a higher rate as soon as he saw the mobile.

It turned out that at 3 months, but not at 2 months, babies' kick rates rose when they were re-exposed to the mobile after a few days. However, the 3-month-old's memory faded completely if a week passed before he saw the mobile again. But even though the baby's memory faded, it could be reactivated when he was allowed to see the mobile. How do we know this? If he saw the mobile after a week, and then still later the ribbon was again attached to his foot, he kicked at a fairly high rate—remarkable skills for a baby only three months old!

Memory is a key component of cognition: memory makes additional learning possible. Fortunately, biological heritage ensures that early in development memory is a part of the baby's bag of skills. We have no way of measuring all that a 3-month-old perceives to determine how much is recorded in memory. We just don't know how much babies actually remember overall. We do know that from the third month onward memory abilities grow rapidly, and this growth provides the basis for the development of other cognitive and social skills.

DEVELOPMENTAL OVERVIEW: BIRTH TO THREE MONTHS

Developmental Highlights

	Early Weeks	1 Month
Motor	Fetal position	Reflex movement
Sensation and Perception	Hears, distinguishes strong visual contrasts	Likes to look at faces; scans visually; differentiates speech from other sounds
Vocalization and Language		Makes soft sounds
Cognition		Can tell difference between bottle nipple, breast nipple, thumb, and pacifier
Social and Emotional	Not sociable; distress cry	Alert when talked to; irritable by late afternoon

HOW TO BE HELPFUL

Do not overstimulate. Use pastel colored sheets. Use one or two toys as opposed to a cribful. Avoid bright lights. Keep TV volume low.

Cuddle and carry the baby when she cries in distress.

Talk to the baby whenever he is alert.

	2 Months	3 Months
Motor	Lifts head and shoulders off mattress	Fingers toys; holds head up for extended time; plays with fingers; kicks actively
Sensation and Perception	Likes to hear sounds with different intonations; tracks objects visually from side to side	Sustains alertness; sees objects clearly; begins to localize sounds
Vocalization and Language	Participates in mini-conversations; imitates a short string of vowel sounds	Coos
Cognition	Anticipates: stops crying at sight of breast/bottle	Recognition (cued) memory; reacts to newness with body stiffening; quiets at sight of interesting toy
Social and Emotional	Makes eye contact; smiles faintly; mildly aroused by sight of toy	Smiles broadly and often; cries when bored

WHEN TO SEEK HELP (BEHAVIORS AT THE END OF 3 MONTHS)

Does not lift head at all

Does not respond at all to social overtures

Makes no facial expressions

Is largely inattentive to objects

Does not respond to any sound

Four to Seven Months
PREVIEW

❧

During this period the baby celebrates the emergence of a whole new dimension of being: his physiological processes are complemented by more capable psychological processes. This change transforms the baby from primarily a physical person with a few hard-earned motor and social skills into a more mentally alert, sociable person who is busy "doing, thinking, and feeling." His curious, attentive, and merry disposition reflect his enthusiasm for his awakening mental abilities. In fact, by the end of this period he is so genuinely delighted by being able to participate in social interactions that he tries to keep these exchanges going.

Improvements in the baby's visual perception make many of these developments possible. A particularly important advance is that his acuity now closely approximates the abilities of an adult. Now that he can actually see clearly, there are many things in his surroundings that he seems to feel he needs to examine more closely. His better sight helps guide his reach so that he can in fact take hold of and investigate objects that interest him. Improved perceptual abilities also help him distinguish familiar people, and he begins to develop a slight preference for his caregivers.

The baby's fine motor skills develop to the point that he can pick up many objects, though small items still elude him.

By the end of this period he can hold a toy in one hand. Gross motor skills are coming on line really rapidly, and by the time he's 7 months old, he can sit unassisted, stand with help, and occasionally crawl for a few moments.

By and large, throughout this period the baby is an enthusiastic explorer, and as he approaches the end of this phase of development, he becomes more receptive to social games. Actively investigating his surroundings and playing games with caregivers helps advance his nascent mental abilities in several ways. His attention improves. Increased sensitivity to his surroundings helps him develop additional expectations about events. He displays very basic communication skills; that is, he is getting better at coordinating gestures and vocalizations to indicate that he wants to be moved or needs something to eat.

The experience of having expectations and the excitement that goes along with being involved in social play make the baby pretty happy. However, his development also gives rise to occasional disappointments. The baby's pleasant disposition sometimes decomposes into anger and frustration when he sees something he wants but cannot get because he is not yet physically adept enough.

At these times his body tenses and quivers in dismay, and he lets out the time-honored caregiver annoyance, the cry. Sometimes during these months, he can be a real stickler about routines, and he frets or whines at disruptions in regularly scheduled events. Fortunately, the baby is easily soothed. So while his displays of discomfort may be more frequent, before the last month in this interval parents' care and comfort can quickly bring them to an end.

Overall, these four months are an exciting time for the baby and for parents. Being able to do more things with his hands, briefly experiencing the thrill of self-locomotion, participating in entertaining social events, and having the ability to get attention when he needs help to reach a toy are all developments that please the baby. From time to time now, there is physical discomfort from teething, and then the usually merry boy can be a testy little person. But with enough emotional support from his caregivers, this little boy is up to facing these physical challenges.

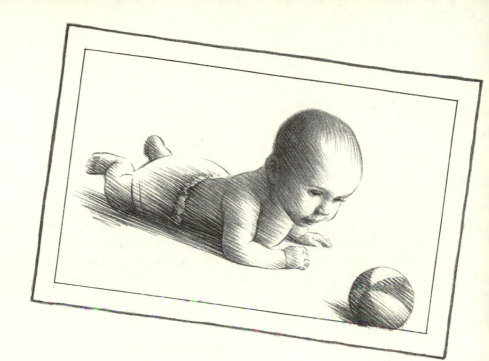

Four Months

rolls from tummy onto back

reaches tentatively

hears soft sounds

initiates smile to familiar people

Average Boy: *Length is 25 inches, with most between 23.5 and 26.5 inches. Weight is 14.5 pounds, with most between 12+ and 17 pounds.*
Average Girl: *Length is 24.5 inches, with most between 22.5+ and 25.5 inches. Weight is 13+ pounds, with most between 11 and 16 pounds.*

❧ Snapshot

Among the changes that occur this month, four stand out: the baby is more energetic; she uses her hands more and more; she holds miniconversations with people and with her toys; she shows definite signs of anger every now and then.

The baby's general peppiness is particularly evident in interactions with people. She stares alertly when talked to, responds with coos, then stops cooing and waits to be talked to again. She's keenly interested in some of her toys and coos to them from time to time. The baby's increased energy and animation result from consistently improving sleep habits and digestion, better vision and hearing, increasing freedom from constraints imposed by reflexes, and greater strength in neck, shoulder, and chest muscles.

Whereas hand play captured the baby's interest last month, attempting to reach for toys is the passion this month. When 4-month-old Ann is propped in her infant seat, her arms lie still at her sides. Her father brings her a small toy rattle and slowly shakes it. Ann's arms pump up and down, her lips open, she breathes heavily, she coos and gurgles, she kicks her legs, and her arms reach out with big, fast movements. She's working out! With help, Ann's hands touch the rattle every so often.

A month earlier, the baby was perfectly content to be held and talked to for hours on end, but now her behaviors show that she wants to do other things as well. While being held, she suddenly squirms, trying to make contact with a toy. It is clear that at this moment she wants to touch a toy more than she wants to coo and smile to a person. The baby's world is expanding. People and toys are both important to her. Parents can help the baby learn more about toys by providing a few interesting playthings and a bright, quiet corner where the baby can reach for and look at her toys. She doesn't want to be left alone, though!

From now on developmental changes assume greater significance. This month a baby's new behaviors are not only specific developmental advances, such as reaching, the advances also support the growth of other behaviors. Improved skill in one area of functioning helps another area become more effective. Each change is a stepping stone for others.

For example, around 4 months head control and visual attention begin to work together and thus improve each skill area even more. It happens this way. This month the baby's head control is quite good, whereas before she really had to work to prevent her head from sagging. She doesn't have to expend as much effort keeping her head up, so she channels this energy elsewhere. Some of the energy goes toward exploring more distant objects in her room. Ann looks intently and repeatedly at the table, a chair, and her windows. As she looks, she's beginning to learn more about the shape and color of the objects in her surrounding space.

Because Ann can hold up her head relatively well, her visual perception gets better. She looks around longer, clearly sees objects that are across the room, and becomes able to distinguish additional shapes and forms. Turning her head this way and that exercises her neck muscles and helps reinforce head control. This cycle of feedbacks continually improves the baby's motor and visual skills. But something else is also happening. Ann is taking in new information; she is learning. Her cognitive skills are improving along with her motor and perceptual skills.

Despite all these behavioral advances, every once in a while 4-month-olds remind us that they are still very, very young. They become overloaded with sights and sounds, and they wear themselves out working so hard to reach their toys. And then they become irritable. Some days they can't seem to maintain their alertness, they don't smile and coo very much, and sleep doesn't come easily. Being held is the only thing that reduces their discomfort, and some nights an extra feeding helps.

❧ *Images of Development*

Motor

Overall, 4-month-olds are much stronger than they were just a month ago. Back muscles are more active, legs are beginning to show some sturdiness, and arms move vigorously when reaching for a toy. In fact, the baby is strong enough now to roll over.

Neck muscles that were so fragile a short time ago are stronger this month, and head control is sustained whether the baby is on his tummy or his back or held upright. On his tummy, Michael raises his head to a 90-degree angle to the mattress and holds this position for minutes at a time. When he is on his back and his arms are gently pulled to raise him into a sitting position, he tries to help by lifting his head and shoulders just a bit.

The baby's trunk muscles are strong enough for him to roll over from his tummy to his back. The first rolling over can happen any time now, so the baby can't be left unattended on a bed. Like most new behaviors, rolling over just happens one day. Michael likes the feel of this new activity and tries to repeat it. After he has repeated it once, he soon gets the hang of it and rolls over often. But once he gets on his back, he's stuck; he doesn't have enough back strength to roll over from back to tummy, and this irritates him.

His back is also still too weak to maintain an unsupported sitting position. His fetal position is gradually disappearing, but just below the shoulder girdle his back is still gently rounded. He needs a bit more lower back strength for unpropped sitting.

At 4 months the baby shows that he is keen to get on with moving all parts of his body on his own. He stretches his legs out when he is lying on his tummy, and he makes slow stair-steplike movements when he is held upright. These stepping movements are far more controlled actions than the reflex movements he displayed as a younger baby.

Michael's reach is guided by his vision: he looks at his hands while they move toward a toy. Later on he will bypass looking at his hands and look directly at the toy he wants. For now, he's taking the time and practice he needs to make his hands and eyes work together efficiently.

About half the time Michael approaches toys with both hands, the other half with either the right or left hand. If he successfully grasps a toy, it may be for just a few seconds. Sometimes he can bring the toy close to his eyes for inspection and then move it to his mouth to suck on it. Other times he holds the toy with one hand and fingers it momentarily with the other, looking all the while. At this age Michael needs to direct all of his visual attention to hold onto the toy. If he is distracted at all, he drops the toy. But he is persistent and tries again, and in a month or two his persistence will pay off. He will be able to hold onto two toys at the same time, although very briefly.

Even though the 4-month-old's grasp is still immature, it is good enough for him to hold on to a 1-inch cube or a small rattle. He primarily uses his palm and cupped fingers. Smaller objects, such as a pellet-sized piece of cracker, still elude him. At 4 months his fingers are not very flexible and his thumb is not yet mobile: it does not move independently of his fingers or hand. Despite these limitations, Michael scratches the

Hint

A few simple toys can help the baby practice his grasp. A small rattle with a handle, a rubber ring that fits into his hand, and a small lightly stuffed doll are examples of toys that encourage grasping in babies of this age.

table top, clutches at a cloth or a part of his body, and rubs his head with his fist. But when he touches and grabs a part of his body, it seems as if he mistakes his body for another toy; he does not seem to understand that it is he that causes the touch.

Sensation and Perception

❧   *Vision.* At 2 months it was necessary to coax the baby into an attentive state in order to get her to look at a toy. Sometimes the enticement worked, other times it did not. Now attention is rapt and sustained for minutes on end. Sometimes attention is so intense that the baby seems to be trying to commit a view to memory.

Looking behavior with toys differs from visual attention to people. Toys elicit sustained concentration, whereas attention to people involves repeated sequences of looks and turning away. There's a reason for the different looking behaviors. A toy has a finite number of stimulating attributes: color, shape, possibly movement, and perhaps a repetitive sound. The baby's visual skills handle these stimuli without any difficulty.

People, on the other hand, represent a complex spectacle made up of ever-changing stimuli. Heads bob up and down, faces smile or frown, mouths show teeth or are closed, and voice sounds are variable—soft, loud, shrill, deep. Even a person's trunk and limbs move periodically, and fingers move constantly. Inadvertently, people can be information overload for a 4-month-old. Babies often turn away briefly simply to take a break from all this sensory stimulation. Once they regain composure, they return to look intently. For the baby a person is the equivalent of a complicated, flashing neon sign that is fun and exciting to look at. But even adults must turn away momentarily from the intensity of neon's color and movement.

A baby of 4 months can see colors, differentiate shapes, distinguish sizes, and detect movement, and now begins to recognize differences in texture. She sees little objects that are nearby and bigger objects that are at a distance. And she seems to prefer red and blue over other colors.

Studies of babies' visual perception show that while 4-month-olds see distinctly, they focus on parts of an object rather than on the whole. The baby will be mesmerized by the face and hair of a rag doll and never attend to its body or feet. The doll for the baby is the head and nothing else.

❧   *Hearing.* This month the baby is better able to hear soft sounds. Ann hears tip-toe steps and the rustle of paper being crumpled. She's curious about sounds and will turn to look at the place where a noise came from.

Ann is a keen listener to human speech and behaves as if she were suddenly aware of the nuances of spoken language. Studies show that she is more responsive to infant-directed speech than to the typical conversational speech adults use with each other. Most of us talk to babies using exaggerated intonations and changes of pitch, a sure way to get their attention.

Vocalizations and Language

The baby now coos often and plays with sounds as if they were toys. She repeats sounds over and over sometimes with minor variations in intonation. This month consonants appear in the baby's speech, primarily *m, k, g, p,* and *b.* There is nothing magical about these letters—they are just the easiest for the baby to produce physically. Sometimes the baby will combine a consonant with a vowel: "Aah, gaa."

Although crying won't disappear for a long time, on balance 4-month-olds cry less than younger babies. One reason is that they are visually and motorically more competent and so are better able to distract themselves. They do cry when bored and frustrated, when they want attention, and when they are just plain overloaded with sights and sounds. Many babies of this age have clearly different cry sounds now for hunger and sleepiness, so it is easier for parents to respond to crying. Whimpers substitute now for coughs and grunts as a means of attracting attention, and seeing mother may elicit a whimper simply because it brings her to the baby.

Cognition

This month, not only does the baby reach out to touch toys, she also begins to use her hands to investigate anything she can touch. Her probes are tentative; she just barely touches the fingertips to a toy. (It will be another four months or so before she engages in sustained play.) As slight as these finger movements are, they help the baby make more discriminations about toys. Touching also benefits her visual explorations because touch and vision combined help her sustain her attention. Toy play gives the baby's nascent cognitive skills daily practice.

Last month the baby showed signs of anticipation when familiar and highly routine events occurred. This month these skills get better. Ann shows anticipation as soon as she sees a cue for an everyday occurrence. She opens her mouth upon seeing a bottle, and she makes wriggling movements when first propped for feeding as if she is itchy for her food.

Social

This month the social smile becomes even more social. The baby consistently smiles in response to another's smile and frequently initiates a smile to a familiar person. When smiling becomes selective, the baby acknowledges that some people are recognized and familiar, a milestone in social awareness.

The first step in feeling close to someone is learning to distinguish one person from another. If Michael sometimes fusses and whimpers when his mother or father leaves him in his crib, he is signaling that he is beginning to understand that some people make him feel good. Moreover, when Michael ever so slightly raises his arms as if inviting someone to lift him, he is indicating that he is becoming tuned in to people. He is beginning to distinguish and seek out social experiences that bring him pleasure.

Michael also begins to initiate a gamelike social interaction. It goes like this. Michael rolls over from tummy to back and then cries because he doesn't like being on his back. At the sound of crying, Michael's mother appears, and seeing the baby on his back, she shifts him onto his stomach. Michael looks at his mother, gives her a little smile, and promptly rolls to his back again. The smile is his way of keeping his mother interested in the game.

Emotions

The baby's range of emotions is expanding. She laughs at certain sounds and tickles, and anticipation of familiar

Hint

Watch for signs of anticipation from your baby. She may open her mouth when she sees you or she may pump her arms. Give her time to display these little anticipatory cues and then talk to her: "Hi, little one. I know you see me and it's time for lunch," and so on. The point is to let her know that you have received her message. She won't understand your words, but she will learn that you are responding to her after she has initiated a signal to you.

events brings happy gurgles. It is not hard to tell when she finds something pleasing. The baby also demonstrates something akin to anger when frustrated.

A 4-month-old also begins to be more aware of others' negative facial expressions. She knits her brows and puts on a downcast expression if she encounters a sad expression when she anticipated a smile. She clearly distinguishes the facial expressions of happy and sad, but this does not mean that she necessarily understands the meaning of these emotions. Researchers are divided on just when a baby begins to comprehend the feelings that accompany facial expressions. Nevertheless, for whatever reason, a familiar caregiver's happy face does seem to make the baby feel good.

❧ Developmental Close-up

Grasping Abilities

Most of us don't think consciously of our hands as tools, but they are. Hundreds of times each day, our hands serve us: they make our bodies presentable to others, assuage our hunger, commit ideas to paper, play chess, knit a sweater, set a table, and give love. Although we share with nonhuman primates the ability to grasp, we are the only species that has a truly opposable thumb, a thumb that can move in an arc around the palm and the tip of which can meet the tip of any one of the fingers. These movements provide the extraordinary hand precision that is a characteristic of many of our everyday activities. We can button the tiniest of buttons, pick up the crumb or bread dropped on the floor, and take hold of the strand of hair that has blown across our eyes.

Let's look at the baby's development of grasp. The story starts with a strong body foundation to support the baby's arm and hand. At around 4 months the baby's shoulder girdle is strong enough to support the combined weight of his arm and hand. His upper trunk is strong enough so that it won't collapse when the baby's arm moves out.

Mechanically, then, the act of reaching is possible. At this time something else occurs that helps the development, and that is the inhibition of the grasp reflex. Now the baby can reach and can also produce on his own a primitive form of grasp. Thus, when toys are dangled in front of him, he is able to reach out and move his fingers over the object. His fingers have very sensitive nerve endings, and they provide feedback about the characteristics of things he touches: this thing is soft, that thing is hard. This kind of feedback helps the baby learn about the properties of objects.

Initially when the baby holds a toy, it is his palms rather than his fingers that do most of the holding. And it is primarily the little finger side of the palm that is involved. This palm grasp is precarious, not very accurate, and requires a great deal of baby energy to use. Gradually the baby's grasp begins to involve more of the thumb side of the palm, and after several weeks the baby actually holds a toy between thumb and palm.

But his grasp looks like the grasp of a chimpanzee: the thumb makes contact with the side rather than the tip of the forefinger. This "scissors grasp" is useful and functional, but it's not perfect. Try picking up a small safety pin with a scissors grasp!

The true finger tip grasp is the most precise grasp of all, enabling us to engage in very precise and delicate tasks. This wonderful fine motor skill, one of the last steps in biology's contribution to grasp development, comes about when the baby's thumb rotates away from his hand and his thumb and forefinger tips can meet, making a letter O—at about 10 to 11 months. Now the baby needs practice to become really skilled in using the fingertip grasp, and he gets it every day by playing with toys and learning to pick up a bit of food and bring it to the mouth.

The development of grasp takes about half a year. As the baby approaches his first birthday, grasp will be accompanied by the ability to voluntarily release objects. These two skills, grasp and release, prepare the baby for learning specific hand skills, such as holding a spoon, cutting with scissors, and building a sand castle. When you look at the dexterity of a 4-year-old as he constructs a toy robot, it can be hard to remember the 4-month-old who struggled so hard to take hold of the mobile in his crib.

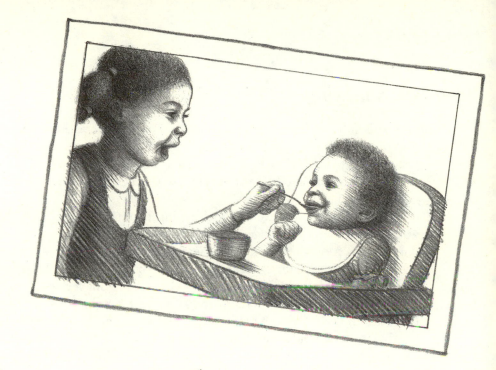

Five Months

wiggles on tummy

makes incipient crawling movements

follows another's gaze

imitates caregiver's vocal intonations

smiles at self in mirror

Average Boy: Length is 26 inches, with most between 24.5 and 27 inches.
Weight is 16+ pounds, with most between 13+ and 18.5 pounds.
Average Girl: Length is 25+ inches, with most between 24 and 26.5 inches.
Weight is 14.5 pounds, with most between 12 and 17 pounds.

❧ Snapshot

The 5-month-old is an explorer, sensitive to and interested in his surroundings. He goes beyond simply looking and touching; he carefully and systematically observes faces and toys. He is equally interested in his own and others' sounds, and he stays quite still so that he can listen closely to the noises around him.

Michael's curiosity extends to learning about his body. He closely watches his hands and fingers as he grasps, rubs, and strokes toys. He purposefully moves the back of his head back and forth against his mattress as if confirming the existence of a body part that he cannot see. He is particularly captivated by his legs, repeatedly raising one leg and then the other when he is held in a standing position. Lying on his back, he sometimes brings his feet toward his face, reaches out and grabs a foot, struggles to bring the foot to his mouth, and occasionally actually nibbles on his toes.

At this age Michael is becoming less distracted by intrusions. Until now his attention was often at the mercy of the comings and goings of his high-spirited sister, and a sisterly disruption meant the end of Michael's self-initiated play. Now he handles her interruptions fairly easily. For example, while Michael flings his arms at a mobile, his sister thrusts a teddy bear in front of his face. He turns toward her, looks at the bear with interest, smiles at his sister, and turns back to his mobile. He can ignore the distraction because of his improved ability to focus and control his attention. When babies control their attention, learning becomes easier.

Michael seems to sense his expanding abilities, and now, when he can't do something, he clearly indicates his frustration. Mentally willing but physically unable to crawl, he is sometimes thwarted in his efforts to get nearer to interesting things he sees. In a valiant effort to get to an interesting toy, he perches on his tummy, elevates his arms and legs, and "swims" rapidly. But this physical exertion is all for naught, and he often breaks out with a loud "Aaaaah." Everything about his actions says, "I want!"

When Michael is relatively calm, he is more skilled at sending signals to others, and at these times he simultaneously seeks eye contact and makes noises (grunts, laughs, coughs) as if to say, "Come here, please!" He is learning that gestures combined with sounds other than cries work well at getting another person's attention.

The 5-month-old seems so capable that it is easy to imagine that he has all kinds of mental abilities. He doesn't. Watch when something appears in a new guise: he is thoroughly bewildered. It takes him a while to realize that his father is the same person even without his mustache or that his sister is still his sister, though her long, straight hair is now a mass of frizzy curls. After drinking orange juice exclusively from a bottle, Michael registers surprise when he is given orange juice in a mug. He seems amazed to discover that orange juice is orange juice, whether it comes in a bottle, cup, or glass.

❧ *Images of Development*

Motor

At this age, the baby's neck, shoulder, and upper chest muscles are sturdy, her back is almost fully straight from head down to hips, and her abdominal muscles are firm to the touch. When 5-month-old Ann lies on her tummy, these strengthened muscles help her support the upper part of her body.

Ann rolls over from tummy to back and back to tummy. She makes incipient crawling movements, precursors of the conventional crawl that will appear at about 7 months. Sitting on her own is still difficult, because she still doesn't have the required trunk strength and postural control. On rare occasions she does manage to sit alone momentarily, but she soon flops over.

Around 5 months of age, reaching is most often accompanied with one arm, although two-arm reaches do still occur. Overall, Ann's reach is less variable this month, in part because it is now almost always visually guided. She still flings her arms now and then because she is not always able to anticipate the minute arm adjustments that are required for a precisely guided reach. Amazingly, though, when she reaches toward a rolling toy car, she is usually fairly adept at adjusting the pace of her reach to the toy's speed. She is beginning to coordinate the act of reaching with her visual awareness of movement.

Ann approaches most toys with a push–pull scraping action, with her palms and fingers cupped as she attempts to adjust her hand to the shape

> ## *Hint*
>
> Play a game with the baby by slowly moving a small ball or toy car along a table top. Sit her comfortably in front of the table top so that she can see the toys clearly and perhaps reach for them as well.

of a toy. She grasps as well as she can and is undeterred by failures. She has considerable difficulty with small objects (a bit of cracker), and although she repeatedly makes scratching movements, her attempts are usually in vain. Uncoordinated finger movements are the reason she cannot pick up small items.

At 5 months, babies are sufficiently skilled in handling toys to free up attention that previously went to monitoring the act of grasping. When Ann succeeds in grasping a toy, she visually inspects it, smiles and talks to it, and then takes it to her mouth for a short examination with her lips. If Ann has two toys in front of her, she manages to hold one while looking at the other. However, this is the limit of her coordination of attention and grasp: if two toys are placed in her hands, she invariably drops one.

Late in the month, Ann begins to transfer a toy from one hand to the other and to lift a cup by wrapping her hands around it. Considering that she only gained control of her hands a short while ago, these actions are quite an achievement and demonstrate the growth of her hand-eye coordination.

These hand activities are important preludes to actual toy play. In about two months Ann will purposefully and gleefully fling toys from a table top. Another month after that she will studiously examine a toy by turning it over and over in her hands.

Sensation and Perception

✿ *Vision.* Vision is still getting sharper and clearer, and the baby begins to pay attention to smaller and less obvious things, such as a little piece of paper lying on the floor or a particular facial feature such as a parent's nose. The baby continues to be fascinated by movement. In fact, movement so intrigues the 5-month-old that, given the choice between an interesting or motionless toy and a less interesting toy that moves, the baby chooses to look at the moving toy.

The baby's perception of depth is also improving. Evidence for this comes from studies that suggest that babies of this age can distinguish a three-dimensional object, for example a teddy bear, from a picture of the object. Other studies show that the baby recognizes a face, whether he observes it in a right-side-up position or upside down. When the baby is able to recognize an object regardless of its spatial orientation, scientists say that the baby has acquired a skill called form constancy.

✿ *Hearing.* The 5-month-old listens quietly to others' conversations, and Michael's attention is easily captured by baby talk that is address specifically to him. Michael also distinguishes between phrases that reflect approval and those that signify disapproval. He invariably reacts with signs of pleasure to positive speech and becomes sober at the sound of negative speech. His different facial expressions reveal that he is discriminating sounds and sights in his surroundings.

Michael's facial responses to different sound qualities may reflect a primitive understanding of emotions or they may simply be a genetically programmed reaction to the more melodious sound features of positive speech. Scientists do not agree about this. In any event, the 5-month-old's attention to the details of speech helps him become familiar with the language used by people in his culture.

Vocalizations and Language

Consonant sounds (*agu, grr*) are more varied and more frequent this month. The baby's vocalizations also show a drift toward the language of the baby's cultural environment; that is, his intonation and the relative length of his utterances sound more and more like those of his caregivers.

Although the changes in the baby's early vocal production are strongly influenced by a biological game plan, the shaping of the baby's actual sounds largely depends on the speech he hears. In other words, without conscious awareness of what he is doing, the baby shapes his vocalizations so that they resemble the rhythm of the sentences spoken by his caregivers. At 5 months of age, a baby reared in the United States by English-speaking parents and a baby reared in China by Chinese-speaking parents both make consonant sounds, but the melody of their vocalizations already differs.

Hint

Talk to your baby, and then talk some more! Give him a chance to join in; hold a brief conversation with him.

Cognition

An interesting behavior emerges this month, in which the baby visually follows an object that moves out of her line of vision. This behavior is seen quite often in the baby's play. Ann is playing with her rattle when it falls out of her hand, and she turns her head to watch the rattle descend to the floor.

Visual pursuit behavior, which seems so simple, suggests that Ann understands that a moving rattle is still a rattle. This intuitive understanding of the constancy of an object when in motion and when still probably helps the baby become more sensitive to specific features of objects and people. We cannot say for certain that this is one value of visual pursuit, but it is true that this behavior emerges at the same time recognition memory time is lengthening. In fact, some studies suggest that babies now remember certain illustrations, such as pictures of faces, as long as two weeks.

Social

A social counterpart to visual pursuit appears now: the baby follows another person's gaze. Ann is sitting on her father's lap, and they are looking at each other. Her father is telling Ann about her new cereal bowl, and, while talking to her, he glances away from her to look at the bowl. Ann has been watching her father's eyes, and as he turns to view the bowl, she shifts her gaze in tandem with his. Gaze following involves attention, and it helps the baby practice controlling her visual focus. This gaze behavior also introduces her to the idea of using her vision to secure information from her caregivers. In a few months babies will unambiguously look to a caregiver's face for cues when they are in new situations.

> ## Hint
>
> Hold the baby in your lap and simultaneously look at something interesting, point to it, and talk about it. Move slowly and try to assist the baby in following your gaze. She'll catch on eventually.

When a 5-month-old matches her looking behavior to that of her caregiver, she signals to others that she can be influenced in a new way. Parents pick up on this cue and make adjustments in their own actions to facilitate the baby's learning. Ann's parents now hold her so that she can look in the same direction as they are looking. They glance more often to an object they are talking about to assist her in making associations between the words they are saying and the object.

One additional social development occurs this month that is important in the overall scheme of things. Now Ann easily perceives the difference between familiar and unfamiliar people. She sometimes becomes quiet and sober at the sight of strangers, although she does not actually cry. In another two or three months, her distress around strangers will have intensified and her response will be stronger. But for now, she simply signals that something is not quite right by being more silent than usual.

Emotions

Last month laughter materialized, and this month unqualified glee appears. Michael's joy is unbridled when he is playing with toys or with his parents. Unfortunately, as signs of intense pleasure surface, signs of greater displeasure also emerge. Michael's anger displays are joined by expressions of frustration.

Frustration appears as the baby senses his own limitations. When Michael is on his back, something fascinating comes into view some distance away, and he tries to reach it. He wriggles and tries to turn over, but he can't, so he kicks his feet and whimpers. This is the turtle frustration fret, so named by one of my assistants. Michael looks like a turtle that has somehow turned over onto its back and can't right itself again. Everything about the baby's actions communicates, "I want to, but I can't."

> *Hint*
> ──────────
> Comfort the baby when he is frustrated. You won't spoil him.

Sense of Self

Ann now smiles at her image in a mirror. Psychologists have different ideas about why this happens. Some say she is simply reacting to another face. Others suggest that she perceives the face as a familiar person (or object) and this brings on her smile. But some scientists regard this display as a precursor of the development of a sense of self: the smile registers the baby's nascent awareness of her own body. Researchers have not figured out a way to test the validity of these different ideas.

While not everyone agrees about why the baby smiles at her self-image, scientists do agree that the onset of a primitive form of resistance (called oppositional behavior) indicates that the baby is beginning to develop some form of self-awareness. Resistance behaviors begin at around 5 months and show up primarily in two forms. One form involves pushing-

Hint

Babies of all ages love
mirrors. Every once in
a while, hold the baby
in front of a mirror
and talk and smile
while she looks. Later
on she'll figure out that
it really is she
in the mirror.

away hand movements; Ann does this
when she is offered food she doesn't like.
The other occurs when Ann clamps her
mouth shut and turns her head to the
side after tasting something that doesn't
appeal to her. Don't let these resistant
behaviors annoy you. They are a sign of
the baby's growth as a person.

🍂 Developmental Close-up

Pushing, Pivoting, Crawling, and Creeping

I sometimes suggest to my students that
one way to gain a sense of a baby's world
is to get down on all fours and creep.
When students actually do this, they invariably comment about how restricted they feel and how glad they are to be able to walk upright. Creeping
is just not very convenient: eye contact is difficult to maintain, transporting
objects is a real challenge, and the pace restricts how far and fast you can go.
While there are drawbacks to this form of locomotion, at least the baby can
get around to explore far corners of rooms. He smiles and grunts as he
edges along, feeling the freedom that self-locomotion brings.

Creeping comes on-line in a series of developments. First it is an abdomen-elbow movement, and it matures into the form where the abdomen is
off the floor and the arms are straight. The various styles of creeping are
called wiggling, which occurs at about 5 months; pivoting, at about $7\frac{1}{2}$
months; crawling, at 7 to 9 months; and creeping, at 9 to 11 months. Babies
vary considerably in the age at which they begin any of these stages, but
most children crawl at around 7 months and begin creeping about two
months later.

Wiggling occurs when the baby, lying on his tummy, inadvertently
moves his body because his legs kick out and his arms move. In contrast,
pivoting is a circular kind of movement the baby makes while lying with
much of his weight supported by knees, abdomen, and chest. The pivot
point is under the abdomen, and it is the baby's vigorous kicking movements that cause him to move in a roundabout fashion and occasionally

forward or backward. Pivoting is not very efficient, but it does let the baby move his whole body a short distance. More important, pivoting is a purposeful movement that occurs when the baby wants a better view of something.

A month or so after pivoting appears, tentative signs of crawling materialize. Crawling labels the motion in which, with abdomen touching or lying slightly above a supporting surface, the body pushes along as a function of alternate, reciprocal movements of elbows and legs. There is a commando version of crawling in which reciprocal movements of the elbows pull the body forward. In contrast to pivoting, crawling produces appreciable forward and backward activity.

In creeping, the baby's hips are bent, his knees are tucked under the lower abdomen, and his straight arms hold his chest and shoulders well above the level of the floor. The baby moves with hands and lower legs touching the floor. (Some babies creep with their buttocks up in the air and with only their hands and feet touching the floor; they look like an inverted U.) Creeping requires good shoulder strength as well as trunk and hip strength to hold the body above the floor in a stable position. Most babies need some practice in the creeping position before they actually begin moving about. Typically, babies try out the creeping position between 9 and 10 months and start to creep about four weeks later.

"Wait a minute," you might be saying to yourself, "I learned that creeping comes before crawling." Yes, some writers do say that creeping precedes crawling. I follow the terminology of the foremost experts of developmental norms, Arnold Gesell and Nancy Bayley, who have described crawling in terms of the baby on his tummy and creeping with the baby on all four limbs (tummy off of the ground).

Over the years a mystique has arisen about crawling and creeping—probably because these are the baby's first forms of independent locomotion. Some professionals claim that crawling/creeping and reading or crawling/creeping and learning are linked. They assert that babies must crawl in order to avoid later problems with cognitive skills. However, there is no scientific evidence supporting an association between crawling and later educational achievement. In fact, a few babies never crawl, and some hitch around on their buttocks. They are just fine developmentally.

Some parents tell me that they've been advised that babies who do not crawl or creep in a certain way may have a serious motor disorder. It is true that a markedly peculiar style of crawling (such as using only one leg for propulsion and dragging the other) may indicate a serious motor problem. But there would usually have to be signs of other developmental lags in head, shoulder, and/or trunk control for a crawling style to be a sign of permanent impairment.

Scientists have recently become interested again in crawling, creeping, and walking. Their renewed research efforts show that all of these forms of self-produced locomotion are important sources of learning. Babies learn about their bodies as they move around in different postures, positions, and situations. These various experiences also force babies to obtain new information about their surroundings; for example, about space and objects (furniture) in space. They begin to pay attention to the rigid boundaries of a table leg in the middle of the floor or the space beneath a table. Often they monitor distance to people and to toys, which translates into the ability to gauge how to avoid bumping into walls. They learn about surfaces that feel good to crawl on (low-pile carpet) and those that are uncomfortable (sidewalk). A whole new world of textures and tactile sensations is opened up to them.

Self-produced locomotion is a source of never-ending pleasure for babies. Crawling and creeping are tools that help babies learn about their surroundings and about their own bodies. It must also provide them with a nascent sense of mastery and independence. Are there other more tangible effects of self-produced locomotion on a baby's overall development? We do know that babies who have limited movement because of physical impairments may be more irritable for a time than babies who can move at will. We also know that early crawling, creeping, and walking are not associated with later intelligence. The early walker may or may not be the bright child.

Six Months

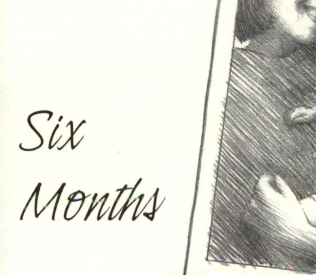

briefly sits without support

transfers toy from hand to hand, and bangs it

develops expectation about familiar event

touches and vocalizes to parent

Average Boy: Length is 26.5+ inches, with most between 25+ and 28 inches.
Weight is 17+ pounds, with most between 14.5 and 20 pounds.
Average Girl: Length is 26 inches, with most between 24.5 and 27+ inches.
Weight is 15.5+ pounds, with most between 13+ and 18.5 pounds.

❧ Snapshot

Every now and then development takes a giant step forward, and the baby suddenly seems far more capable than before. This month is one of these times. There is all-around growth in the baby's skills. The 6-month-old is definitely growing up and is also fun to be around.

Baby Ann is a happy little girl who rejoices exuberantly at the many new things she can do. She chirps, laughs, and often delights others with her cheerful mood and new competencies. Why is she excited? Well, these are her achievements this month:

- rolls over easily and inches forward on her belly
- sits alone momentarily
- supports herself in a standing position when assisted
- distinguishes between male and female voices
- makes sounds that bear resemblance to speech
- learns behaviors that characterize familiar people
- sees almost everything with good vision
- whines for attention

This impressive list of behaviors is ample evidence for labeling this month a pivotal age in early development, but there are even more changes afoot.

Ann's behaviors show that she is learning to integrate her knowledge. She is beginning to make connections between what she sees and what she touches. She has a rudimentary ability to understand and carry out very simple action plans. Ann modulates her own emotions so that they mirror what she sees in familiar people. She watches caregivers' actions and begins to imitate some of their simpler movements. Overall, mental savvy is developing in the 6-month-old at the speed of an SST.

One example of the baby's new competence is her increasing precision at sending messages about what she wants. Now Ann not only recognizes what she wants, she demonstrates from time to time that she can figure out what she needs to do to get what she wants and does it. For example, while Ann is sitting on her mother's lap, she looks directly at her, then at the toy she is holding, and then she lightly touches her mother's hand. Ann is telling her mother that she wants the toy. When her mother responds to her gestures by offering the toy to her, Ann smiles broadly.

Ann's cousin is also up to new tricks. He loves to eat, and now when he's hungry he frets, looks at his mother, and pulls on her shirt if she is nearby. This is a whole new set of behaviors for him, and he displays them only near mealtime. Also when he wants to hear the song "Itsy-Bitsy Spider," while looking at his mother he makes *eh, eh* sounds and raises one of his hands ever so slightly.

Still, at the age of 6 months Ann and her cousin are fairly inexperienced at communication, and sometimes they don't send messages when their parents expect them to. The timing of their messages is sometimes a little off. But it is pretty amazing that they use gestures, eye contact, and nonfretful vocalizations to make their wants known, when just a few months ago the only way they could communicate was to cry.

While the 6-month-old is usually happy, she does cry and shed genuine tears when upset or in pain. Right now teething causes Ann some distress, and this leads to crying during the day as well as to difficulty with nighttime sleep. At this age Ann is intolerant of being kept waiting, and she also becomes distressed when her newly formed expectations about events do not come to pass (for example, mealtime is delayed even though she is already in her feeding chair). On these occasions the baby whines, but thankfully she is still receptive to parents' attempts to comfort her.

All in all, this is an age marked by tremendous growth in the number and complexity of the baby's abilities. Behaviors that seemed to be several months away when the baby was 5 months old suddenly burst onto the scene at 6 months.

Do keep in mind that as more and more behaviors develop, the degree of variability in babies increases. Not every 6-month-old baby shows all the behaviors I describe, and some 6-month-old babies will do things that I haven't mentioned. That's all right. Variability is just part of development.

❧ *Images of Development*

Motor

At 6 months, the baby's trunk is strong enough to support rolling over from back to tummy. He also has the strength to sit alone momentarily, provided he leans forward and plants his arms on the floor to maintain his equilibrium. By the end of the month, his balance improves and he sits straighter and for longer periods of time, sometimes even holding a toy, without falling over. He stands with assistance and supports most of his body weight on his legs. If he feels secure while he is being held upright, he bounces up and down and makes gleeful noises.

Grasp now requires less conscious effort. The baby reaches eagerly for toys, and his efforts invoke fewer extraneous body movements. Michael makes anticipatory adjustments of his hand so that his grasp accommodates the size and shape of objects. He sometimes miscalculates where he should be reaching, but he persists in his efforts until he is able to grasp the object he wants. Michael can now hold onto a toy in each hand and easily transfers toys from one hand to the other.

Hint

Provide a few toys that have different shapes, sizes, and textures. Rotate some of the toys every week or so; babies of this age get bored with the same playthings. Make sure that none of the toys can be swallowed. A rule of thumb is that no toy should be smaller than the baby's fist.

At the beginning of the month, grasp primarily involves holding a toy between the first and second fingers and the palm. As the month progresses, Michael begins to use his thumb in concert with his fingers, but small objects still elude his grasp; he resorts to scooping at small objects with his whole hand.

As Michael's hand coordination improves, he is even more inclined to try to bring objects to his mouth. While this creates parent concerns about safety, oral exploration is a source of many learning experiences. The lips and tongue have sensitive nerve endings, and the baby can get to know the finer features of texture and shape by mouthing objects. Since the baby attempts this maneuver with anything he can grasp, parents have to take special precautions to see that small objects are out of his reaching range.

Sensation and Perception

Vision. For a while now, 6-month-old Ann has been able to visually discriminate the boundary of a toy (the outline of a teddy bear) as well as some of the toy's characteristics (teddy's ears), but she's had difficulty taking on both kinds of information at the same time. Studies show that babies of 6 months easily do this, and researchers infer from the behavior that babies are now beginning to form whole pictures of objects.

With ever-increasing visual skills, babies recognize familiar people more clearly. Accompanying this development, they begin to display mild fretting if a stranger approaches too closely or too quickly. This negative response is often quite brief.

Depth perception has come a long way, and babies of this age readily respond to differences in the distance to objects that surround them. They are also skilled in figuring out the orientation of objects (up, down, or sideways). Overall, researchers have found that the 6-month-old can distinguish one visual pattern from another in a matter of seconds and store this information for periods as long as a few weeks.

Equally impressive is the 6-month-old's ability to combine different kinds of information. The baby makes a connection between the input she receives when looking at an object and the information she gets by touching the same object. In one study babies were given a small square block, but they were prevented from seeing the block in their hand. While they were holding the block, they were shown drawings of a square and a circle. The babies looked more often at the drawing of the square than the drawing of the circle, suggesting that they recognized that this image resembled the object they held. This coordination of vision and touch means that the baby no longer always has to look at the things she handles to figure out what they are.

🌿 *Hearing.* At 6 months, babies have a keen interest in a variety of sounds. Babies seem most attuned to loudness, intonation, and other acoustic cues. Because music has complex sounds, babies tend to listen intently to nursery songs, music on the radio and TV, and the sounds of instruments.

The baby also distinguishes male and female voices; she expects a female voice to go with a female person and a male voice to go with a male person. If this doesn't happen, she registers surprise. The 6-month-old is also remarkably good at identifying the vocal signature of the people who are most often around her.

This sensitivity to everyday sounds has developmental implications for language. The baby's hearing is becoming fine-tuned in a manner that makes her most receptive to the speech sounds of her family's language. For example, Ann lives in an English-speaking family. She hears people around her say words such as *cat* and *tack*, but Ann is not exposed to people speaking Arabic words that include the sound of *tca*. At around 6 months, this lack of exposure has an effect. If we studied Ann's response to sounds,

Hint

One of the best vocal and action games for babies of this age is a performance of "Itsy-Bitsy Spider." Babies enjoy the melody and hand movements.

we would find that she is losing the ability to discriminate the sound *tca*, a sound she had the potential to recognize in earlier months.

This fine-tuning progression happens with babies around the world. Japanese babies, for example, become less able to discriminate *r* sounds because *r* is not a sound in the Japanese language.

Vocalizations and Language

Losing the ability to make certain sound discriminations also fosters the baby's responsiveness to the sounds of his own family's language. This process of sound discrimination contributes to the baby's later productions of sounds that mimic the intonation qualities of the family's language.

The "talk" of babies of about $6\frac{1}{2}$ months is called canonical babbling. It consists of vowels and consonants in a sequence such as *da-da-ga-ga*. The consonants most often used at this age are *g, k, l,* and *d*. Each syllable in a string of babbles is clearly defined and articulated.

Babbles sound like adult conversational speech in both intonation and "sentence" length, and this indicates that the baby is definitely listening to the speech around him. As far as we can tell, babbles do not have any meaning, but obviously babbling is one way for babies to practice forming sounds. Some scientists believe that babbling prepares the baby for speech production by helping him become better aware of his own sounds and how he can make his sounds vary.

Cognition

The 6-month-old has an active mind, and he is busy making many new associations and expectations about his surroundings. For one thing, the baby is constructing an image of a whole person, an image that is more than one or two surface characteristics. Ann knows her father by a combination of his appearance and walk and his voice, touch, and scent. She adores him and his laugh, and she makes special babble sounds that are just for him. Ann greets him with these sounds when he is dressed in jeans, a suit, or a bathrobe and whether he is smiling or frowning.

Much to Ann's surprise, her father approaches her crib one morning without his mustache. It takes her a little while to adjust. Ann is solemn at first and does not utter her usual greeting. After a few minutes she becomes more like her chirpy self, but those who know her well can tell that something is still amiss. Ann needs time to reconfigure her mental picture of her father; after two days, she behaves with her father as she had before he shaved off his mustache.

At 6 months the baby remembers physical features of objects and people. This month she begins to focus on learning how others act and react and how they generally go about doing things. The baby is acquiring knowledge about sequences of behaviors. In a parallel development, the baby is also learning to remember the broad outline of an everyday routine such as mealtime or bathing. We know this learning is taking place because she reacts to changes in scheduled events.

In fact, the 6-month-old is a stickler for routines. Ann has learned when to expect some events to happen, and when they don't, she's not very forgiving. She knows that waking up in the morning is followed by a bottle, a bath, and then breakfast. If these events don't happen this way, Ann frets. She also knows that when she wakes up from her afternoon nap her sister will be there to greet her. Her sister invariably cuddles Ann and plays with her, if only briefly. When her sister stays after school one day for a soccer game, Ann is irritable all afternoon. Her carefully constructed expectations about her sister's homecoming and hugs haven't been realized.

Finally, the awakening of an adaptable intelligence is demonstrated this month by the way the baby uses specific behaviors to express her wants and to get her wants met. The touches, nascent gestures, vocalizations, and body movements the baby uses show that she is beginning to acquire a primitive ability to understand, plan, and execute actions.

Hint

Watch for subtle cues from the baby. Show her that you understand by responding to her signals. This definitely makes her feel good. If she taps your hand, ask yourself if she wants the toy you are holding, or for you to do something with the toy, or to caress her. If she turns to look at you, talk and smile. Let her know the message is received.

Social

At 5 months of age the baby visually followed another person's gaze to an object held in a hand, and now at 6 months he follows another's gaze to an interesting object that is farther away. This activity is the beginning of the development of joint attention and is made possible by the baby's ability to pick up and utilize cues from another person's gaze. Joint attention paves the way for more efficient learning and for sharing more social experiences. "Look at the car," you say to the baby while you point to a car. Your familiar voice causes the baby to stop and pay attention, and now the direction of your head tells him where you want him to focus his gaze. You don't have to physically move the baby to the car so that he will look at it.

The age of 6 months also marks the onset of an elementary form of social imitation. If you bang a toy on a table, the baby will bang a toy. (Babies of this age love to bang toys.) If you smile and move your body toward him, he moves his body ever so slightly toward you. Mimicry behavior develops rapidly over the next six months, and all of it evolves from these first tentative efforts by the baby to be like you.

Emotions

The baby is now beginning to match his emotions to others' emotions. If mother is sad, then the baby is likely to project sadness. The baby probably doesn't know what it means to be sad, but he can perceive and reciprocate the facial expressions associated with this emotion. This coordination of behavior is another example of the baby's overall mental development: he can integrate what he perceives about others' feelings with how he acts.

In terms of a 6-month-old's own emotional displays, he is characteristically a happy little child and wonderfully responsive to people who please him. He shows his pleasure with glee (rocking back and forth, smiling, and laughing), performing solely to make his favorite people also laugh.

His ability to clearly distinguish familiar people makes him a bit more wary of strangers. By and large, though, he doesn't fret in the presence of strangers as long as the situation he's in is familiar or family members are present.

Sense of Self

The baby's self-awareness gets a boost with his focus on lower body parts. Michael kicks his feet and looks at his legs while they move. Or he holds a foot up in the air and carefully inspects it. All the while, his attention is intense, as if he is creating an internal model of his own body. Of course, we cannot know what the 6-month-old is actually thinking; scientists can only speculate about the baby's actions and the development of self.

❧ Developmental Close-up

Developing an Expectation About an Event

When a sequence of events occurs regularly, we begin to anticipate a particular order for these events. Most of the mundane events in our lives—waking up, bathing, dressing, mealtimes, the drive to work—occur in a well-established sequence. We expect these routines to happen in a set way, and we use them to help organize our lives. Routines also reduce the cognitive effort we have to devote to some tasks, freeing up mental energy that can be used to address other issues.

> ## *Hint*
>
> Babies love the freedom of movement when they have no clothes on. Try to provide some no-clothes time for kicking and exploring. (You may want to keep the baby's diaper on!) Make sure the room is warm enough when you do this.

Some of our expectations come from the natural world, and others have been created for us. We expect that day will follow night and that work will be compensated. Most of our expectations develop out of our accumulated experiences, and, if our expectations are violated consistently, we become inconvenienced and downright upset.

Most of the young baby's expectations develop from the world caregivers create for her. In other words, when parents provide sameness in the baby's day, for example, recurring and consistent periods of physical care, play, and rest, they lay important groundwork for helping babies learn behavioral routines. Similarly, when parents structure the baby's immediate living area into places to sit, lie down, and move about, they pave the way for the baby to learn about space and the events that occur in each niche of living space. Additionally, parents help the baby develop social expectations when they are available consistently for play or when they regularly provide soothing in times of fatigue and hurt.

The baby's initial expectations emerge with the development of certain perceptual and social skills. Around 3 months, the baby begins to smile in response to another person's smile on a regular basis. At 4 months of age, the baby holds simplified, turn-taking conversations and is differentially responsive to facial expressions. The 5-month-old starts to send signals that indicate that she wants attention, and she also accepts something akin to instruction in shifting her gaze to look in the direction that a caregiver looks.

Now at 6 months the baby is able to coordinate these specific skills and to discern the totality of a brief everyday routine. Mother, for example, fills the tub with water, gets a towel, assembles fresh clothes, and then puts the baby in the tub. When an infant is able to remember the sequence of an event—bathtime—on the basis of a cue that starts the sequence (water in the tub), the logical next step for the baby is to develop an expectation, also called an anticipation, for the event. Mother running the bath water means that a bath will follow. Babies show that they are beginning to expect different events, that is, to be fed by certain people and in a certain way, to see certain people when they wake up, and to see caregivers react in certain ways to the babies' own actions. If expectations are not met, the baby will likely show a behavior akin to disappointment.

The positive side of this growth is that the baby increasingly discerns routines and regularities. The baby's anticipations mean that she is employing a form of memory strategy. But there is a slight negative side as well. The baby is quick to notice differences between familiar and unfamiliar events, and she becomes upset when something dramatically new enters her life (a new babysitter, a relocation of the place where her diaper is changed).

It is unrealistic to expect that every aspect of the baby's regular routine can be rigidly adhered to every day, but total regimentation is undesirable, anyway. The baby needs to have new experiences to learn from. When changes in the baby's routines are necessary, sensitive parents can ease the baby's adjustment by introducing them slowly.

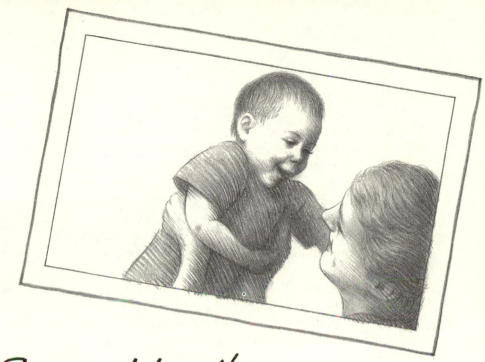

Seven Months

crawls

investigates toys by dropping them
from heights

enjoys social interactions

enjoys familiar caregivers

Average Boy: Length is 27.5 inches, with most between
26 and 28.5 inches. Weight is 18.5+ pounds, with most
between 15.5 and 21+ pounds.
Average Girl: Length is 26.5 inches, with most between
25 and 28 inches. Weight is 16.5+ pounds, with most between 14.5 and 19.5 pounds.

❧ Snapshot

In regard to family routines and activities, at 7 months, babies are well on their way to sociability. During the past few months there's been steady growth in behaviors that are important for social interactions.

- At 2 months, the baby made eye contact.
- At 3 months, he blossomed with a social smile.
- At 4 months, he wanted company and stopped crying if he saw you.
- At 5 months, he showed he wanted attention by coughing or grunting, or with body language or direct eye contact.
- At 6 months, his bids were more specific; when he wanted a toy, he looked at you, lightly touched your hand, and looked again at your face. More than in any previous month, he was happy when you laughed and played with him.

In the next few months these foundation behaviors are combined and used to create richer forms of sociability. Playing social games is an example. The 7-month-old begins to sense that a social game such as pat-a-cake is different from just sitting on his father's lap and playing with his fingers. He stares, makes barely perceptible movements, and utters a few sounds as his father coaxes him to play pat-a-cake. By 8 months, he's more sure about the fun involved in games and he loves "I'm going to getcha!", "*Peek*-a-boo," and "Where *aarrre* you?" Pleading for repetitions, he laughs, tugs at parents' hands or clothing, and babbles away in the hopes that the games will continue. In a matter of weeks he gets better at game participation, and he also shows other signs of sociability, such as initiating a wave for good-bye, throwing kisses, and pointing to something for others to observe. Still later, babies intentionally invite others to join in their toy play.

In contrast to the mutual pleasures of sociability, socialization is arduous for both parents and baby. Babies are basically unsocialized and probably do not recognize the need to change their ways. Socialization demands specific kinds of input (do's and don'ts) from parents and ultimate acceptance by children. Input starts in babyhood. Sure it's fun to pull mom's hair, but it hurts! Dad's new wire-rimmed glasses are intriguing, but they don't stand up too well when flung to the floor. The baby learns to recognize that his parents feel strongly about certain situations. However, mere recognition is insufficient. At some point, even a young child has to learn parents' lessons.

Although 7-month-olds are too cognitively immature to deal with socialization demands, important precursor behaviors emerge at this age.

One of these involves the unmistakable discrimination of and preference for familiar caregivers. Caring about someone means that the baby is more likely to feel badly when he sees that his action annoys his caregivers. His remorse eventually helps bring about compliant behavior.

Another emerging socialization precursor is the baby's ability to distinguish a happy facial expression from one that is sad. Being able to interpret his parents' facial expressions helps compensate for the fact that he cannot comprehend speech. In the months ahead, his ability to "read" faces will also help him learn which behaviors are acceptable and which cause distress.

The social arena is not the only domain where there are important changes in abilities. Some form of crawling often appears this month. The baby, tummy touching the floor, propels himself clumsily forward using arms and legs. Babies seemingly love the sense of moving on their own. Even though they may only be able to crawl a distance of three or four inches before collapsing, they determinedly practice crawling for minutes, even hours, at a time. This practice will pay off in a few weeks; then the baby will easily cover a distance of twenty feet.

Crawling opens up new adventures for the baby that include cupboards, furniture, and table legs. It also ushers in new concerns for caregivers. The crawling baby is a curious animal who pulls on electric cords, reaches into low shelves, and knocks over the dog's dish as he vigorously explores his environment. Baby-proofing floor space is parents' only alternative to constant vigilance. Ideas for keeping your baby safe are listed on page261.

❧ *Images of Development*

Motor

At 7 months Ann's shoulders, chest, abdomen, and hips are sturdy enough to support sitting alone and crawling. She is not quite ready to stand alone because her body is still bent slightly forward at the hips. But the baby's legs are developing strength, and already her legs support her full weight when she's held in a standing position. Not only is Ann stronger now, but her body is still remarkably flexible. She easily brings a leg to her chest, grabs hold of a foot, and puts a toe in her mouth!

If Ann is placed in a sitting position, she can maintain the position for minutes at a time, though she sometimes leans forward on her arms and hands to stabilize her balance. Soon she will try to get into a sitting position on her own, but this month Ann is not adept enough to move from lying down to sitting. This movement involves a complicated sequence of maneuvers that are still a bit beyond her capabilities.

One new aspect of behavior is the baby's greater tendency to use one hand instead of both hands when reaching or grasping. This one-handed reach gives Ann more opportunities for learning. She holds a toy doll in one hand and strokes the doll's head with her other hand, simultaneously learning about variations in sizes, shapes, and textures. Once again, a stepping-stone effect is in action: improvements in the baby's use of her hands as tools also promotes Ann's cognitive development and vice versa.

This month grasp involves mostly the baby's thumb and the first or second finger. This type of grasp permits picking up small objects (pellet size), which 7-month-olds do relatively quickly and easily. However, the baby still isn't able to bring the tips of her thumb and first finger together like adults do; instead, she grasps by using her thumb against the side of her forefinger. In a matter of weeks, play with toys will have strengthened the baby's fingers, and the adult grasp will increasingly materialize. But for now, the challenge is to get grasp down pat. Parents helps by providing small pieces of cracker for practice in self-feeding skills, which coincidentally also improves grasp.

There is some clumsiness in the 7-month-old's grasp. Ann often drops the toy she is holding, yet she reaches out for it again and again. She may not be able to hold on to anything for very long, but this doesn't discourage her from persisting in exercising her new skills. She is unabashedly enthusiastic in her play and obviously enthralled with the idea that her arms and hands are terrific tools. Between crawling and working with their hands, babies keep very busy.

Sensation and Perception

Vision. The baby's ability to perceive differences takes several steps forward at this age. Researchers have demonstrated that the 7-month-old can distinguish between male and female faces, detect the difference between a smile and a frown, recognize a distinctive feature of a face such as a bushy eyebrow or a crooked nose, and remember a face for as long as a week. All these skills help the baby identify familiar and unfamiliar faces and thereby assist in the process of socialization.

Babies of 7 months are so intrigued by what they see that they sometimes stop playing to stare at a face. Their gaze is intense, as if trying to etch a face into memory. The baby's visual attention is also intense when playing with toys. He keenly observes how a wheel moves if it is touched, or that a toy drops if he pushes it off the table.

Studies also show that the baby is now sensitive to spatial layouts. We can see this at home as Michael crawls. He rarely bumps into furniture and detours around a box left in the middle of the room. He also seems to have a good sense of the path from his room to another nearby room.

♣ *Hearing.* The baby listens more selectively to often-heard words such as "mommy" or "daddy." She may hold her body very still or change her facial expression to register her attentiveness. This focused listening prepares Ann for understanding the relationship between the sound of a word and a gesture. The fruits of this exertion will be exhibited in a month or two when she waves as she hears someone say "Bye-bye."

Michael's enthusiastic play is also beginning to teach him that his actions can bring about sound. When he hits the truck on the table there's a loud bang. When he rolls his toy car on the floor, there is a hum. Associations of sounds and his actions are now becoming part of his knowledge.

> ## Hint
>
> Encourage the baby to crawl from room to room, provided it is safe and you are there to follow him. He practices crawling and also learns about space.

Vocalizations and Language

Most babies of 7 months babble repeatedly when they are content and in familiar settings. In contrast, they have a tendency to be very quiet when exposed to new situations. This was vividly demonstrated by a 7-month-old who recently visited my class. Her mother described the baby's frequent singing and babbling and said that the baby even made loud noises while cheerfully watching the play of her three-year-old brother and his friends. Yet in class, she barely murmured a single sound. Her silence indicated an appreciation of this unfamiliar setting—and her uneasiness with it.

The vowel and consonant sounds Michael utters and his intonations continue to drift toward the patterns of the language spoken in his immediate surroundings. He has also invented his own sound for when he is happy and another sound for when he is displeased. Michael's mother relates how he expels a low moan when he is crawling back from an excursion to a far corner of the room. She says he sounds as if he recognizes that the distance he has left to cover will take every bit of his strength.

Hint

Pushing or dropping toys from a tabletop is a game to the baby, much like pat-a-cake, only in this instance she is the initiator of the game. Play this game with her. True, picking up toys is tiring for you, but the game won't last very long. And babies just love to toss things from heights.

Cognition

The 7-month-old is keen to study things other than her own body. Ann flings herself at her rattles and persists in trying to reach them if they are beyond her grasp. She constantly manipulates the toy she holds, sliding it this way and that or rubbing, banging, or chewing it. Her behavior is purposeful; her attention does not stray. All the while she is collecting information about the relations between her actions and objects. There is a mind at work here, an intelligence that is blossoming!

One of the most fascinating types of exploring at this age is dropping toys from a height. When Ann is sitting in her high chair, the tray is her favorite launching pad. This activity helps her develop a representation of the properties of an object. When Ann drops her rattle from the high chair, it makes a different sound than when her rag doll hits the floor. After hearing the sound and seeing the toy on the floor, Ann will soon recognize that the toy on the floor is the same toy that was just on her tray. Soon she will learn to remember objects, even though they are no longer actually visible.

Social

At this age babies reveal their genuine enjoyment in social interactions. Their bodies quiver with excitement when greeting a familiar person. Arms are raised in a pick-me-up gesture. And if they feel that they are not receiving a sufficient amount of attention, they cough or make babbling sounds.

At 7 months, babies have learned to recognize the behaviors that make a favored caregiver laugh. Swaying to the sound of music is a common one.

This is also the age when babies begin to be receptive to social games such as peek-a-boo and pat-a-cake. Although their facial expressions show that they are puzzled about the ins and outs of games, they enjoy this kind of social play. They even try to muster an appropriate hand response to pat-a-cake but are largely unsuccessful. By 8 months, they have become willing and delighted partners.

Emotions

This month the most noticeable change in the baby's emotions is the display of negative feelings. Body movements signal fear and anger as well as pleasure. Michael's emotional responses are clearly and appropriately tied to events. A looming object arouses fearfulness, toys elicit pleasure, the sight of a needle at the doctor's office brings tears, and when it is time to put on an over-the-head shirt he tenses, knowing that his arms may be briefly confined. Once in a great while, Michael's cries resemble a fit of anger. For a brief time, he is unresponsive to his parents' efforts to soothe his distress. Michael may display a facial expression that resembles hurt feelings, where the lip quivers and the eyes become downcast and teary. He may have a wary expression in the presence of strangers, which usually conveys not anxiety but rather puzzlement brought about by uncertain surroundings.

Sense of Self

Playing social games provides Michael with an introduction to the world of rules and social roles. The baby dimly recognizes that there are certain expectations of him and that his actions precipitate specific reactions. At this age, however, his image of a social self is very immature.

Hint

Because babies of this age are so friendly to familiar people, it is easy to forget that they can be wary of unfamiliar people. They may need a little extra comforting in these situations.

Knowledge of the body as a whole is barely evident. One of my students observed a 7-month-old who had been crawling for about two weeks. Although the baby seemed to make discoveries every day, he did not yet understand how his body related to a tight-fitting space. This is what happened. The baby managed to crawl under the coffee table, but, as he tried to move around, he hit his head. He cried. His father came to the rescue. The baby would not be deterred and immediately crawled back under the table, only to hit his head again. His father retrieved him again. Back again under the table with the same result! His parents then blocked access to the table. Would the baby ever learn to protect his head? Of course, given additional practice time, he probably would have been an expert in a couple of days—if his parents had been keen on the idea.

❧ Developmental Close-up

Attachment and Day Care

Attachment is the term used to identify the need to affiliate with certain individuals. This need is strongest in times of stress and uncertainty. Attachment also refers to the feeling of security we have with these people.

John Bowlby introduced the theme of attachment. Bowlby agreed with Freud's view that mothers are primary forces in babies' lives, but he went even further. He claimed that human babies and their mothers are biologically endowed with behaviors that foster close interaction.

What forces pull a mother to her baby? Hormone release at the time of birth? Feelings of closeness that started during pregnancy? These are probable factors. Mothers and other adults are also attracted to babies because babies are inherently cute. In this case, cuteness derives from certain physical characteristics babies are born with: they have relatively large heads in relation to their body size, they have broad foreheads, their eyes are big relative to facial size, and nose and mouth are relatively small. It is a given, then, that adults are attracted to babies and that parents in particular develop an attachment to their babies. But the emotion goes both ways: babies develop an attachment to their caregivers. For Bowlby, this starts with the baby's attraction to her mother and comes about this way. Initially the baby's mother feeds and cares for her. Around 6 months or so, the baby begins to discriminate her mother from unfamiliar people. In Bowlby's scheme, this is followed by the development of the baby's wariness toward strangers. The next step is that the baby seeks her mother when something new and strange occurs, and, around the end of the first year, this behavior occurs with some regularity. Bowlby used the term "proximity seeking" to describe the baby's desire to be close to mother when something unsettling occurs. Much of his scheme (except for the emphasis on a baby's attachment solely to her mother) makes sense and goes along with what we know about development.

Enter Mary Ainsworth, a developmental psychologist who studied with Bowlby and was eager to apply his ideas to real babies. Whereas Bowlby had laid out the theory of attachment, Ainsworth wanted to measure it and find out how and why babies differ in attachment relationships. In time Ainsworth and her colleagues devised a series of observations in order to measure attachment in babies, including a test of the proximity phase of attachment; this test is called the "strange situation," or SS. The SS consists of a brief series of episodes in which mother and baby are joined by a stranger, and then the mother and stranger take turns leaving the baby with the other. The SS generally lasts about twenty minutes.

At the conclusion of the SS, the baby's reactions to being reunited with mother are evaluated. Most babies seek contact with mother, and they are classified as being securely attached. Some babies avoid their mothers, and others alternate between seeking and resisting their mothers. These babies are considered to be insecurely attached. Approximately 30 percent of babies in the United States are classified in the latter two groups.

Researchers who are proponents of attachment theory argue that Ainsworth's scheme for assessing the degree of attachment is valid. Of equal importance, some report research that shows that secure attachment stems from sensitive caregiving. They further report that secure attachment in infancy leads to significantly more competent children than avoidant or resistant behavior.

Other researchers do not question the concept of attachment relationships but ask if the SS is the best way to measure attachment. Some critics say that the test is too brief and that it does not consider behaviors mothers exhibit during the assessment. Others state that the SS measure is nothing more than a reflection of the baby's temperament. Still others contend that babies have multiple attachments, and the SS is therefore an inadequate test of the baby's closeness to significant others. There's also a question about the role of culture and the patterns of interactions between mothers and babies. Babies from other cultures who are tested with the SS often show a higher proportion of insecure attachment relationships than do babies tested in the United States, indicating that cultural factors play a role in how babies respond to separations and to strangers.

Where do I stand? I recognize the value of the concept of attachment; I think of it as a caring bond between the baby and one or more of her caregivers. I also agree that the responsiveness of babies to their caregivers partly depends on quality of caring that has been provided. However, I think attachment also depends on the ability and desire of a baby to receive and to give affection. Some perfectly healthy babies are just not interested. I am also impressed with the studies that clearly reveal that babies can form multiple attachment relationships, albeit the manifestations of attachment can vary somewhat. For example, many babies form attachments to their fathers that differ slightly from those with their mothers. Overall, my strongest disagreement with attachment researchers concerns their use of a brief situation to represent the sum of a baby's experiences with a parent. I have difficulty accepting the idea that behaviors demonstrated during one brief event can be a good predictor of overall developmental outcomes.

A few years ago, media interest in attachment was sparked by a contentious debate among psychologists regarding the effects of day care on caregiver (especially mother) attachment. Some scientists claimed that a secure attachment with mother is at the core of all future social, emotional, and cognitive competencies, and they argued that out-of-home care takes the baby away from the very person who is the baby's bedrock. Psychologists who subscribed to this view pointed to data from a number of studies that showed a greater number of insecure babies among infants who attended day care than among home-reared babies.

However, another group of scientists has aggressively attacked these conclusions. These scientists emphasize that a baby's early development hinges on the quality of the environment that the baby is reared in. Whether in a home or day-care setting, a caring, educated, sensitive caregiver helps a baby learn and develop. These scientists have also described the conditions that ought to be present in a quality day-care setting: adequate safety precautions; access to age-appropriate toys; trained staff; and the organization of the baby's day while in day care. These are important things to look for, because there is evidence that demonstrates the negative effects of low-quality day care on early development. Clouding the picture still further is recent information that suggests that the effects of day care may simply reflect the influence of heretofore unmeasured family factors.

Because of many unanswered questions, a major national day-care study has been initiated of many hundreds of children from different parts of the country. A great deal of information is being collected about the children, their day-care settings, and their families. This study should provide answers to difficult questions.

Without doubt the arguments about day care and attachment are relevant to the lives of millions of working mothers who wonder what will happen to their babies in day care. In my view, working parents can and should make informed and sensible decisions about day care. They must take time to ask important questions. Is the surrogate caregiver intelligent, sensitive, and knowledgeable about babies? Is the setting where the baby will be safe? If a caregiver takes care of several children, how many children does he or she care for, and how many babies are involved? If the baby will go to a day-care facility, is it licensed, and what is the training of the director and the staff? Trust your intuitions as well. Do you feel right about the setting and the people, or do you have a vague sense of discomfort? If the latter is the case, start looking again.

In addition, working parents can do their best to respond sensitively and caringly to their babies. Although this can be difficult after many hours of work, quality time does make a difference. But even very young children are resilient and can manage if once in a while you are too tired to play with them.

DEVELOPMENTAL OVERVIEW: FOUR TO SEVEN MONTHS

Developmental Highlights

	4 Months	5 Months
Motor	Briefly holds a small toy; sustains head control; rolls from tummy onto back; reach is guided by vision	Approaches toys with a push-pull scraping action; back almost straight from head to hips; rolls from back to tummy; makes incipient crawling movements
Sensation and Perception	More alert looking; distinguishes colors, shapes, sizes; hears soft sounds; responds to speech; coordinates looking and listening	Attends to smaller objects; better depth perception; listens quietly to speech and shows signs of pleasure; greater interest in sounds; recognizes a face even if upside down
Vocalization and Language	Plays with sounds; vocalizes consonants *m, b, k, g, p*	Makes more consonant sounds and says consonants more often; intonations move toward speech most often heard

	4 Months	5 Months
Cognition	Begins to reach out and gently probe objects; immediate anticipation; opens mouth at sight of bottle	Visually follows an object as it is moved out of direct line of vision; remembers pictures of faces
Social	Consistently directs a smile at familiar people; initiates social interction; fusses when familiar people leave	Follows another's gaze to an object that is held in hand; shows some recognition of the unfamiliar by quieting
Emotion and Self	Crying decreases; laughs at certain sounds; gurgles with pleasure; shows nascent anger	Usually gleeful and pleased but sometimes frustrated; smiles at own image in mirror; shows primitive resistant behaviors: turns head from disliked food

	6 Months	7 Months
Motor	Reaches eagerly for toys; inches forward on belly; sits alone momentarily; stands with assistance; adjusts hand to shape of toy; transfers toy from one hand to the other	Sits alone for minutes at a time; picks up a toy with thumb and side of the forefinger; holds toy in one hand
Sensation and Perception	Distinguishes male and female voices; recognizes familiar people quickly and easily; loses ability to make certain sounds	Distinguishes male and female faces; listens keenly to often-heard words; frowns; sensitive to spatial layouts; distinguishes features of faces; attentive to movements
Vocalization and Language	Sounds bear resemblance to speech; canonical babbling— strings of vowels and consonants	Babbles repeatedly in familiar places; can be quiet in unfamiliar settings; may invent sound for happy and another for sad

HOW TO BE HELPFUL

Talk to the baby; if he coos and babbles back to you, pause and listen.

Find simple, colorful toys that fit in his hand. If possible, select rattles and toys that differ in shape and texture.

Get the baby a crib mobile that makes a sound when touched.

Do not leave the baby alone on beds, couches, or chairs.

	6 Months	7 Months
Cognition	Learns behaviors of familiar people; reacts to changes in familiar events	Explores objects by manipulations; drops objects from heights; attention strays less easily when playing
Social	Sends signals better; follows another's gaze to object that is farther away; shows elementary social imitations	Joins others in swaying to music; quivers in excitement at sight of familiar people or toys; makes pick-me-up gesture; greets others with babbling sounds; receptive to simple social games
Emotion and Self	Whines; matches emotions to others; performs to make others laugh	Unabashedly enthusiastic in play; sometimes harder to comfort; shows fear and anger; makes facial expressions that indicate hurt feelings

WHEN TO ASK FOR HELP (BEHAVIORS AT THE END OF 7 MONTHS)

Never smiles or otherwise shows pleasure

No day-night sleep pattern

Tonic neck reflex persists

Is totally inattentive to toys and people

Does not localize sounds

Does not engage in experimental sound play

Eight to Twelve Months

PREVIEW

❧

From a developmental standpoint, this five-month period is full of significant events. However, before we take a look at specific advances, we need to step back and talk about how development in this period differs in general from that of earlier months. First, while there continue to be important changes in physical abilities, increasingly growth involves the baby's mental abilities. The baby isn't able to tell us about these psychological events. Therefore, to understand just what type of mental development is taking place, we have to carefully observe and interpret various behaviors. Second, improvements in mental skills more often than not involve new combinations of increasingly complex behaviors. These changes in the content and nature of development mean that, to picture what is happening developmentally, we need fuller descriptions of behaviors. From here on, at each age level, I spend less time describing the growth of a specific behavior and more time discussing behavioral sequences and their implications.

Let's take a look at some of the specific developments that take place during this five-month period. Two milestones occur in motor development. By the end of this period, the baby has both the uniquely human gross and fine motor skills—the ability to walk upright and the mature pincer grasp. Dramatic developments occur in language comprehension and speech production: the baby begins to understand a few words, and near the end of this period she might say her first words.

The baby's social skills also surge ahead. In the first seven months, the baby has been steadily accumulating a stock of behaviors that are basic to human social interaction. Now she learns to combine these foundation behaviors (making eye contact, smiling, gesturing, and so on) into more complex social skills. These complex behaviors support her participation in richer forms of social activity. Social play such as pat-a-cake games, caregiver attachments, imitation of others' behaviors, and initiation of interactions with body gestures are examples of social competencies that mature during this period.

And if these developments are not enough, several new behaviors emerge in the areas of cognition and emotion. Cognitive development is wide-ranging and includes improved problem-solving skills, memory skills that do not rely on cues, and the ability to better control and direct attention. Emotions now include feelings of fear and jealousy. In addition, a baby can not only 'read' others' facial expressions, she sometimes adjusts her mood so that it is compatible with her caregivers' emotional state.

Whew! What a program! Fortunately, there are some months during this period when the baby slows down and gathers herself for the next phase of concerted growth. For some babies, at around 8 months and 11 months, there may be a period of two to three weeks when the pace of development slows down a bit. Overall development picks up appreciably between 9 and 12 months.

With so much happening, it's no wonder that the baby is overwhelmed from time to time and needs comforting and reassurance. Fortunately, during these months she learns where to look for assistance, how to communicate her needs with gestures and vocalizations, and how to interpret caregivers' responses to her requests for aid. Overall in this period, there is a marvelous balance between the baby's accumulation of skills that will support greater independence in the second year and the acquisition of behaviors that help her solicit/ secure the assistance she needs. There can be some glorious surges and a few bounces as baby and parent rocket through this period of wondrous development.

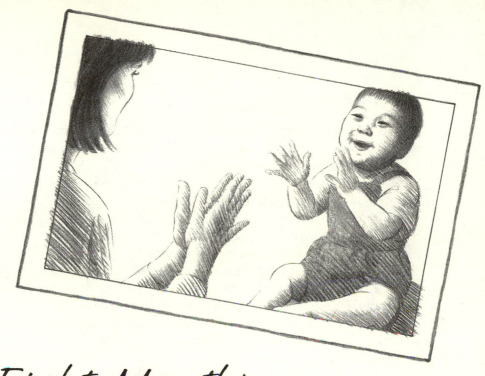

Eight Months

gets into a sit without help

turns objects with hands

mouthing of objects peaks

associates words with events

shows wariness to unfamiliar people

Average Boy: Length is 28 inches, with most between 26.5 and 29+ inches.
Weight is 19.5 pounds, with most between 16.5+ and 22 pounds.
Average Girl: Length is 27+ inches, with most between 25+ and 28+ inches.
Weight is 18 pounds, with most between 15.5 and 20.5+ pounds.

❧ Snapshot

This month body gestures, vocalizations, and pleading looks communicate babies' strong desire to be social, saying "Look at me!" "Talk to me!", "Pick me up!" "Play with me!" When his father enters his room, Michael jams his body against the side of his crib, squeals "Aahrahaa," and stretches his arms toward his father. He tugs at his mother's jeans and makes babbling noises when he wants something. Ann, in her highchair, leans toward her brother's plate of food and frets until he puts small pieces of bread on the highchair tray. Ann cuddles up to her father while they sit on the couch. Taking one of his hands, she moves it toward the other, saying "Uh, uh, uh," which is her way of telling him that she wants to play pat-a-cake. Being able to communicate clearly is an impressive achievement. But being able to communicate to someone you care about is even better. Ann smilingly wraps her arms around her father's legs when she crawls to him. Quite the opposite happens with the baby's responses to unfamiliar people. With increasingly better visual perception skills, babies are able to compare somebody who is new with people who are familiar. They hold back until better acquainted.

The refinements in visual perception that contribute to comparisons of faces also account for the remarkable fascination 8-month-olds have for the things and events in their environment. They peer out of car windows as if studying other cars, people, trees, anything. Sensitivity to sound also increases at this age. Babies of 8 months listen carefully to various sounds, enjoy songs and music, and play with sounds as they try to imitate them.

At this age cognitive abilities are in a period of relative consolidation as skills are pulled together in play resulting in new learning experiences. Michael sits on the floor entertaining himself with a pile of blocks before him. He picks one up and bangs it on the floor. Then he slides the block along the floor, stretches his arm so that he holds the block way out in front of him, inspects the block from afar, and brings it near his eyes and turns it around in his hands and examines it closely. Next he stretches his arm out and intentionally lets the block go. He giggles as the block makes noise when it hits the floor. He picks up another block and drops it as he did the first. He does this again, babbling as each block strikes the floor. Michael's purposeful and systematic play represents the beginnings of the sustained and intricate exploration of toys that will appear in the coming months.

This month is the age when many babies reach a peak in bringing toys and other things to their mouths; the behavior increases and then subsides. The increase may occur because babies have good control of their arms and hands and can hold and move toys fairly easily. In addition, they have discovered the exquisite sensitivity of their lips and tongue. So they deftly bring a toy to mouth and explore it with their lips and tongues solely for the sake of learning. Information from mouthing is added to information gained from touching and visually inspecting the toy. The frequency of mouthing diminishes after 8 months because babies become more efficient in moving around and therefore find other intriguing things to do.

Parents may object to mouthing because of fears about safety. Small, unsanitary, or otherwise unsafe objects should be kept away from babies. Some parents also object to mouthing because of family or cultural beliefs. Here parents should follow their own inclinations; a baby's development will not be impeded because he doesn't mouth toys.

❧ *Images of Development*

Motor

Improvements in sitting and crawling and the beginning of creeping and standing with assistance are big motor achievements this month. All of these gross motor movements require a sturdy trunk that can support the upper body. The trunk must also be limber enough to allow the baby to pivot from a side position when he is lying flat and then rotate up into a sitting position. Muscles are now strong enough for these movements to occur.

In addition, getting into a creeping posture demands that the muscles around critical joints lock in place. For example, as a baby moves to a creeping posture, his hip joints have to lock so that his legs do not collapse from under him. In order for the baby to maintain the all-fours position, his shoulders and hips must function as skeletal supports and his trunk must stay firm and straight. Think of a suspension bridge: the baby's arms and legs are the foundation supports, and the baby's trunk and back make up the bridge.

Later in this month babies pull themselves to a tentative standing position and make stepping movements. As with the onset of crawling and creeping, standing upright delights the baby and is often accompanied with whoops and hollers. Early on, most babies do not know how to get down from a standing position. Sometimes they let go and fall, and other times they remain standing and wail for help.

Individual variations in motor skills are increasingly apparent although the end result is the same. Michael sits by first rolling onto his stomach, then he gets into a crawling position, and finally he twists his upper trunk around and up while simultaneously moving his legs out in front. Using another technique, Ann rolls on her side, braces her hands against the floor, and she pushes her trunk upright, using her outstretched arms as levers. However a baby reaches a sitting position, when he gets there, he may rest quietly for a few seconds as if replenishing his energy.

Differences are also apparent in the ways babies crawl and creep. Ann moves around the floor by pivoting on her belly and propelling herself on her elbows, occasionally showing a primitive form of creeping on all fours. Her creeping is not yet particularly effective in terms of speed or distance, but it pleases her enough to shout with glee.

In contrast, Michael creeps with ease; he crawled only briefly a month or so ago and then quickly moved on to creeping. He reconnoiters as if he were a commando scouting the lay of the land. He moves anywhere in open space and pokes his fingers into anything that has an opening for tiny fingers. He pulls on everything that seems pullable. But unlike a commando, Michael does not heed caution signals. He does not understand the difference between safe and unsafe or right and wrong, and he can be quite a menace to himself. He does stop moving when a sharp "No!" or a loud "MICHAEL!" is directed at him, but moments later he is likely to go back to the same place and poke or pull at the prohibited item. His parents have learned that floor-level hazards have to be covered or removed and floor-level breakables protected from the 8-month-old's explorations.

A new variation in hand behaviors emerges this month, enabling the baby to turn a small toy around in his hands. This behavior is called examining. The baby's actions resemble the hand movements a coin collector makes when he scrutinizes a brand new penny. Examining toys is not trivial from a developmental standpoint; it is an example of sustained attention to objects, which enhances learning.

Hint

Examining has lots of developmental benefits—eye-hand coordination, attention, learning. In my lab we painted small blocks (about an inch and a half square) bright red and then added one or two white dots on each side. Babies loved them. (Use nontoxic and lead-free paint.)

All these motor skills that make 8-month-olds far more independent than before also have other developmental ramifications. Babies are able to engage in more sustained play and social interactions because they no longer have to contend with minor irritations that disrupted their play activities in earlier months. Before, fingers could go every which way just when they were needed to pick up a toy. Sitting balance could be upset and PLOP—that was the end of toy play. Sometimes crawling to a toy was so exhausting that the baby had no energy for social play. Freedom from these kinds of interruptions makes it possible for a baby to string actions together into useful behavior sequences. Now 8-month-old Ann crawls across the room to get to the toy her father holds, changes from a crawling position to a sit, grasps the toy, and babbles to her father, telling him about it.

The baby's new vigorous motor activity may bring on a weight spurt. Exercise turns fatty tissue into muscle tissue, and muscle tissue weighs more than fatty tissue.

Perception

✤ *Vision.* At about 8 months, the baby's visual receptors are becoming more sensitive to relatively distant objects and events. The behavior of an 8-month-old who visited one of my classes illustrates this nicely. The classroom had about five rows of chairs with each row having about six seats. The baby, ignoring students sitting right in front of her, was especially fascinated with two students in the back row who had particularly animated facial expressions, and she studied them for minutes. Her preference for the distant faces indicated that she saw them clearly. Babies do not acquire all of the principal components of adult vision until they are 7 or 8 months old. Then they can see clearly both close up and farther away.

✤ *Hearing.* Babies' improved visual discrimination of gestures is matched by an increasing sensitivity to sounds. Babies listen intently as others talk as if studying different words, which may explain why babies of this age are able to distinguish between different speech intonations. For example, babies in English-speaking environments are able to distinguish the difference in melody and word accents between the question "Is Michael going home?" and the statement "Michael is going home."

The 8-month-old also loves songs and music. He may show preferences for some songs and playfully imitate the cadence of a favorite song, capturing the many sounds in it.

Vocalizations and Language

This month the baby definitely begins to associate a word with an event. Bye-bye and a wave go together; "pat-a-cake" and claps go together. The baby also begins to recognize that a particular gesture means the same thing to other people as it does to her. She signals that she wants to be picked up by raising her arms, and she assumes that other people know what the gesture means.

Similarly, when the 8-month-old regularly produces a particular sound, such as "mamamama" for a familiar person or "buh" for a ball, she has learned an important function of speech: people repeatedly use a specific word to refer to a specific thing. "Ball" is the word people use for the round thing that rolls. "Milk" is the word for the thing that goes into the bottle.

> ## Hint
> ───────────────
> There are some really fine audio tapes of nursery rhymes. Babies enjoy the rhythm of these songs and learn sounds as well.

The ability to associate a spoken word and an action often manifests itself quite suddenly, but as with almost all aspects of development, this skill has been gradually evolving for some time. Months earlier, for example, the baby's learning involved the association of two events that occur close together. At 5 months a bib signaled that food was on the way; if an adult put on a coat, then the door would soon open. At 7 months, associative learning took another step forward as the baby began to connect sound with an event. For example, Ann invariably stopped playing when the phone rang, waiting for someone to pick up it up. Similarly, she crawled toward the bathroom when she heard water running in the tub. At 8 months, the fruits of these preparations are becoming apparent in the baby's use of a sound to refer to a specific object.

Some of the babies' babbles now sound almost like real words, another step in the progress toward actual speech. This advance is helped along by two phenomena. First, the baby increasingly plays with sounds. She might experiment for minutes at a time with making the *b* sound in *bye*, as if attempting to reproduce the word itself. Second, she often imitates the mouth and jaw movements of her caregivers as they speak, and this helps her learn about the actions she has to take to produce words.

Cognition

This month a few behaviors emerge that foreshadow the extensive cognitive growth that takes place between 9 and 12 months. First, the baby displays some primitive problem-solving aptitudes. If given a string that is attached to a toy, he fingers the string inquisitively, experiments tentatively with pulling it, and watches to see if anything happens to the toy. The 8-month-old seems to have a vague notion that the string and the toy are somehow causally related. Through repetitions of his explorations with the string, he soon learns that it can be used to make the toy move.

Second, there is a good amount of shaking, dangling, and banging toys this month. Michael seems to be purposefully investigating what happens when he strikes his truck on the table. His behaviors suggest that he has already acquired an ability, albeit a limited one, to engage in a goal-directed activity.

> ## *Hint*
>
> Social games such as pat-a-cake and peek-a-boo are fun for babies and parents. Games also help babies' social skills, language, and comprehension of gestures.

Social

The 8-month-old focuses affection on one or two individuals, usually one or both parents, though it is not uncommon for a sibling or other family member to be a primary target. Michael's person of choice is his sister. If she is playing nearby, he wriggles, crawls, creeps, rolls—does anything he can—to make his way to her. The baby doesn't exclude other people from his affection, rather, he simply gives one or two people more attention than he gives others.

As Michael's preferences intensify, his wariness toward unfamiliar people increases correspondingly. Sober facial expressions appear when an unfamiliar person comes too close, and sometimes he clings to a caregiver to offset his fear. This increasing discomfort in strange situations comes about because of the baby's growing ability to compare and contrast new environmental features with familiar settings as well as new faces from faces of known persons.

Emotions

Not all 8-month-old babies have the same wary reactions to strangers. A baby's response to unfamiliarity is influenced by her temperament and the extent of her exposure to novel situations. A friendly, relaxed baby accustomed to the comings and goings of many family members might show wariness only for a brief period, if at all. After only a short time, she may even flirt with a stranger to get the newcomer's attention. On the other hand, a subdued baby reared in a small family might show intense wariness that verges on anxiety for an extended period of time. Differences in the babies' responses to newness do not appear to have long-term developmental consequences. Different responses merely reflect the emergence of babies' individual styles: their personalities are beginning to form.

At 8 months other features of the baby's individuality are becoming evident. In 8-month-olds, differences in wanting cuddliness, tolerance for dirty fingers, patience, delight in manipulating toys, and the pleasure derived from social interactions are common indicators of this variability. This month parents are likely to comment on the baby's style and draw personality comparisons with another family member. "Laura is just like my mother, stubborn!" said a mother as she likened her own cute 8-month-old to the baby's grandmother. (In the Close-up for 11 months, I describe these and other core elements of the baby's personality.)

Sense of Self

Babies of 8 months are acutely aware of their various body parts and actively engage in exploration of and experimentation with their bodies. They massage their arms, run their hands inquiringly over their tummies, squeeze the flesh on the back of their legs, and poke fingers into ears. Babies are investigating what their bodies can do and which actions make them feel good and which hurt.

Sometimes babies get up on all fours and sway back and forth in a trancelike state. This behavior is part of learning about the body, and much to parents' relief, it eventually stops! Babies also get into a creeping position, hitch their rears up an inch or two, and peer out between their legs.

❧ Developmental Close-up

Social Play

At 8 months the baby's interest in social play increases. The baby's receptivity to social events promotes her parents' interest in bringing her into more frequent social interaction, and her parents now insert more social games into everyday activities. Perhaps they do this because they sense the baby's renewed interest in people, in contrast to her recent single-minded preoccupation with her toys. Whatever the reason for her parents' greater use of games, these delightful exchanges encourage the baby's joy in performing for others.

Social play is not only fun, it provides the 8-month-old with important learning opportunities. Social play has specific characteristics that distinguish it from the baby's other social interactions. First, in social play there is a designated role for each participant and the roles of the various players need to be coordinated. Ann's father introduces her to the game of pat-a-cake, and she soon learns that she is expected to respond. Ann also learns that if she does interact, her father will repeat the game. She anticipates his actions with glee, and her own role-playing also seems to bring her much pleasure. In another form of social play, Ann reaches her arms out to her father while simultaneously engaging him in eye contact. She expects him to respond to this signal by picking her up. If her father acts as expected, Ann is delighted, but if he fails to perform his role, she wails inconsolably.

In both these forms of play, the baby learns that social behaviors are not just random events. They involve actions that are quite specific, and the actions proceed in an orderly fashion. If a particular sequence of behavior does not come to pass, the baby begins to realize that other anticipated events do not materialize.

A second feature of social games is rule structure. A game of pat-a-cake involves hand clapping and rhyme, but it does not include waving goodbye. The baby learns that disruptions of rules (a goodbye wave inserted in pat-a-cake) are greeted with expressions of disapproval and dismissive gestures. The third characteristic of social play is that it contains repetitive sequences often woven together into longer sequences. Repetitions provide the baby with numerous opportunities to work on receiving and responding to cues.

The fact that parents enjoy social games is enough reason for them to take place. Indeed, parents probably don't consciously approach social play and social games as teaching tools. Nevertheless, studies show that the three types of games that parents of 8-month-olds tend to play with their babies provide learning opportunities for the baby. The game that most resembles teaching is where parents playfully make sounds and encourage the baby to reproduce these sounds. Babies love to play with sound, and this game is inherently attractive to them. Participation is also relatively easy to sustain.

A second kind of game incorporates movement and requires the baby's visual and auditory attention. Examples include pat-a-cake and peek-a-boo, the most popular games of all at this age. Each of these games has its own rhyme, specific physical movements, and rules for the adult and the baby. Babies have to not only pay attention in order to participate but also coordinate what they see with what they hear and both of these with how they move their bodies. These games also help babies learn that some behaviors must be executed before other behaviors can be performed.

The last group of games is largely physical. It includes "I'm gonna getcha" games in which the parent playfully approaches the baby and rubs or hugs her, and "horsie" games, in which the baby rides on the adult's knee. Here the baby learns to anticipate the physical tickling, hugging, or rocking that accompanies a verbal cue.

Studies of babies' game participation skills show that at 8 months the baby is mostly just learning the rules and tends to observe rather than actively participate. By 9 months of age the baby joins in games on a fairly regular basis, and in each succeeding month he gets better at being a fully involved partner in these games.

Social Bids

Social bids take many forms: a wave, "come sit by me," an embrace, "see you tonight?" Whatever their form, the bid provides an overt signal of wanting to share another's company. For months now, the baby has shown enjoyment when around others. By seven or eight months, his social bid gestures are clear. More and more he recognizes those people he wants to be with, and he has the motor skills (gestures) to communicate his desires.

According to some researchers, babies offer three kinds of social bids to other people. The first kind is labeled social interactions. Here the baby's goal is to draw attention to himself. He uses eye contact, sounds, or hand gestures to attract notice, to solicit comfort, or to request participating in a social game. Sometimes the baby will issue an appeal for help with a brief hand movement.

A particular kind of bid for attention is teasing. This behavior is most often observed in children 13 to 14 months of age. In teasing, the baby clearly wants an adult to look at what he is doing; teasing may also be an attempt to find out if a behavior is acceptable. At any rate, teasing frequently involves activities that have already been prohibited. If the baby has heard "Don't touch the phone!" often enough, he will just as often seek eye contact with a parent before moving toward a phone.

The second type of social bid is described as an initiative for securing joint attention between baby and adult. Here the baby tries to direct another person's visual attention to a particular object or event that is interesting to the baby. A behavioral sequence in a joint attention bid may go like this. The baby looks at a toy and then at his father's face while pointing to the toy. If his father fails to respond to his actions, the baby will repeat them again because he perceives there is something amiss in his father's lack of response. These overtures may be a bit vague at this age, so even an attentive parent may not see or register the bid; and even when the baby repeats it, it may not be understood.

A third category of social bid involves the baby's attempt to share or give things to another person. My colleagues and I saw a great deal of this type of activity when we were studying the play of one-year-olds. The babies were seated on the floor with their mothers nearby. A small basket of toys was set down beside them. The most common behavior was that the baby picked up a toy, looked at it, perhaps played with it briefly, and then took the toy to his mother for her to see. Notably, the baby merely held the toy out to his mother; he did not actually try to get her to take hold of the toy. As soon as his mother looked at the toy, the baby crept or walked back to the basket and sat down to play alone with the toy.

In summary, in this second part of the first year babies' social interactions become rich with game play, and in the games parents help babies learn the structure of certain social interactions. This learning lays the foundation for later play with peers, when parents are not around to help.

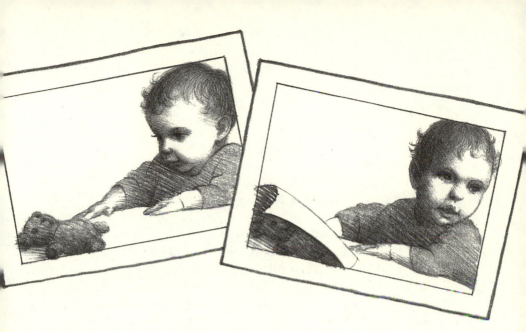

Nine Months

shows signs of intelligent behavior

makes speechlike vocalizations

recognizes simple cause-and-effect
relationships

tries to influence social interactions

frowns when displeased

feeds self finger foods

Average Boy: Length is 28.5 inches, with most between 27 and 29.5+ inches.
Weight is 20+ pounds, with most between 17.5+ and 23 pounds.
Average Girl: Length is 27.5 inches, with most between 26.5 and 29+ inches.
Weight is 18.5+ pounds, with most between 16 and 21.5 pounds.

❧ Snapshot

At 9 months the baby suddenly seems more mature and more capable. There are obvious changes in his motor and language abilities. He stands without assistance and begins to create word sounds—"mabama," "bad-aba,"—that have no meaning but are precursors to real words.

These manifested behavioral changes are so distinctive that it is easy to overlook the less obvious but dramatic surge in cognitive capabilities also occuring this month. The 9-month-old is far more mentally competent than he was just a month ago. All along the baby has been building his fund of information—how people and objects look, how people treat him, how people use objects, how a room looks, how sounds come from some things and not from others. Now, at 9 months, the baby begins to devise new ways of dealing with the world using his store of knowledge. He is acting intelligently.

What does intelligence mean? Well, intelligence among older children and adults is defined in terms of the ability to solve problems, make decisions, and engage in planned behavior as opposed to spur-of-the-moment actions. In short, intelligence is effective adaptive behavior. Babies' first displays of intelligence involve attempts to do something about events that are not to their liking; they begin to act adaptively.

Let's see what intelligence is all about for the 9-month-old. Michael is sitting in a corner of the living room playing with his truck. His brother and a friend enter the room and go behind a couch to play. Michael sees only the tops of their heads from where he sits, but he hears their whispers clearly. He wants to join them, so he starts to crawl toward the sounds made by the two boys at play. Michael soon encounters the couch and finds himself with a problem: how can he get to the boys with this obstacle in his way? Two months ago he might have simply stopped and cried when his path was blocked. Now he calmly assesses the situation. He uses information he already has: the sound of his brother's voice, the location of the boys, the location of the couch, the space around the couch, and his ability to move on his own. With this knowledge, Michael devises a plan to circumvent the obstacle that prevents him from reaching his goal and neatly crawls around the couch. Michael is being intelligent; he is solving problems with plans and actions he generates himself.

Another characteristic of babies' emerging intelligence is the ability to use an intermediary to achieve a goal. The 9-month-old might spontaneously take hold of a parent's hand and move the hand to a toy (such as a jack-in-the-box) to make the toy "act." Intermediaries are not always people. One 9-month-old finds her toys on top of her blanket and pulls the blanket toward herself to bring the toys within reach. Another baby uses his foot as a tool to pull a toy closer.

The 6-month-old baby barely touched a parent's hand to send a message. At 9 months Michael's touch is firm and clearly directed to a goal. When babies intentionally bring others into their own miniworlds, they demonstrate a primitive understanding of forces and actions that are independent of themselves, that is, they are beginning to recognize that they are a part, rather than the total, of a physical and social world.

The 9-month-old's intelligence is helped along by the emergence of recall memory. In particular, a form of recall memory called object permanence is evident this month (see the Close-up). Unlike recognition memory, which relies on the availability of visual or auditory cues to trigger a recollection (seeing a face triggers memory of a person's name), there are no immediate cues in recall memory. In recall we rely on our mind's card file. Because the baby's card file is so limited, he starts to remember by generating his own cues from some kind of an event. When he sees the wheels of a toy truck, the rest of which is hidden under his blanket, he remembers that the wheels are part of his toy and retrieves the truck from under his blanket.

How does recall memory help babies solve problems more quickly and more effectively? Well, babies are now better able to store information for slightly longer periods of time, and among the pieces of information they store and recall are solutions to problems. As recall memory develops, the baby becomes more skilled at recognizing similarities in problems and at retrieving stored solutions to solve them. Once the baby has figured out that he can crawl behind the couch to get to his brother, he can adopt the same strategy to find a ball that has rolled behind a chair.

This month cognitive development also involves improvement in the baby's capacity to distribute her attention effectively and engage multiple tasks. In other words, she does not become distracted when many different events are happening. Look at Ann, who is sitting comfortably in her stroller. While she sits, Ann eats from the spoon her mother touches to her lips, fingers her doll tenderly, and keeps an eye on her brother playing nearby. Periodically, she babbles musically to herself. Not very long ago Ann needed to focus all of her attention on just one task in order to do it well.

Also this month, Michael starts to move with restraint rather than impulsively as he reaches for a toy. The prudent reserve he now displays contrasts sharply with his behavior just two months ago. Then Michael grabbed at almost anything, but now he pauses and looks before he touches and focuses on the object of interest. What is this thing? What can I do with it? This reflective behavior promotes planned action and problem solving.

Overall, this month is a time of dramatic developments. Why? Many scientists think that the mental growth of babies during the last part of the first year is linked to increasing maturation of neuronal networks in the front part of the brain, called the association cortex. This brain area is known to be involved in certain kinds of cognitive activity (for example, planning), as well as behavioral inhibition (control of impulsive behaviors) in older children and adults.

Whatever the origins of change, the growth of babies' capabilities in this and ensuing months has profound effects upon parents. Parents see the baby as different, as increasingly capable, and they modify the ways they interact with their babies. They begin to provide additional lessons, mostly informal, about toys and other things that surround the baby. They extend their sentences and use complex words and phrases to describe how a toy such as a jack-in-the-box operates. Parents also gradually begin to direct the baby's attention to what is safe, nice, dirty, and so on, and even begin to issue directives ("No!" when the baby crawls to an electric outlet). Parents' changed behaviors contribute to the baby's increasing attention and memory and help move the baby out of babyhood.

Lest we forget, though, the 9-month-old is still a baby. Irritability and sleep upsets may reappear this month. According to some studies, about a third of babies who have been good nighttime sleepers now wake up and cry. Several reasons have been put forth as explanations—for example, teething, physiological growth, and the onset of dreaming—but scientists are not really sure why sleep disruptions happen. Combined with the tendency to occasionally resist soothing that emerged two months ago, these upsets can produce some sleepless nights as parents try to comfort a distraught, overtired baby; but within weeks most of these upsets disappear just as inexplicably as they came on.

❧ Images of Development

Motor

Overall, 9-month-olds have better control of their bodies; their gross motor movements are mobile, efficient, and quick. In addition, their grasp is purposeful and largely coordinated; their fingers adapt to objects of different size, shape, and weight.

Sitting is balanced and steady, and the baby can maintain a seated position for many minutes. Ann can lean forward to pick up a toy and then easily reerect to a well-balanced sit. Last month she sometimes struggled to get into a sit from a lying down position, but this month she adeptly moves from lying down to sitting and back. She spends time pulling herself to a standing position and standing. Her legs easily support her entire weight, but she needs to hold on to maintain her standing balance. Ann pulls herself up as often as possible throughout the day, even though she has difficulty getting down and often falls.

Reaching and grasping skills include new movements. The baby easily picks up a small block by neatly folding her hand around the object. She uses her thumb with her first and second fingers to execute this maneuver. Ann's fingers are also becoming more independent of one another. She can now use her index finger by itself to poke at small objects. These improvements in fine motor skills enhance the quality of explorations. The 9-month-old investigates the smallest features of toys and traces the properties of an object with much precision. Sensitive finger probes provide added learning experiences.

> ## *Hint*
>
> Toys that attach to the rails of the baby's crib entice the baby to cruise around the crib. A crib is among the safest places to practice cruising, because the mattress provides a cushion when the baby falls.

All along, as the baby's grasp has been becoming more refined, she has not been able to release objects when and where she wants. When she has lost interest in a toy, she has just let go of it. At 9 months the last major component of grasp, the voluntary release of objects, emerges. As with most motor skills, this new ability is at first crude and clumsy, and the released toy may not land where the baby intends. But at this age the baby releases a toy by extending her fingers just a bit rather than flinging the toy, and her ability improves quickly. Voluntary grasp and release moves the baby farther along in her quest for knowledge: in a few months she will stack blocks and look at the tower she has just built. She will also put pieces in puzzles where they should go.

Perception

❧ *Vision.* Now the baby is likely to notice a small object, such as a small piece of cracker that is lying next to a whole cracker, and he processes this

Hint

You can help the baby's development of voluntary release by giving her small blocks and a wide-mouthed plastic jar. Most babies of this age love to dump blocks into a see-through jar and watch them fall.

information relatively quickly. In fact, the 9-month-old often finds tiny objects irresistible. A 9-month-old visiting my class ignored his father's efforts to entice him with a doll to creep a short distance. He had spied a small piece of paper lying about three feet away from his father and crept swiftly to it, picked it up, and put it in his mouth.

Vocalizations and Language

At 9 months, babies are clearly moving nearer to producing spoken language. The baby has been combining vowels and consonants in babble for several months now. The mixture of sounds and the length of vocalizations makes some babbles sound almost like sentences. "Gaga dah dahdah mmmm ummm" can almost be mistaken for a chant in a foreign language. Some 9-month-olds also make sounds that closely approximate real words: *mamama, dadada, baba.*

Many of the wordlike sounds that babies produce are not directed at a specific object or event, so they are really only precursors to words. However, a few babies produce specific sounds for particular items much as an adult would use a word to distinguish an object. A baby may use one sound to call a parent (*mmm*) and another for the puppy (*gaga*). Some 9-month-old babies can actually produce an approximation of a real word or two. In these instances, the baby does not know the real meaning of the word he produces. He has learned an association of the sound of the word with an object. *Bah* stands for *bottle*, the word he associates with his bottle.

Most 9-month-olds gleefully imitate sounds produced by others. They are also more skilled at reading gestures, and they try to imitate some of them, as well.

Cognition

In addition to changes in the baby's problem-solving skills, recall memory, and attention control (see the Snapshot), there are other developments this month. For one, the baby displays more curiosity; she peers and pokes at anything and everything. She also seems to be more aware that her own actions can make something happen. Ann creeps to her basket of toys and pulls out a push-pull toy with a long handle. She sits on the floor and uses the handle to push the toy away from her, listening intently to the sounds the bell in the toy makes. When she pulls the toy toward her, the bell rings again. Ann stops moving the toy, and the bell stops. Next Ann drops the handle and extends her arm. She looks at her arm, but the bell does not ring. Ann has just learned that it is the effect of her arm on the toy that makes the bell in the toy ring.

> *Hint*
>
> This is a good age to begin reading aloud books that contain brightly colored, simple pictures of objects and animals.

Other behaviors attest to a primitive awareness of cause-and-effect relationships. One day Ann tries to drink from her bottle while clamping the nipple tightly in her teeth and elevating the bottle slightly with her open palm. With barely a pause, Ann tips the bottle more and relaxes her tooth grip. Obviously there were two problems that Ann recognized: the milk could not flow through a clenched nipple and could not reach the nipple unless the bottle was raised higher. Knowledge of cause-and-effect relationships is tenuous at 9 months, but even a sketchy understanding of the concept is another milestone in babies' mental lives.

Knowledge of cause-and-effect is also directly linked to the baby's increasing understanding of goals. In particular this month she begins to recognize that there can be more that one way to achieve a goal. I demonstrate this in class by placing a 9-month-old's favorite toy inside a ring and attaching a string to the ring. I set the ring with the toy inside it a few feet from the baby and extend the string toward her so that it is just within her reach. The baby can crawl to get the toy or pull on the string to bring the toy to her. At 7 months babies invariably crawl to the toy, but many 9-month-olds reach out and pull on the string to get the toy.

When babies use alternative approaches, or when they use intermediaries such as the string, they are taking apart, or decomposing, a situation. By separating each piece of an event, they show that they recognize a means to an end (one part of an event) as well as the end itself (another part of the event). This development is another important precursor to further development of more complex reasoning skills.

Social

The baby is intent this month on exercising control over his social interactions. When he wants to get a parent or his sister to play with him, he can now move to them on his own. He may try to direct a parent's gaze to something of interest by looking back and forth from object to parent, and he occasionally insists on eating the same food as his parents at dinner. Controlling a social situation sometimes involves exclusion rather than inclusion: when Michael's mother reprimands him, he sometimes turns his head away as if he doesn't want to hear.

This month babies show increasing affection for specific individuals. Ann shows her feelings for her father by pursing her lips whenever he approaches, a precursor to throwing him a kiss. Some 9-month-olds become subdued when a favored person leaves and may cry if left with even a familiar substitute caregiver.

Emotions

The baby's increased interest in controlling his own activities occasionally produces some difficult moments for parents. Suddenly the baby protests lying down for diapering. Wriggles turn into frets that lead to wails and uncooperative thrashing about.

The 9-month-old is developing a real frown, which he displays when he is unhappy about something. Because 9-month-olds remember schedules with greater ease, they frown and cry when everyday routines do not go as expected. Other events elicit frowns. Michael recently had a cold and a bad cough, and the family doctor prescribed a mild cough syrup. Michael took it the first time, making a face that he did not like it; and he accepted the medicine the second time his mother gave it to him. Not so the third time! As he saw his mother approaching with the spoon, he frowned, turned away, and clamped his lips tightly.

Babies of 9 months strive to exert some independence, but their efforts occasionally remind us that they are after all babies. When Ann is tired or bored, she seeks comfort by insisting that her

> ### Hint
>
> Don't fuss when your baby shows resistant behavior. He really doesn't understand what he's doing.

mother or father hold her bottle even though she easily holds it herself. Sometimes when fatigue overwhelms her, she just wants to be held, even if her parents are occupied with something else.

Sense of Self

The baby feeds herself finger foods, indicating a rudimentary sense of independence. Also, increased control over body movements, in combination with improved recall memory skills, means that she has more knowledge of her own body. She doesn't actually have to move

or to feel a body part to know it exists. Researchers suggest that at 9 months she is able to recognize herself and her mother in a mirror and that she responds slightly differently to her own image. In addition, placing a hand on her father's to get him to give her a toy or frowning to indicate displeasure are early manifestations of psychological self.

❧ Developmental Close-up

Recall Memory

The first type of memory that babies develop is called recognition memory because the sight of an object or the sound of a word cues memory. I often describe recognition memory using this example. There's a program on TV that you plan to watch. It sounds interesting, and you haven't seen it before—or so you think. About ten minutes into the show, you suddenly recognize a scene. "Oh, I've seen this program!" you exclaim. In a matter of minutes, you mentally reconstruct the entire plot of the show.

Many of our everyday activities provide us with cues that spur memory. For example, driving past a filling station, you suddenly remember that you are almost out of gas. You see a person walking across the street, and you move closer to see her face because her coat looks like one an old friend used to wear.

Most of us would find it difficult to function in a world in which we relied solely on immediate cues to remember. Fortunately, we have another kind of memory, which scientists call recall memory. Recall memory allows us to access the information that is stored in our heads. Names, dates, formulas, the route to work, and the bids at last night's bridge game can all be retrieved by recall memory. Many scientists believe that recall memory is developmental, maturing after it first emerges. During the first few years, memory capacity expands, and children become more efficient in accessing memory. Of course, increasing language skills and intelligence help immeasurably.

Object permanence is a rudimentary kind of recall memory. Object permanence means that a baby remembers an object even when it is hidden from view—a doll covered by a blanket, for example. Typically, this occurs at about 9 months of age. When the baby actively removes the blanket to retrieve the doll, he shows that he remembers the toy and that he saw the toy being covered. Researchers confirm the emergence of object permanence by three behaviors: the baby's act of uncovering the toy, his immediate discard of the cloth that covered the toy, and his unhesitating reach for the toy. Initially, the baby's recall memory works to retrieve only very recent information, information stored seconds rather minutes or hours ago. Yet even these moments are an important development.

A number of years ago, my colleagues and I studied the development of object permanence in a group of babies from the time they were 7 months of age until they were about two years old. We used pieces of felt about eight inches square and an interesting flat toy. When the babies were younger, we hid the toy under a pad and waited for them to reach for the pad, discard it, and grasp the toy. As the babies grew older, we made the task more complicated by scattering several pads on the table and hiding the toy under one of them, making the object permanence task particularly challenging: the babies had to remember not only the toy but also the specific pad that covered the toy. Later we made the task even more difficult by putting the toy inside a cup, moving the cup under the pads, leaving the toy under one of the pads, and then presenting the cup to the baby. At about 18 months most babies were no longer fooled by the cup and multiple pads and quickly discarded the pad that covered the toy.

Overall, our studies showed that it took slightly less than a year for the baby to move from success with a single pad to conquering the cup and multiple pad challenge. This study not only confirmed the notion of object permanence, it had everyday implications as well. Around the middle of the second year, toddlers' recall memories are improving rapidly for simple everyday objects and routine events.

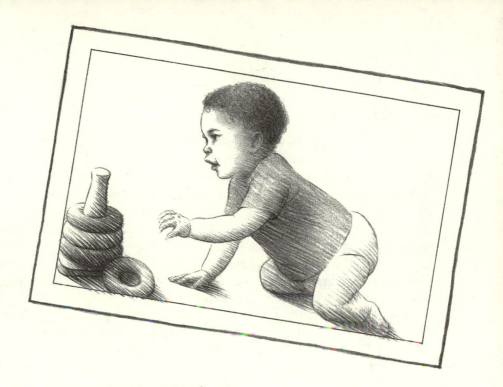

Ten Months

creeps, stands alone

holds toys, implements by handles

begins to group similar objects visually

looks at parent for visual cue

Average Boy: *Length is 28.5+ inches, with most between 27.5 and 30+ inches.*
Weight is 21+ pounds, with most between 18.5 and 23.5+ pounds.
Average Girl: *Length is 28+ inches, with most between 26.5+ and 29.5+ inches.*
Weight is 19.5+ pounds, with most between 16.5+ and 22.5+ pounds.

❧ *Snapshot*

Last month the baby showed new skills in dealing with everyday predicaments in her physical world. This month she displays a similar resourcefulness in her dealings with the social world; her social intelligence is emerging. She figures out better ways of picking up information from her parents, and she gets better at communicating her wants. These growing social competencies have an effect on others. Her parents increasingly view her as a social partner as opposed to a social rookie. Parents often reduce their use of baby talk, playfully ask for specific kinds of responses ("Wave bye-bye to grandma"), and sometimes consciously hold back assistance, watching to see what the baby can do on her own.

Let's look at an example of the 10-month-old's social intelligence. It's a warm spring day, and Ann's mother opens the back door to let in air. Ann follows her, crawling to the threshold. "Should I go farther?" she seems to ask as she turns and looks at her mother's face. Her mother frowns and says, "No, Ann!" Ann's eyes never leave her mother's face. She sees the frown, registers it, pauses, and then crawls back into the kitchen. Another day, Ann's brother brings her a new bright green rubber turtle. Her eyes open wide, acknowledging her fascination with this strange new thing. Something holds her back; she's not sure what she should do. She turns to her mother who is standing nearby and looks at her face. Her mother smiles, and Ann reaches for the turtle. Ann is engaging in social referencing, intentionally looking to others for information (see the Close-up).

The act of turning to another person to find solutions is not only adaptive behavior, it also represents a milestone in socialization. The baby is on her way to understanding that others can help—she's not in this alone. As babies learn that others have value, it becomes easier to socialize them. Babies, just like adults, do not want to lose the support of people who can help and reward.

Ann's discovery of her mother's and father's facial expressions as a source of information goes along with her discovery of details she has not appreciated until now. She is absorbed by the small design on a piece of cloth, the tiny wheels on a miniature toy train, the texture of her applesauce, the lines on an animal cracker, and the mole on her father's face. The 10-month-old stares, touches, and pokes, all the while seeming to ask, "What is this?" Michael, the same age as Ann, loves books. He peers intently at pictures in an alphabet book as if studying the different shapes and colors of the letters. Although his interest in each page is relatively short-lived, his overall attention indicates that he differentiates one picture from another. Michael is also beginning to show interest in simple puzzles. He moves a round block toward a puzzle that has a circular cutout, seemingly aware that they go together.

Let's look at the 10-month-old's efforts to communicate her needs and wants. She turns her head to and fro to indicate "No," "Maybe," "Yes." Then she occasionally uses a languid finger point, not fully developed as yet, to call attention to something she wants her parents to look at. Recall that last month the baby began to use index-finger probes. Well, this month she is able to combine the acts of extending her index finger and extending her arm, which results in a point. As she gets better control of the point and recognizes its social and communicative value, she'll use it more forcefully and more often.

At 10 months babies are also learning that certain sounds—that is, words—go with specific people, objects, and happenings; and now they repeatedly use sounds to identify similar kinds of objects. One 10-month-old created a sound that stood for her toys. One day she said "yass" to a toy in her hand. Several days later she handed a toy to a boy in her play group and said "yass." A week later she said "yass" while watching the mobile in her crib spin around.

Elementary vocal classification includes events as well as objects. Ann mutters "Ghhghh" when her play is suspended for a diaper change. She makes the same sound when her mother temporarily stops feeding her to wipe her chin or when her mother pulls her away from an electrical outlet. These three events have the common theme of interruption of a pleasurable event.

The 10-month-old's efforts to make herself clear to others are helped along by her parents' emotional displays. Their smiles, verbal encouragements, and waves greet each success. On the other hand, even the most loving parents emit groans, frown, or issue sharply worded commands to tell the baby that some activities are taboo.

This month the baby is less likely to put toys and other things into her mouth than she was a month or two ago, although parental vigilance is still necessary. If she does mouth her toys, she's likely to look at them first as if checking them out.

❧ Images of Development

Motor

Down on the floor on all fours, Michael demonstrates his expertise in the science of creeping. He has become a brilliant technician in finding out-of-the-way places to explore. Fortunately, this month he is more inclined to stop, at least momentarily, at a sharply worded "No!"

Michael stands in his crib holding onto the rail. He loves being able to stand and babbles cheerfully as he peers around. While he stands, he often practices lifting one foot and then the other, although sometimes he just stands in place and perches precariously on his toes. He also cruises, that is, he walks around his crib or playpen holding onto the rail. Toward the end of the month Michael gingerly lets go of the rail and briefly, albeit unsteadily, stands alone. Overall, the pace of gross motor development seems to slow down this month, as if the baby were getting ready for the big leap to walking.

Around 10 months, fine motor enhancements involve tuning the precision of grasp and extending the ways grasp can be used with everyday implements. Michael picks up a spoon, scrutinizes it, and purposefully bangs it against the side of a bowl. Although his movements with objects are not terribly effective, Michael is learning to use his hands as instruments for doing specific tasks.

> ## Hint
>
> Babies are more likely to practice standing alone when they feel a solid support under their feet. That's why they prefer a dense low-pile carpet to a shaggy rug or a lawn.

This month another kind of fine tuning occurs that has to do with how the baby picks up objects that have a handle. At 6 months the baby picked up a bell by wrapping his hand around the base of the handle. When he was 8 months, his hold on the bell was unchanged, but he investigated the bell's clapper and purposefully shook the bell to make it ring. This month Michael's sharpened perceptual skills let him see the bell anew. He now understands that a handle makes it much easier to hold and ring the bell, provided the handle is grasped at the top. With this in mind, he intentionally grasps the top of the handle, rings the bell, and babbles contentedly at his own cleverness.

By this age, Michael may begin to exhibit a preference for using either his left or his right hand in his bell-ringing play. In the months ahead, the baby's hand preference will slowly become more pronounced, but it will be some time before he opts exclusively for one hand over the other.

Perception

🌿 *Vision.* Discrimination abilities are continuing to develop. If presented with a very small, clear plastic bottle that contains a small piece of food (perhaps a cooked green pea), the 10-month-old will point at the pea through the bottle's sides. She may also try to reach the pea by poking or shaking the bottle. Her actions indicate that she is aware that the pea is separate and distinct from the bottle itself.

Hint

Break up a cracker and let the baby drop the pieces into plastic bottles of different sizes and shapes.

Laboratory studies show that if a 10-month-old is shown a picture that contains sketches of birds that have slightly different features along with a drawing of a rabbit. She ignores the rabbit. She also looks at each of the birds as if she is visually grouping them, demonstrating that she is now able to ignore irrelevant details (for example, different-shaped beaks) when making a classification. Because this ability is so new, babies make perceptual groupings of this kind only after previous, repeated exposures to each of the objects displayed in the stimulus. Why do we care about these early forms of classification skills? The ability to classify represents an efficient way to store a lot of information with a minimal amount of effort.

Babies who effectively make comparisons between two objects are necessarily proficient at managing visual attention, and at 10 months, babies show that they are adept at shifting attention from one object to another. Ann looks at a toy, looks at her dad, glances again at the toy, and then stares at her father's hand. This social invitation indicates that Ann's attention control is improving; each of her actions is well-defined, and she moves comfortably from signal to signal.

Vocalizations and Language

Along with development of finer sound discriminations, babies are adding to the associations that they can make between words and actions. Michael recognizes that the phrase "Clap hands" means to bring his hands together. He also knows that "Give it to me!" means let go of what you're holding or watch mother take it from your hand.

Vocal acts are now a regular part of the baby's everyday behavior. Michael produces a string of vocalizations whether he is playing alone or with others. At this age babies imitate new sounds, such as trills, and experiment with "cuh" for cookie and "bah" for bye. The baby vocalizes new word sounds fairly regularly, and most of them comprise syllables in the language the baby regularly hears.

Cognition

This month, everyday play is composed of the same types of actions as it was last month—touching, shaking, dangling, throwing, biting, and rubbing—but now the baby expands her applications of these techniques. One new type of exploration is demonstrated when the baby rubs her fingers around the inner surfaces of cups; the notion of inside and outside is a fascinating new discovery.

A noticeable new play behavior is the baby's use of specific sequences of actions over and over again. These repetitions of sequences illustrate her ability to organize her behaviors to meet a goal (for example, learning all about her toys) and to remember the action plan she has developed. Ann picks up a tinkly soft ball, brings it to her lips briefly, turns it in her hands, shakes it vigorously, and then sets it down. Then she picks up a hard block and repeats exactly the same sequence of actions. She then tries out the sequence with a doll, and then goes back to her ball. This systematic exploration of toys helps sharpen her knowledge of shape, texture, and sound. There is another benefit as well: the repetition of hand movements helps refine her fine motor skills.

> ### Hint
>
> Introduce some toys that are variations of a common theme: three or four different kinds of cars or toy animals or small dolls.

Social

The 10-month-old clearly recognizes that he needs to communicate to others, and he effectively uses gestures to overcome his inability to produce comprehensible language. One of my colleagues shared the observations she had made of the gestures of her young son, David. Her son's behaviors graphically illustrate sociability, emotional range, and the ongoing mastery of social communication.

Before David was 10 months old, he had already learned several gestures. He waved at "hi" and "bye" on request and played pat-a-cake with his sister. Around the time he was 10 months old, he started to shake his head from side to side as an adult does, to indicate "No." (Shaking the head to indicate "No" is one of the earliest gestures babies make.) As far as David's mother knew, he discovered head shaking all by himself.

David's head shaking was done so regularly and deliberately at 10 months that it was possible to identify its three distinct meanings. First, David shook his head from side to side as a sign of displeasure. This was the scene. At 10 months he was an extremely messy eater and invariably deposited food on his chin, chest, and elbows as he ate. After each meal his mother went to the sink, picked up a damp washcloth, and walked toward David to begin the clean-up routine. One day he actively shook his head as his mother approached, as if to say "No! Get that thing away from me!" Thereafter, he would shake his head as soon as he saw the washcloth in his mother's hand.

David also used head shaking as a cue to himself to control his own behavior. Like most 10-month-olds, he loved to play with telephones. The one that appealed to him most was the phone on his mother's bedside table. Whenever he headed for this phone, his mother would call sharply to him. As soon as she had his attention, she would say, "Not for David." One day as he crept toward the phone, his mother called out, "No, David." He stopped, looked at her solemnly, shook his head, and briefly suspended his movement toward the phone. His mother was convinced that David was dimly aware that he was not to touch the phone.

David's third use of head shaking was in a game he invented. While sitting in his highchair, he would look at one of his parents or his older sister until he established eye contact. Then he would rapidly shake his head back and forth, laughing all the while. The game was best with his older sister; if she shook her head, he repeated his head shaking and laughed with glee. At the time, David's mother wrote, "I can't think of any other give-and-take game that he plays with such obvious pleasure, although he does smile and occasionally chortle with pat-a-cake."

Emotions

The 10-month-old can be an intensely emotional baby. Our grandson Andrew began to greet his grandfather with loud shouts of glee when we visited in our red truck. He seemed to adore truck and grandfather equally. Andrew's negative emotions could be comparably as strong. He would actively turn away from people visiting our home who were unfamiliar to him. When one friend tried to approach him with outstretched arms Andrew did not move, but he cried bitterly in protest.

Sense of Self

Being able to stand alone evokes a series of adjustments in the baby's image of his own body and its relation to his surroundings. His whole perspective on the world begins to change as he no longer has to look up to almost everything. Now he's on an even level with more of the world, and he can even look down on the family cat. What an ego boost!

The 10-month-old loves to imitate body actions. His father covers his ear with his hand, the baby tries to do the same. Stretch a leg, the baby imitates.

Babies of 10 months seem to have an understanding of their own mirror reflections. Michael looks at a mirror and sees a toy close by; still looking in the mirror, he picks up the toy and plays with it. In all, the baby shows growing awareness of the physical side of his selfhood.

✿ *Developmental Close-up*

Social Referencing

Early in the child's second year of life, parents begin to issue firm do's and don'ts, usually with an eye to protecting the child from harm or the family's possessions from the child. These socialization lessons are based on the child's recognition and acceptance of others' wants, feelings, and abilities. Social referencing—looking to another person for guidance in an unclear situation—is a precursor behavior that shows that babies are becoming sensitive to other people's knowledge.

Social referencing is a universal behavior; that is, it is a common form of information seeking among older babies, toddlers, children, and adults. Just as a ten-year-old may sneak a quick look at the face of a trusted buddy rather than admit that she doesn't know what to do next in a board game, the 10-month-old looks at a familiar caregiver's face when she isn't sure whether to explore a new toy.

A social reference has a very specific purpose. Its goal is to obtain information by using nonverbal cues. However, social referencing involves more than reading cues, it implies that each participant has some key knowledge. First, both the seeker of information and the holder of information recognize that facial expressions and gestures convey meanings. Second, both parties know the meanings of certain expressions (a smile says "All is well," a frown says "I don't like . . ."). Third, the seeker of information has learned to interpret the expression whether it occurs at home, in a store, or in a park. Given this complexity of interpretive demands, the fact that 10-month-olds engage in social referencing is additional testimony to their burgeoning mental activity.

Social referencing as an area of research has sprouted and blossomed in the last ten to fifteen years; even the term does not appear in twenty-year-old textbooks. What happened? A few researchers noticed that babies showed questioning glances at times of uncertainty. The researchers started to describe details of these interesting behaviors. Before long, others began to study the kinds of events that led to social referencing, how parents responded to these kinds of babies' glances, and how babies reacted to different kinds of adult facial expressions.

Several ingenious studies were devised to examine the phenomenon of social referencing. One of the earliest and most notable was conducted by Joseph Campos and his colleagues. Their research used a variation of a technique called the visual cliff that had been devised years ago by researchers who studied babies' depth perception. The visual cliff is basically a large wooden box that has a sturdy glass top as a cover. One half of the bottom of the box is painted with large black and white checks and the other half is painted with small black and white checks. The result when looking down is an optical illusion: at first glance it looks as if there is a steep drop-off at the intersection of the large and small checks. Scientists reasoned that a baby's hesitation to cross to the illusionary drop-off side indicated awareness of depth.

In the social referencing studies initiated by the Campos group, the baby was placed on top of the glass at the end that had large checks (the "shallow" end). The baby's mother was instructed to encourage her baby to crawl across the glass that covered the seemingly treacherous drop. However, the mother was to give an additional signal. Sometimes the mother was to smile when she encouraged her baby, and other times she was to frown. The study showed that babies took their cues from their mothers' facial expressions, most often venturing across the "deep" end when their mothers smiled.

Other studies have used unfamiliar toys and unfamiliar people and have obtained results that confirm the Campos data. Overall, research shows that babies are most inclined to confront an ambiguous or fearful situation when they see a reassuring facial expression from a familiar adult.

As with most developmental processes, social referencing comes about in a gradual fashion. Babies first learn to discriminate others' facial expressions. Next they learn to associate a happy expression with one meaning and an angry expression with another meaning. Then, they learn to respond appropriately to another's emotional expression. The last step in this learning process involves using another's emotional expression to guide behavior.

Some scientists view social referencing in terms of opportunities for infants to obtain answers to immediate problems. Others contend that babies also reap long-term benefits from social referencing, because these behaviors develop the baby's ability to achieve goals on her own. In this view, social referencing has dual value: it promotes an immediate experience of self as well as a later self-sufficiency.

Whether or not social referencing actually has a long-term developmental role, the behavior does confirm that the baby is an active and avid information seeker even in times of uncertainty. This aptitude is critical for learning. Research may eventually reveal whether the baby who engages in appreciable amounts of social referencing encounters fewer difficulties later on in reading others' cues and in developing her own social skills.

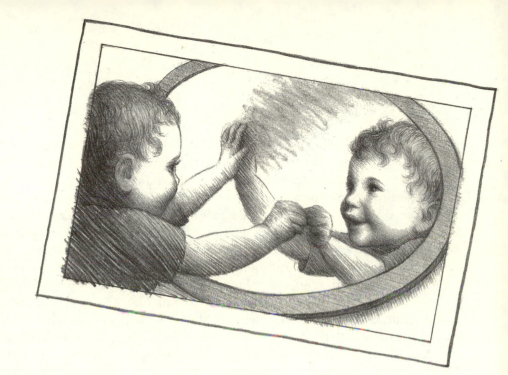

Eleven Months

walks holding on

releases objects voluntarily

temperament more pronounced

recognizes alternative means to an end

Average Boy: Length is 29.5 inches, with most between 28 and 31 inches. Weight is 21.5+ pounds, with most between 18.5+ and 24.5 pounds.
Average Girl: Length is 28.5 inches, with most between 27+ and 30+ inches. Weight is 20+ pounds, with most between 17 and 23.5 pounds.

❧ Snapshot

The 11-month-old is preoccupied and at times downright obsessed with learning to walk. He spends a good part of the day preparing himself for walking by practicing his standing skills and walking holding on. He enthusiastically cruises around his crib, along the couch, and down one side of parents' bed and up the other side. He's so insistent about standing and cruising that he is often unwilling to sit or lie down. Much to the chagrin of his parents, he struggles to stand while in his highchair. He stands in his crib calling out word sounds long after his established bedtime. Life with an 11-month-old is suddenly a little more trying for parents!

The 11-month-old's determination to walk fuels his desire to exercise his independence and motivates him to try new ways of doing things. He experiments with taking big steps and small steps and holding onto the rail with his left or his right hand. His understanding that there is more than one way to do things is improving; and as he has more experiences, his actions become more planned. For instance, Michael is cruising in his crib and comes to his teddy bear, which is resting against the crib rails, blocking his path. Without a moment's pause he drops down, creeps around the bear, grabs hold of the rail, pulls himself up to a standing position, and resumes cruising around the crib.

Michael's interest in walking seems to make him more interested in all kinds of movement. He deliberately jiggles a bell's clapper as if wondering how this movement produces sound. He sits on the floor and rolls his ball repeatedly, studying its easy motion. His eyes are riveted on the movements of his father's keys as he dangles and shakes them. He even accents his favorite forms of communication with motion; he vigorously nods when he laughs and shakes his head when he says "No!"

The 11-month-old's gross motor activities are dominant this month, but fine motor skills show changes as well. Most important, babies are better able to release toys easily. Although this development may not seem profound, a coordinated release is a momentous precursor to more sophisticated forms of play. Without it, the baby would find it difficult to build with blocks, fit puzzle pieces into a puzzle, or put pegs into a peg board. Of course, a coordinated release is also useful for putting a spoon back into the soup bowl or putting the toothbrush into its holder.

There are also modest though important gains in language skills this month. Babies seem to understand a few of the words that are directed to them, and they associate a person or an object with a word. *Mama, Dada,* and *bear* now seem to have meaning. The baby also produces more sounds that are like real words and some sounds that are actual words.

Overall, 11 months is an age at which important achievements occur, even though changes may not be particularly dramatic. A variety of subtle developments are happening, including maturation of skills (the ability to voluntarily release a toy), integration of skills (maintaining balance when upright), and consolidation of skills in preparation for new abilities (cruising prior to walking).

✿ *Images of Development*

Motor

At 11 months, Ann holds onto the railing and cruises around the edge of her crib or playpen until she literally collapses from exhaustion. Her pacing helps improve her control of body movements when she is in an upright position and clarifies her sense of where her body is in space. Remember that she is used to navigating by creeping on the floor, so her view of near and far space, room arrangements, and even people is changing as she moves about standing up. Cribs and playpens are great practice areas for her because they offer a confined, safe space while she gets used to moving her body in relation to her surroundings.

At this age differences in babies' movement styles are apparent. Ann loves to stand and to cruise as much as Michael does, but she shows less abandon than he and is methodical and tactical in her prewalking practice. Her movements look like a carefully choreographed dance, while his look like a spontaneous, old-fashioned hoedown. Increasingly parents will notice considerable variation in both the nature and the content of the skill of babies of the same age.

Ann is relatively adept at gross motor movements, and possibly because of her skill she approaches some of her practice sessions as if she has a plan in mind. She often uses a child-sized chair to support her rise into a standing position. She kneels and places both hands palm down on the chair seat. When she is set, she deliberately raises one knee so that she can set her foot firmly on the floor. Next she pushes off with that foot and her hands so that she rises slowly into a stooped-over position. Then she slides one hand to the chair back and finally pulls up with this hand while pushing with her other hand until she gets into a standing position. After she is in a standing position, she sometimes holds onto the back of the chair and pushes it along in front of her. It provides the support she needs for cruising. Her movements are synchronized, and her actions are as fluid as a modern dance. She also shows nice coordination of problem-solving abilities and motor skills!

As careful as Ann is as she practices her walking, she occasionally shows a wonderful freedom with her body. She is trying to get onto a low chair, but as agile as she is, she can't raise her leg high enough to climb onto the seat. She leaves the chair and stretches herself as tall as she can get and tries to reach the toys in her toy basket. A doll on the bottom of the basket is just out of her reach. As she tries to climb over the side of the basket to get the doll, the basket tips over. All of a sudden, she is sitting under the basket, and the doll she wanted is now lying beside her right hand! She gets out from under the basket, picks up her doll, and plays happily.

Overall, fine motor skills are steadily improving. When Ann is given a cup and a half dozen one-inch blocks, she is now able to place the blocks carefully in the cup. She plays with her toys by holding and looking at them, tapping them with her hands, and throwing them. Sometimes she runs her fingers over them as if scratching them; she's probably determining their texture and feel.

Improvement in grasp and voluntary release leads to a big change in babies' eating habits. They often use the thumb-forefinger grasp to pick up and feed themselves large and small pieces of cookie. The 11-month-old sets a cookie down on her highchair tray, whereas a month ago her efforts might have resulted in the cookie bouncing off the tray and onto the floor. Sometimes she's even able to set her cup down without launching juice all over the highchair tray.

Language

🍂*Comprehension.* In the last few months babies have learned to figure out some of their parents' gestures, facial expressions, and intonations. Some clever researchers have shown that there is a definite increase in the number of words the baby comprehends at 12 months versus 9 months, so it is likely that an 11-month-old does make associations between a few words and objects or people. In fact, numerous parents have reported that at 11 months the baby is more responsive to a phrase such as "Give it to me!" or the word "No!" than last month. The baby is also more likely to react to his name. Sometimes, though, it is difficult to tell if the 11-month-old actually understands that a specific word names a specific thing (person, object) or if his response is based on his recognition of parents' gestures, body language, and speech intonations.

Overall, comprehension seems to be quite limited at this age. One study that involved slightly older babies showed they understood fewer than 25 percent of the simple nouns and verbs their mothers used while playing with them. Another researcher showed that babies and toddlers use a lot of guesswork in their efforts to understand words and phrases.

Production. Determining how the baby's speech production skills are changing is not as difficult as trying to find out what he understands. In casual observation, it is clear that this month the baby directs more of his word sounds at specific objects, people, or events (*du* for daddy, *buh* with a wave for bye-bye). He sometimes combines these sounds with appropriate affective expressions; for instance, *buh* may be accompanied by a facial expression of expectation and a gaze at the door. Babies of this age also work on learning to speak by closely watching the mouths of older children and moving their own mouths in imitation of their speech.

Even during this early period of speech acquisition, differences begin to appear in the number of words babies produce. Some babies say a half dozen words, while others do not produce one. Michael says only one word, "Uh." He mostly utters this word softly, but when he points to his spilled juice, he yells "Uh, uh, uh!" No matter how many words the baby speaks, he invariably says fewer words than he understands. His word comprehension will continue to exceed his word production for the next year or so of language development.

One word that some 11-month-olds have in their vocabularies is "No," which they often accompany with head shakes. Sometimes they even nod their heads and say "No" when they want to communicate agreement rather than dissent. They do this because they don't have a *yes* word. First, the word *yes* is too hard for them to pronounce. Second, the 11-month-old usually has no understanding of *yes* because it is a word not commonly used by parents. To express positiveness, parents don't often say "Yes" to their baby; they are more likely to say "Good baby" or a similar phrase. So it is not too surprising that an 11-month-old says "No!" to a cookie even though he loves cookies and dearly wants one. The *no* is his universal action verb; he now recognizes that something will or should happen whenever he uses this word, even though what that something is not always clear to him.

The *no* of 11-month-old babies is quite unlike the *no* of 18- or 24-month-old toddlers. The older toddler's *no* signals self-assertion and resistance to a parent's request. Sometimes the need to assert himself is so strong that a two-year-old also says "No!" when he really means "Yes." At this older age the baby knows how to say "Yes," but he may be so set on having his way that he will not say what he really means.

Cognition

This month babies appear to catch on to the notion that there is more than one way to be entertained; they are likely to try another tactic when a first choice is not available. For example, Ann has been playing with her father's keys. Now he needs them. Unlike earlier months, she is easily mollified when dad replaces the keys with a magazine. She busies herself right away with turning pages and making word sounds at some of the pictures. Continuing with her play despite the loss of the keys indicates that Ann's adaptiveness is continuing to evolve.

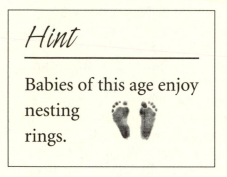

Hint

Babies of this age enjoy nesting rings.

The 11-month-old is also moving toward a greater appreciation of the characteristics of objects. If given a set of nesting objects like the old-fashioned Russian dolls that fit inside each other, she will attempt to nest them. At this age she sometimes correctly fits one object into another, but she is usually unsuccessful at fitting the whole set together. When given a narrow rod six to eight inches long, she uses the rod as a pointer and taps a nearby toy. With this simple action, the baby shows that she recognizes a functional use for the rod.

Social

This month, the difference in toy play of boys and girls is apparent. Even though their parents have been rearing them in nonsexist environments, many babies show gender-related toy preferences. Many girl babies prefer soft, cuddly toys, while boy babies often display a preference for "action" toys. By this age boy babies begin to move around more actively than girls, and girl babies tend to exhibit more curiosity than boys by performing longer or more intricate toy examinations. A number of scientists believe that some biological influence is at work here. Whatever biology's role and despite often observed gender predispositions, it is important to remember that many normally developing girl babies enjoy playing with action toys and many normally developing boy babies favor cuddly toys.

Better skills and greater participation in social games is a byproduct of the 11-month-old's improved balance and fascination with motion. Two months ago Ann merely tolerated being bounced on her father's knee, but now she shrieks and laughs gleefully, and she often tugs on her father's pant leg begging for a ride.

One other interesting social development occurs this month: the baby begins to respond warmly to a greater number of people. Her various interests support affectionate attachments to people who play various roles in her life. It is not uncommon for the 11-month-old to form special relationships with her father, a friendly next-door teenager, a grandfather, and so on. She knows that each one acts and reacts to her in different ways, and she obviously enjoys these differences.

At 11 months babies are exposed to other babies in greater numbers than ever before. Many mothers participate in some kind of Mommy and Me program, and some working parents place their baby in group baby care. By and large, in a group situation, the 11-month-old simply goes about entertaining herself with her own toys. Nevertheless, babies' social skills seem to be given a slight boost by exposure to other babies. The 11-month-old doesn't show prolonged interest in other babies, but she does creep toward another baby, sit close to him, and sometimes even hold out a toy to him. Though more contact with other babies does not seem to have a dramatic immediate impact on social interaction skills, some researchers suggest that early peer exposure paves the way for easier preschool peer relations. Only more research will tell; right now there is not enough data to support this suggestion conclusively.

Emotions

The 11-month-old has his emotional ups and downs, but on balance his mood is buoyed by increased independence and the thrill of moving about in an upright position. Despite his generally positive disposition, there can be some rough moments this month. Anger appears every so often, as babies seem to become easily frustrated at this age. Different babies' ways of handling frustrations differ greatly. Some express these emotions with physical acts, like the son of the great scientist Darwin, who beat a toy he didn't want! Others might react to an unwanted toy by crying, forcing a parent to intervene.

Some babies are cautious now about venturing into new space, while others forge ahead into unknown areas. Ann is generally serious and quiet when she plays alone, but Michael grins and babbles incessantly whenever he has a toy in hand. Michael loves being near his sister and inches close to her, but Ann generally ignores her brother. Ann no longer accepts a bit of cracker to eat—she insists on the whole thing—but Michael is content to eat whatever he is offered. Michael starts to fret when his father puts on his coat, but Ann waves merrily as her father walks out the door. All in all, around this age each baby is beginning to show individuality; the baby's personality is emerging.

Sense of Self

Moving about in an upright position strengthens the baby's sense of the independence of her physical self. She is becoming more aware that her body is under her control and she can move it wherever she wants. With so much attention focused on her body and movement, it is not surprising that Ann quickly learns the names of parts of her body. When her parents ask, "Where is . . .?" she points correctly to her nose, tummy, and toes. She also loves to watch herself in the mirror, waving her hand at her mirror image, and then trying to pat it. This, too, helps her learn about her body.

This month the baby's improved ability to carry out her role in more social games reinforces her sense of mastery. She can be quite insistent this month about feeding herself; she doesn't mind that her clumsiness with spoons and cups leads to a mess!

Hint

Although the 11-month-old is messy with spoons, she is effectively feeding herself finger foods, such as cooked peas, carrots, bits of potato, and pieces of pancake. Try letting her feed herself finger foods at the beginning of her mealtime and introducing a spoon after a while.

❦ *Developmental Close-up*

Temperament

Almost everyone knows individuals who are easy-going, who don't get upset about day-to-day irritations, are generally calm and happy, and like being with people. Then there are the opposites, people who are jumpy, irritable when the unexpected arises, moody, and often want to be alone. The combined individual peculiarities in a person's behavioral style are called temperament.

Variations in temperament have long been studied in adults, and researchers have asked many questions. Does temperament play a role in mental illness? In some circumstances, it does. Does it have anything to do with intelligence? Generally not. Are temperamental characteristics inherited? Studies have shown that there are predispositions to inherit some temperamental characteristics, but exact copies of temperaments are not handed down from one generation to the next.

In the 1950s and 1960s, two child psychiatrists, Alexander Thomas and Stella Chess, began to ask if children's temperaments could be a factor in the ways children develop. They were impressed with the variability in children's moods, adaptability, and activity levels, and were equally impressed with how easy it was to rear some children and how challenging it was to rear others. Could these differences be important? Thomas and Chess went on to describe three kinds of children. The easy child often shows positive mood, is adaptable, and is mild to moderate in intensity of response. The difficult child has a tendency to show up and down moods, withdraws from stimuli such as new experiences, has low adaptability, and shows high negative affect. The slow-to-warm-up child is inactive and uncomfortable in new situations and tends to withdraw from them.

Having identified these styles, Thomas and Chess launched a major study of temperament that followed babies into childhood and then into adolescence. (Colleagues would extend the follow-up into adulthood.) Their early findings showed that most temperament qualities do not remain stable from infancy into childhood. Indeed, the only temperament quality that showed stability was intensity of response. They also found that children with difficult temperaments are more challenging to rear than other children, but that the baby's temperament alone is not the only factor in children's emotional and social well-being. Much depends on whether the temperaments of parents and children can adapt to each other. This potential mutual adaptation is called goodness of fit. Thus, easy-going parents might be able to adapt to a baby who does not sleep and eat well, is often irritable, and does not easily tolerate even minor changes in everyday routines. But trouble lurks if both parents and child are nonadaptable, tense, irritable, and moody. The point is that effective parenting of a somewhat difficult baby can make his entry into the social world a little easier.

Chess and Thomas defined temperament as having several core characteristics: approach and withdrawal to stimuli, activity level, general emotional tone, distractability, intensity of response, reactive threshold, rhythmicity, and soothability. More recent researchers define temperament with fewer dimensions than Chess and Thomas did, and they do not always agree on which dimensions are important. For instance, Jack Bates emphasized that temperament is manifested largely in social interactions and is most often thought of in terms of emotion, attention, or activity. Other researchers include intensity of emotional response, and still others talk about emotion and physiological arousability and regulation. Regardless of differences in definitions of temperament, almost all researchers agree that temperament is a result of a person's genetic makeup. They also agree that it is important to be sensitive to variations in temperament because these differences influence social interactions with parents, peers, teachers, and others.

What does recent research tell us about temperament? Well, temperament research on sets of identical twins confirms that genetic background plays an important role in at least the activity level dimension of temperament. If parents are active and on the go every minute, it is unlikely (though not impossible) that their baby will be quiet, slow-moving, and placid. In addition, researchers have found that genetic influences on temperament are not very strong in the newborn period. Said differently, the temperament characteristics babies display in very early life are not necessarily the ones they will show later on. However, by the end of the first year, temperament features begin to become more pronounced. Finally, research shows that stable dimensions of temperament include activity level, emotional tone, and inhibitory control. However, stability does not mean "permanent"; a child's temperamental predispositions can be modified as a result of his experiences. Research suggests that it is probable that an active child will be an active adolescent, but this outcome is by no means certain.

The practical implication of temperament studies is that parents shouldn't be overly critical of their child-care skills. Some children are incredibly active by nature. It is not your fault if an active child can't sit still in a restaurant. Distract him by bringing along a book or two and a few small toys.

Twelve Months

walks alone

combines two toys in play

speaks a few words

holds toy out to parent

forms attachments

Average Boy: Length is 28.5 inches, with most between 27 and 29.5+ inches.
Weight is 20+ pounds, with most between 17.5+ and 23 pounds.
Average Girl: Length is 27.5 inches, with most between 26.5 and 29+ inches.
Weight is 18.5+ pounds, with most between 16 and 21.5 pounds.

❧ Snapshot

The 12-month-old straddles a developmental threshold: she is no longer a dependent baby, but she is not yet a full-fledged toddler; she requires a few more months to develop the complex social and language capabilities and sense of self that we associate with toddlerhood. Overall, this is a wonderful time for the tyro toddler. She is inquisitive and has a wide-eyed appreciation of her surroundings that speaks to an ever-growing intelligence. Her pleasure in her locomotive independence seems to know few bounds. The one-year-old enjoys herself and her parents enjoy her, even though they may not be sure if they are dealing with a baby or a child.

The first birthday is a major milestone, and the one-year-old has good reason to celebrate this occasion. Twelve months ago she was a helpless fretting newborn. Six months ago, though chirpy and happy, she couldn't get around on her own and sometimes had difficulty showing people what she wanted. Now she walks a bit, says a few words, and uses her hands to communicate and play. Her accomplishments are quite impressive and will serve as vital building blocks for development during her second year.

The birthday girl is hard at work. For one thing, she eagerly continues to practice her walking skills. Unassisted walking is a source of amusement for her, and even a brief stroll broadens her field of exploration and increases opportunities for learning. In addition, walking frees her arms and hands whenever she moves; before, they had to be used in crawling and creeping. So now she uses her hands for moving toys from place to place, another big step in the transition from babyhood to childhood.

Walking is a developmental event that parents of the one-year-old view with mixed feelings. It signals the end of needing to attend to her every wish, but it also marks the beginning of a long period when they will have to monitor her wanderings. As soon as children begin to walk easily, they no longer like to spend time cooped up in playpens. They would much rather be walking in the kitchen, living room, and other places where there are enticing things to get into. Parents have to increase their vigilance.

Walking is the big event this month, but there are other important changes afoot as well. For the first time the baby is able to exquisitely coordinate her attention control, her problem-solving skills, and her ability to use her hands as tools. While Ann is sitting on her mother's lap in my classroom, I set a cardboard tube about five inches long on the table and drape a chain made of a dozen or so paper clips across the tube. Ann looks intently at the tube and chain. Then she rolls the tube on the table and stands it on end. Next she picks up the chain with one hand and tries to insert it into the end of the tube, which she holds more or less steady with the other hand. She sees a potential connection between tube and chain and tries to make it happen. She's not coordinated enough to succeed every time at what she tries, but she repeatedly attempts to accomplish this and other new tasks.

The 12-month-old's play shows off other kinds of improved cognitive and perceptual skills. She makes a collection of a ball and colored rings, presumably because all of them are round. She puts all her yellow blocks into her toy basket, leaving out all blocks of other colors. In addition, her play includes multiple examinations of a toy. She pokes, fingers, inspects, scratches, mouths, and rolls a toy. She repeats these maneuvers time and time again until satisfied. These repetitions are not stereotyped; she deliberately introduces variations into her routines. What happens if I push the truck? If I pull the truck? If I push the truck on the carpet rather than on the wood floor? Finally, she demonstrates sharpened visual perception skills as she fits covers onto jars, removes a round puzzle piece from its circular hole, and attempts to insert different-size toys into a plastic jar (some fit and some do not).

Although the one-year-old seems to relish playing in her own way with her own toys, she is also eager to bring others into her play. Sometimes all the toddler wants is acknowledgment of a toy. Ann takes a preferred pull toy to her mother as if inviting her mother's participation; she pulls the toy away as soon as her mother reaches for it. Ann's message is "Tell me you see me and my toy." She drags a favored doll to her older sister when she comes home from school. A 12-month-old who has been reared in a family that emphasizes reading often tows a picturebook around, hoping somebody will read to her or at least point out pictures.

> ## *Hint*
>
> Children of this age enjoy novelty in books. Keep the old favorites and get a few new ones. Look for colorful and simple content matter.

Overall, there are many little ways the 12-month-old shows she is beginning to develop assertiveness and possessiveness. These new behaviors are due partly to the pleasure she gains from being in control and doing things on her own. Shrugging away assistance, she devotes many minutes to trying to remove her shoe. She perseveres at feeding herself, although eating without help means that she sometimes drops the best piece of cookie on the floor. She walks by herself despite frequent falls. Walking, playing, or talking serve handsomely as sources of satisfaction: she is performing them without any assistance. The one-year-old is well on her way to developing her own identity.

Children of this age are fun, but they do present challenges. Young toddlers are so busy that they often collapse with fatigue, and at the end of the day they need structure and attention. They also need monitoring when the family social scene gets busy. Children of this age love to be with others, but their tolerance for other children, family friends, and visiting relatives can be measured in minutes rather than hours.

In all, the first birthday closes out a year of acquiring many basic skills. It also opens the door to a period when these foundation behaviors are used to develop more complex skills and to establish independence. From now on, more and more childlike behaviors will be evident.

❧ Images of Development

Motor

Around a year of age young toddlers stand on their own and walk independently. The characteristic gait of toddlerhood is wide-based, that is, the feet are spread apart. This posture lowers the body's center of gravity and increases stability, which is just what the beginning walker needs. In fact, the designation toddler comes from the word toddle, which literally means to move unsteadily. Whether he has been walking for a week or for a month, the one-year-old is still unsteady on his feet. Walking demands a great deal of his attention; he checks where his feet are and where his body is in relation to a room and its furniture.

Because Michael's balance is initially very precarious, at first he walks holding onto a support with both hands, then he holds on with one hand, and finally he walks without assistance. The pace of growth in self-locomotion skills picks up rapidly after walking is achieved, and in the next few months young toddlers learn to walk backwards, run, and jump. Just six months from now parents will be admonishing, "No running in the house!"

At this age fine motor skills are fairly well developed. Michael adeptly holds a string of beads, and his fingers move methodically over each bead. While performing this deliberate investigation, he intermittently points to the dog. Michael easily goes back and forth between bending his fingers to inspect the beads and straightening his fingers to point at the dog. He never once looks directly at his hands.

Hands are coordinated enough for stacking small objects and placing very simple puzzle pieces. Michael now easily reaches, grasps, and releases with either of his hands, so he can use one hand to hold a toy and the other to perform some action on it: he holds his pegboard with his left hand and tries to insert the pegs into the board with the right hand.

> *Hint*
>
> Give the baby a dozen or so well-sanded blocks and a couple of plastic jars of different sizes that he can dump blocks into.

Perception

Sometimes development involves losing an ability so that a new, more mature form can take its place. Toward the end of the first year babies are less able to discriminate sounds that are not in the language of their primary caregivers. One study showed that year-old babies reared in the United States had difficulty discriminating various *t* sounds common to Hindi. What this means is that babies are becoming more sensitive to sounds and words of their own culture.

Language

Comprehension. At 12 or 13 months there is a dramatic upswing in understanding word sounds. Just a month or two ago the baby only seemed to comprehend only one or two words. Now the young toddler generally responds appropriately to twenty to fifty words. She nods her head, points, and runs to carry out commands such as "Show me . . . ," "Get the . . . ," and "Where is . . . ?" The first words that are usually recognized refer to the people, toys, objects, animals, or activities a 12-month-old regularly comes in contact with. Words she initially understands usually include *sleep, kiss, look, come, get, dolly, bear, ball, car, shoe, bottle, no,* and *doggy* (or the dog's name).

There is, however, a substantial amount of variability in comprehension skills at this age; some 12-month-olds understand as few as three words and others more than a hundred. Family makeup may be a factor. For example, babies who have older siblings are exposed to far more spoken and gestural language than are only children. Research also suggests that at this age girls understand more words than boys. This gender difference may be due to slightly faster biological maturation; however, studies show that little girls tend to be talked to somewhat more than little boys, and this increased experience may account for the differences.

When I describe comprehension at this age, I do not mean to imply that the young toddler understands the definition of words such as *shoe, ball,* and *teddy bear.* Whereas to his older sister a shoe represents a piece of apparel made of certain materials and having a specific style, to Michael a shoe is simply something that is put on a foot, whether it is a shoe, slipper, or boot. Similarly, in the world of the one-year-old, anything that moves on four legs and is furry is likely to be thought of as a dog, whether it is a dog, a cat, or a tiger at the zoo.

Occasionally 12-month-olds inadvertently fool their parents about the words they understand. Sometimes they produce a proper response to a request because they really do understand. Other times they guess right on the basis of a look or a gesture that accompanies the request.

Production. At this age language comprehension skills are typically more advanced than language production abilities. The 12-month-old routinely says fewer than a dozen words, and it is not uncommon for a total vocabulary to consist of only two or three words. As with comprehension, there is considerable variability in the language production of year-old children. I once evaluated a 12-month-old girl who had a documented vocabulary of five hundred words. She had begun to talk at 8 months. I also saw a boy of the same age who had a vocabulary of a hundred words. But these children are rare. Scientists are not sure why there is such developmental variation in language production. Familial inheritance, the presence of siblings and other relatives, the nature of caregiving, and patterns of parent conversations to the baby are all factors that researchers are continuing to study.

Words that include *m, b, d,* and *w* sounds seem to be easiest to say at this age. That's why *mama, baba* (for bottle), *da-da, buh* (ball), and *wah* (water) are often among the first spoken words. Besides their own real words, young toddlers often mimic the speech of others. Put a toy telephone receiver in their hands and they jabber away, mimicking the sounds of conversation.

First words are little more than word sounds that the 12-month-old has laboriously matched to objects and people. Michael calls his mother

Mama, but he also uses this word to address other females. Michael uses *sh* to refer to something that goes on his foot and *baba* to denote anything to drink. He talks all the time, even though he does not have many real words. His speech is a combination of real words and nonsense sounds, technically called jargon. "Mmabahgon," he said one day, which sounded a lot like "Ma, my bottle is gone." It's not certain that that was what he meant, but his intonation was just right.

Cognition

Imitative learning is common at this age and helps generate new forms of play. Ann bangs a spoon on a bowl, imitating her sister eating ice cream. Michael holds his toy hammer by the handle and pounds away just like his father. Unfortunately, he doesn't yet realize that he should be selective about where he pounds.

A great deal of trial-and-error exploration goes on this month. While this is an important form of learning, problems can arise when the 12-month-old explores in ways that are potentially harmful. He stretches so that he can reach the stove knobs and turn them, he goes over to the VCR and gleefully punches all the buttons, he pushes and tugs at the funny-looking plant that stands on the floor. Parents have to find a balance between encouraging their child's need to explore and protecting him and the family possessions.

> *Hint*
>
> Now is the time to provide some play-size cups, mugs, dishes, and pots. Make sure these toys are solidly constructed so that they don't break if accidentally stepped on.

Memory skills again improve this month. Whereas the 9-month-old solves object permanence tasks that involve one hiding place, the 12-month-old manages to remember when the hiding task is more complex. For example, Ann takes a small car, puts the car into a small box, removes the car, and then places it under a piece of cloth. The task not only involves multiple stimuli, it also demands spatial awareness as the object is moved about. The year-old generally finds the car.

Studies show that year-old children have what is called cross-modal recognition memory. This complicated term means that a child can hold an object in his hands and, without seeing the object, correctly select a drawing that matches the object. Michael's crib behavior illustrates this capability. He likes to look at and cuddle his soft toy rabbit before going to sleep. During the night Michael wakes up and gropes for the rabbit in the dark room. He immediately recognizes it when he touches it. Because vision and touch are now linked, Michael does not have to wait until daylight when he can see the rabbit to make sure that it is in his crib.

A current research interest is evaluating a young toddler's ability to understand sequences and to recognize hierarchies, for example, to array objects from small to large size. At 12 months, the toddler is just beginning to arrange objects by size. He repeatedly attempts, in a process of trial and error, to arrange the rings of his stacking cone and the pieces of his nesting toy in order. Success will come in a couple of months as the toddler figures out spatial configurations, size, and sequences.

Social

The one-year-old dearly loves toys, but this love is matched by his affection for people. He is particularly affectionate toward a few people. He runs to his father and kisses him when he gets home. When his father sees a helicopter in the sky and points to it, Michael looks up. He recognizes at some level that his father wants him to share this experience with him.

Michael also imitates his parents' daily activities. Small household items that fit in his hand (spoons, cups, combs) provide ample opportunities for his imitative inclinations. In the morning he reaches for a toothbrush and holds it against his mouth.

Changes in social behaviors also include the development of more attachments. Michael forms multiple attachments because different people offer him various kinds of enjoyable experiences. His older brother plays rough-and-tumble games with him, an older sister adopts Michael as her toy soldier, and his grandfather gives Michael rides on a bright red truck. Multiple attachments also increase the 12-month-old's willingness to explore; he has any number of people to turn to for comfort and reassurance.

Also at this age, children assume greater control in social games. During object permanence studies I was involved with, many a one-year-old child viewed the tasks as a game. They began to assign new roles to my colleagues and me. They would take the toy that was being hidden, hide it under one of the felt pads, and look expectantly for a response from us. Of course, we played along with much glee and laughter, acknowledging a nice example of the inter-relationship of cognitive and social skills.

This month parents find it necessary to introduce a few more simple rules to help keep the child safe and the family's possessions intact. Sometimes the one-year-old responds appropriately to commands such as "No!" or "Don't touch!" However, compliance is inconsistent often due to a lack of understanding and sometimes to resistance. A parent's gentle assertiveness, monitoring, and consistency are essential for learning, and eventually even a young toddler gets some of the messages.

Emotions

The year-old child is emotionally aroused by others' distress and may cry if she hears someone crying. She doesn't make any attempt to offer help or comfort; she simply acknowledges the other's misery with her own cries. The young toddler also cries when something happens that is not to her liking, such as being refused more ice cream or being exposed to a situation that was fearful to her at another time (the doctor's office). The 12-month-old also laughs a lot this month, at her own cleverness, at her own jokes, and in play. She even acts as if she's beginning to develop a sense of humor.

In some children signs of jealousy appear at this age. Jealousy is an interesting emotion developmentally because scientists are not sure about its origins, why it appears at about a year, and why not every 12-month-old displays it. In some cases, jealousy is most apparent when siblings are present who demand/need parent time, but it can even surface with pets. Ann's family just brought home a puppy. Ann clearly loves this new family member, and she's often down on the floor petting the puppy and stroking its fur. However, Ann frowns and frets when her father pets the puppy,

> *Hint*
>
> Early signs of jealousy are relatively common. The 12-month-old doesn't understand others' affectional relationships. Because of her cognitive immaturity, it doesn't pay to make an issue of these behaviors. Just give her lots of love and affection.

and she tries to insert herself between her father and the dog. She doesn't yet understand that her father's affection for the puppy in no way lessens her father's love for her.

Self

One psychoanalyst described this month as a time when the toddler begins "a love affair with the world." Walking and the ability to use words to express thoughts and feelings contribute to the love affair; they are also the cornerstones of what will be the toddler's sense of personal identity. The world is hers to master and to conquer. Every once in a while she stops to peer at herself in a mirror as if to say, "This is me!"

Also, the one-year-old's increased efforts to include others in her experiences and her imitation of others may signal that changes are taking place in her awareness of self. At some level she seems to recognize that "belonging" has something to do with knowing about others, knowing about her own separation, her own existence, and recognizing that it is others who often make us feel good and occasionally make us feel sad.

❧ Developmental Close-up

Speech Acquisition

I find the acquisition of speech one of the most extraordinary accomplishments of early development. The transition from no speech to words is sudden and dramatic, although of course the baby has been preparing himself to learn language from birth. One week the baby makes sounds that have no meaning to us, and then suddenly he says a word that is comprehensible. "Puppy," Andrew declared at 13 months when he looked at Natasha, the family's short-haired Doberman. "Puppy," Andrew said two weeks later when he saw Charlie, our small, shaggy cocker-poodle. Actually, neither dog was a puppy, but that did not matter: Andrew was speaking; he was saying words.

Why did Andrew select *puppy* as one of his first words? Lois Bloom, a noted researcher of babies' and toddlers' language, says that children's first words refer to things they know best and that are interesting. That is why words such as *mama, dada, doggie, bye,* and *gone* are common first words. Natasha played a major role in Andrew's family life, and she was also a big dog.

Interestingly, Andrew's father occasionally called Natasha *puppy,* although more often he called her Natty or Natasha. Somehow Andrew sorted out these words and realized that *puppy* applied to both his dog and our dog. I never heard Andrew refer to Natasha as Charlie or vice versa. Remarkable indeed.

How speech develops and grows is a tantalizing question. Several ideas have been proposed. Bloom suggests that speech comes after babies develop an understanding of people, events, and situations. Recall that between 9 and 12 months, babies begin to remember objects and people even when they are out of sight. Also around this age babies detect commonalities in characteristics, such as birdness or dogness. Babies also distinguish between familiar and new faces. They are building a storehouse of knowledge that Bloom believes is a prerequisite to language development.

Others do not agree. For a long time some scientists believed that babies learn language solely by imitating the speech of others. This idea began to be rejected when language researchers like Bloom recorded sentences that were true baby creations. Imitation could not be a reasonable explanation for toddlers' phrases such as "Mommy sock" or "No dirty soap." In contrast to the theory that imitation is the source of language learning, Noam Chomsky argued that the principles of speech for all languages are innate: a genetic blueprint lets a toddler reared in an English-speaking household innately derive information about English grammar, such as that nouns typically precede verbs in a sentence. Chomsky viewed environmental influences as switches that set universal principles in motion; otherwise, he did not think they had much of a role in language acquisition. Today, only diehards reject the importance of the language that a child hears in his everyday experiences.

The most popular current view of speech acquisition is a modified biological-environmental one. Yes, the premise goes, there is some kind of biological basis for language because children learn words without being taught. They also eventually put words together to make a sentence without being taught. But language acquisition and growth are helped immeasurably by other people who are in the child's social milieu. It is a fact that children who are deprived of social interaction have less robust language skills. Alternatively, routine parental conversation with infants and toddlers, Bloom suggests, facilitates all kinds of language learning.

From a developmental standpoint, one of the most interesting aspects of speech acquisition is the variability observed among same-age children. At 15 months, some children still do not speak, others speak half a dozen words, and a few have a vocabulary of fifty or more words. Of course, parents do become concerned if their three-year-old does not speak, but it pays to remember that several immensely gifted children, including Einstein, did not speak until past two years of age.

While most of us tend to think of language development in terms of the number of words a toddler utters at one or another age, scientists who study the growth of speech consider many other issues. For example, they ask whether the words that are produced are single words, two-word sentences, or sentences of three or more words. Typically, single words characterize the speech of children who are between 12 and 24 months, whereas two- to three-word sentences are often used by many two-year-olds ("Mommy tummy hurt").

Language researchers are also concerned with word meaning. When do children use words that are appropriate to an event? Even novice speakers do so surprisingly often. When does word imitation occur? It seems that children echo words they are in the process of learning, not the words they know well. "Feeway," two-year-old Andrew would say when I announced that we were going to drive on the freeway.

New words, Bloom says, cost the child cognitive effort. Here is an example one of my colleagues related about her toddler daughter. When Giuliana was 16 months old, she pooped in her diaper when she and her mother were in a department store. My colleague rushed to the ladies' room, only to find it closed for cleaning. Repeatedly, she knocked on the door, loudly calling "Miss! Miss! Miss!" When the cleaning woman opened the door, my colleague thanked her profusely. Shortly thereafter Giuliana was given a new doll, which she promptly named Miss. The department store episode had obviously made a big impression on her. Fast forward to Guiliana at 21 months. Every evening when she came home from day care, her mother would greet her with "I missed you!" One night Giuliana picked up her doll and said, "Miss, I missed you!" No sooner had she uttered the words than she turned to her mother with a stricken expression on her face as if to say, "I don't understand what I'm saying." Her mother comforted her and explained as well as she could why a word could be a name and also refer to a feeling of loss.

Sometimes a stressful situation brings on a struggle with words. If the cognitive effort is disproportionately high, the child reverts to imitation. Consider an example. The mother of three-year-old Sam and five-year-old Bruce has reminded them about inside and outside toys. While playing outside, Bruce mounts Sam's tricycle. Enraged, Sam can only manage to pull a familiar phrase from memory. "That's not an outside toy," he yells. Bruce gets the message even though the words are not quite right.

Language researchers also consider speech in terms of its grammatical construction. Children show marked variability in the elements they use in a sentence and in sentence construction. Differences include the use of prepositions, tenses, singular and plural forms, negations, and contractions. The question for the researcher is what kind of sentence can children produce when they are two or three or four years old?

Another researcher and her colleagues recorded and analyzed the crib monologues of Emily, a remarkably precocious two-year-old. Emily's sentences were long, contained complex clauses, and were replete with adjectives. Yet Emily's monologues rarely contained *ing* endings, possessives, articles, or the third-person singular. At 21 months, Emily said, "So my daddy went in the meeting in the car." This is a complex sentence for a two-year-old to produce. Two months later she produced this very awkward sentence: "On Saturday go Childworld buy diaper for Emily." This sentence tells us that mature forms of speech can be interspersed with immature speech forms during the course of language development. Young children can get tongue-tied just like grown-ups!

Speech for the child is fundamentally a tool for communication. Children use words to tell others about who they are—their activities and their feelings, desires, knowledge, and caring. Here are some examples.

Commands to others

24 months, Ann to her father while sitting at the table: "Daddy eat."

24 months, Michael greeting his grandmother with a football: "Grandma, tackle me!"

Understanding past tense

27 months, Andrew to his mother after she gives him a cold drink: "I was thirsty."

Pleasure at achievement

30 months, Michael to his grandfather after he had erected a tower of blocks: "I did it!"

Attempts to understand

30 months, Allie to her mother while raking leaves: "Why don't leaves turn blue or purple in the fall?"

33 months, Neal to his mother while in the park: "Why can't you pick up a hole?"

DEVELOPMENTAL OVERVIEW: EIGHT TO TWELVE MONTHS

Developmental Highlights

	8 Months	9 Months
Motor	Begins creeping; pulls up into unsteady stand, can't get back down; examines objects by peering intently; overall better body control; not interrupted as often by unintended movements	Sitting is balanced and steady; easily moves between sitting and lying; pulls into a stand more often; more easily picks up small objects; pokes at objects with forefinger; deliberate quality to some movements; voluntary release begins to emerge
Perception	More interested in distant objects; quiets when others talk; distinguishes between questions and declarative statements	More visually aware of tiny objects; if given choice of picking up a small or large object, will pick up smaller item
Vocalization and Language	Associates a word with an object or event; produces a sound for a toy or person; experiments with sounds	Sentencelike quality to babbles; may produce a wordlike sound for an object or person; may "say" a word—*bah* for bottle

	8 Months	9 Months
Cognition	Displays primitive problem-solving abilities; attentive to play—shakes, banks, and dangles toys; often mouths toys as a way of exploring	Begins to remember without cues; uses knowledge to solve problems; aware of cause and effect; recognizes that own actions may effect outcomes; distributes attention between events; "uses" people to make things happen
Social	Affectionate to specific people; more responsive to social games; increased wariness to un-familiar people or situ-ations; makes more social bids	Tries to direct another's gaze to a specific object; wants to be like parents and may insist on eating same food; specific affectionate displays—purses lips
Emotion and Self	Individual style may be more apparent; rubs and explores body parts; likes to sway on all fours	Shows negative emotions when restrained; frowns when annoyed; actively seeks others' comfort when tired; recognizes self in mirror; nighttime crying may reappear

	10 Months	11 Months
Motor	May show right or left hand preference; stands alone unsteadily; begins cruising; stands on toes while holding on; grasp is more fine-tuned; begins to use some household implements (spoons)	Experiments with steps; obsessed with learning to walk—cruises until exhausted; volitional release—can set things down without dropping; feeds self with thumb and forefinger; variability in motor skills is greater
Perception	Discriminates an object within an object—a pea in a jar; begins to visually group similar objects	
Vocalization and Language	Elementary comprehension of gestures and phrases; experiments with new words—*cuh* for cookie	Word comprehension increases significantly; may say one or two words; may say "No" but doesn't always mean no

	10 Months	11 Months
Cognition	Explores inside and outside surfaces of toys; repeats play sequences with different toys; investigates textures, designs, or parts of toys; peers intently at pictures	Uses props as aids (a chair to stand); more adaptive in play and more easily entertained; begins to put knowledge of an "inside" to use—tries to stack cups
Social	Uses gestures to communicate likes and dislikes; looks to others for help—social referencing; makes a languid finger point	Gender-based toy preferences emerge; some interest in age-mates; affectionate to several people ; more physically adept—better at social games
Emotion and Self	Intense positive and negative emotions; occasionally testy; uses reflection in mirror—may see toy and move over to it	Greater variability in emotions—temperament is more evident; learning to associate names of body parts; may insist on feeding self

12 Months

Motor	Stands alone; walks without assistance; uses wide-based gait; grasp and release more coordinated, stacks two blocks; may try to insert a peg into a pegboard
Perception	Puts covers onto jars; checks feet when walking; groups toys with like features—shape or color; no longer discriminates speech sounds not in parents' language(s)
Vocalization and Language	Responds to two- or three-word commands; comprehension is improving—but does a lot of guessing about word meanings; usually says two or three words, but there is considerable variability in production; uses same word for a group of items—*wah* may mean water and milk

HOW TO BE HELPFUL

Play peek-a-boo, where's baby gone, pat-a-cake, and how big is baby.

Find a safe, warm place for baby to practice crawling and creeping.

Hang a play box from the rails of the crib.

Introduce story time with simple picture books.

Childproof electrical outlets and remove hanging lamp cords.

12 Months

Cognition	Partially stacks cones and nests cups; comprehensively examines objects; uses imitative learning; deliberately introduces variations into play sequences; memory better and includes cross-modal recognition memory
Social	Imitates simple behaviors; enjoys participating in turn-taking; shows toys to others; forms multiple attachments; may respond to simple rules; loves to be read to
Emotion and Self	Becomes distressed when others are distressed; cries when something is not to liking; may show signs of jealousy; laughs often at own cleverness; loves to look at self in mirror; struts/preens when walking; wants to show mastery—plays on own

WHEN TO SEEK HELP
(BEHAVIORS AT THE END OF TWELVE MONTHS)

No grasping skill

Cannot sustain a sit

Does not discriminate people

Inattentive to gesture

Totally uninterested in social games

Makes no vowel or consonant sounds

Is unconsolable

The Second Year
PREVIEW

☙

*T*he terrible two's! Myth or reality? In jest, but with more than a grain of truth, psychologists Joseph Stone and Joseph Church described toddlerhood as the first adolescence. At both ages, mood swings and emotional outbursts appear unpredictably. Unreasonableness, self-centered behaviors, and stubbornness are common. Emotional upheavals are often due to major developmental transitions, particularly those that involve selfhood. The toddler, just beginning to understand his own body and his own identity, is easily threatened by a perceived psychological or physical intrusion. Another source of stress in the second year is increasing social demands to conform and to cooperate.

Major transitions are rarely easy for anybody. Church commented that times of major change are often accompanied by "disruption and turbulence." Many developmental scientists, myself included, agree—and the second year vividly demonstrates this point—the extraordinary development in these twelve months does create rough spots for toddlers and parents, but it is also the source of many richly rewarding experiences.

I sometimes think that whoever coined the term terrible two's was like the person who talks about the one rainy day that is forecast for the week ahead instead of the rest of the days, which are supposed to be sunny and mild. There are many more positive developments than instances of disruptive behavior during the second year. Take motor development. Most toddlers enter this period just able to take a few tentative steps; yet by 24 months they walk and climb and run and jump effortlessly, and bend, stretch, and squat comfortably. The 12-month-old handles his toys precariously, and a year later he uses spoons, crayons, and other household tools. Throughout this year parents and toddlers alike are entertained and delighted by these evolving motor abilities.

So much dramatic and far-reaching development takes place during this period that it is useful to organize it around four benchmarks: thinking in terms of ideas, pretend play, using two- or three-word sentences, and exercising autonomy. The interplay of these cognitive, language, and self-concept milestones greatly influences behavior in the second year. In fact, a good deal of the emotional instability that arises during this period can be linked to differing rates of growth in these four capabilities. As a consequence, one minute the child can be absorbed in play, but the next minute he can be throwing a violent tantrum. Let's see how this comes about.

During this period the toddler learns to think in terms of ideas, to remember ideas, and to apply ideas. By ideas, I mean a mental or verbal image of objects and people without a thing or a person being present. The toddler's forms of play (functional, pretend) in the second year demonstrate these types of cognitive growth. One of the toddler's foremost ideas is an increasing understanding of his own identity and self-hood. In turn, a burgeoning sense of self leads to feelings of autonomy and independence.

Toddlers are keen to exert their new sense of autonomy. However, they do not yet understand that they are members of a society and that being a member of a society means that there are certain things they are not supposed to do. As a result of conflicting individual and social wants and needs, toddlers often find themselves frustrated in their attempts to explore their environment on their own terms. The limits that parents often place on the toddler are one source of frustration. Another comes from his inability to make the world of objects do his bidding. If the tower he is building falls down, he perceives it as a defeat, and frets, cries, and tantrums frequently result. Compounding the young toddler's frustration is the fact that, although word comprehension is generally keeping pace with new mental skills, ability to say words and sentences lag behind. The gap between what he would like to talk about (events, objects, and feelings) and what he is able to say makes it harder for the toddler to deal with his environment. Sometimes his only resource is to cry; he doesn't know how else to express his confusion.

Emotional displays are a distinctive feature of this age, but not all emotional developments in this period are disruptive. For example, the toddler is definitely more concerned about others' feelings, develops a nascent form of shame that helps him learn about do's and don'ts, and displays a delightful sense of humor.

That's a panoramic view of development in the second year. What about some age-specific behavior characteristics? Well, the 15-month-old climbs and explores, is fascinated with toys and their characteristics, teases and tests parents, and seeks help for others in distress. The 18-month-old is more self-absorbed because of his growing self-awareness. His vocabulary may have grown to 50 or even 100 words, but his cognitive and memory skills have outstripped his spoken language, and the gap between his comprehension and speech production actually widens this month. For these reasons and others that we don't fully understand, many 18-month-olds are restless, irritable, and stubborn from time to time.

At 21 months the toddler is emotionally calmer but more exacting. He has begun to develop a sense of how things "should be," and his requests can be incredibly specific: he wants to wear this shirt, not the other. Fortunately, he is beginning to use two- and three-word sentences, so he can make more of his thoughts known. He also often tries to use the ideas he has acquired. His play reveals that he remembers elaborate sequences of events.

By the end of the second year, the toddler easily entertains himself and in turn is easily entertained by his surroundings. He has an increased interest in agemates, his pretend play is more complex, he shows that he understands family members' roles, and his language skills are less of an impediment now and cause less frustration. However, he has developed a more structured idea of the world, and he can be contrary when he is unable to impose his viewpoint on others. When he doesn't get his way, tantrums may result. Change is upsetting at this age, and for parents it can be especially trying to move, to have new babysitters, or to take the child on a long trip.

Learning to be your own person isn't easy. Balancing self-desires with social demands can be challenging. I don't make excuses for toddlers; they can be a real pain. Even I sometimes contemplated returning my grandson to his parents not long after they dropped him off for a weekend. But parents who focus on the times when things are going smoothly rather than on the willful displays or emotional outbursts will find that, overall, this is an exciting stage in their child's development. The child's willfulness is a sign of growth, not a sign of spiteful action.

Fifteen Months

climbs

loves to explore

engages in functional play with toys

teases others

tries to help

Average Boy: Height is 31.5 inches, with most between 30 and 32.5+ inches.
Weight is 24 pounds, with most between 21 and 27+ pounds.
Average Girl: Height is 30.5+ inches, with most between 29+ and 32+ inches.
Weight is 22.5 pounds, with most between 19.5 and 25.5 pounds.

❧ Snapshot

The 15-month-old is a toddler on the move, poking into things as if his curiosity knows no bounds. In the home, everything the toddler encounters is fair game: drawers, the laundry basket, cupboards, closets, books, the vacuum cleaner, and the water in the toilet bowl. Many toddlers engage in persistent and repetitive behaviors as they set about learning all about an object.

I had been studying Tim's cognitive development for a number of months. When he was about 15 months old, I presented him with some familiar cognitive play tasks. One task involved figuring out how to get a cookie placed on the far side of a lazy Susan. Unlike in previous visits, this time Tim discovered that he could turn the lazy Susan on his own to get the cookie. Suddenly Tim gave the Susan a spin, then he spun it again and spun it again. He slowed the Susan down and turned it slowly, and then he speeded it up again. His eyes grew big, his cheeks became flushed, and he breathed heavily. In his eagerness Tim forgot all about the cookie. The lazy Susan, which had been the means to reach a goal, had become the all-absorbing interest.

Another 15-month-old, Noah, showed a similar preoccupation with repeated explorations, although the circumstances were quite different. Noah's mother was teaching him how to put big plastic keys into a toy keybox. As they sat on the floor together, Noah watched his mother intently for several minutes. Then he suddenly stood up and swiftly taking a green key ran to the door of the playroom. He touched the toy key to the keyhole. Then he dashed from room to room in his large, rambling house, at each room touching the key to a doorknob. His mother and I trailed behind him, but he never saw us, indeed, he never glanced at anything other than the key and the doors.

The intensity of toddlers' curiosity means that they want to touch virtually everything they can get their hands into and onto. True, the toddler is learning, but parents are rightly concerned about protecting their child from harm and keeping family possessions intact. The result is an increase in parents' do's and don'ts. "Ann, the TV is a no-no, don't touch." "Michael, hold my hand as we go up the stairs!" "Andrew, you may not bite me!" At this age, the toddler may blithely go on his way after a reprimand or cry to the point of needing comforting.

Overall, 15-month-olds do not take prohibitions and restrictions easily. Many times they ignore a parent's request, once in a while they comply, and often they tease. Their teasing is not malicious; rather it seems to be a way of checking whether parents really mean what they say. Dad says don't touch the VCR. What will happen if I do? If I shake my head no when Mom offers me a spoonful of my favorite fruit, will she let me eat it anyway? The cat sits on the coffee table and Mom doesn't say anything. Can I sit on the coffee table?

Negative emotions are often on display this month, and sometimes the toddler is more forceful than he has been. Partly this is due to the imbalance between what he can understand and the ways he can talk about his needs. Yet the behaviors are also manifestations of a new assertiveness as the 15-month-old becomes more independent and sure of himself. Woe to the parent who interrupts his toy play for something as mundane as a diaper change: protests and squirming result. Screams may greet the parent who won't let the toddler stand in a high chair. The 15-month-old cries as if in deep despair, and ten seconds later he tries to stand again. Does he understand safety? No. Does he understand that he is being ornery? No. Is he a challenge? Yes.

On the other hand, the 15-month-old is more expressive about his caring for others. In particular, he begins to show a new kind of sensitivity to others' sadness and distress. For several months now Michael has shown concern when his mother or father seems sad, but now he offers a pat or a hug to show that he not only cares but wants to help. Michael's caring is not restricted to adults: he invariably pulls a grown-up over when a child in his play group starts to cry.

Contrasting behaviors are reflected in other activities of 15-month-olds. On the one hand they are usually in perpetual motion—up the bottom step, down, up, down, and on and on; dragging, climbing, and rolling off the footstool. On the other hand they have an increasing desire for routine and sameness. Ann wants to brush her teeth every morning, no matter what. She feels the same way about her afternoon walk. She is also finicky about the food she eats and the clothes her mother picks out for her to wear. In their own way, children of this age signal that they need structure and control at the same time they need freedom to explore.

The 15-month-old's desire to exercise her mobility is another source of parental pleasure—and challenge—this month. Parents enjoy watching the 15-month-old walk, sway, dance, and otherwise carry on, but they are dismayed with her insistence on physical freedom and her passion for climbing. Ann dislikes any hint of physical constraints and sometimes toddles away at diapering time or resists her mother's efforts to put on her sweater or socks. She also dearly loves to climb up onto the back of the couch. When her father says "No!", she stops momentarily, smiles cheerfully, and resumes climbing to her perch. Her father groans, reaches to pull her down, and moves her elsewhere.

Overall, this month interactions between parent and young child take on new dimensions. Parents introduce more informal lessons ("See, this is the way to tie your shoe"), raise their expectations about appropriate behavior, and increase their displays of disapproval for "misbehavior." Parents are increasingly challenged to be flexible and adaptive in dealing with the transition between babyhood and childhood, and parenting this month and for several months to come is a precarious balancing act.

Behavior is increasingly complex and rich at 15 months, but the highlights mentioned here are general trends, and there is much variation among toddlers. Toddlers vary widely in temperament, their need to explore, their language skills, and their tolerance for frustration.

✥ Images of Development

Motor

Children of 15 months still keep their feet spread apart in the characteristic gait of toddlerhood. Every so often they fall, but they ignore these interruptions and go on. And they hardly ever creep.

> ### Hint
>
> Try to be firm and consistent about climbing in unsafe situations (counter tops, back of chairs). Young children love to climb but must learn when climbing is a safe activity and when it is not.

This month's primary new motor activity is climbing. Trying to climb out of the crib is relatively common, and chairs, tables, stepladders, patio benches, and couches are also particularly irresistible lures. Climbing up is accomplished fairly handily, but getting down unassisted is another story. At this age most toddlers do not have the balance to retrace their movements and get safely off the couch or table. For this reason, parents and toddler often have a standoff or two about where climbing is allowed.

An occasional clumsiness at this age is a reminder that some motor skills are still recent accomplishments. Rising from a sit to a stand is an example. Ann's balance is still imperfect and her legs are not strong enough to maintain a squatting position, so to get up she rolls from a sit into a creeping position, raises her rump into the air, and then uses her hands to push up into a stand. Not surprisingly, she teeters a bit when she's upright, but she usually manages to maintain her standing balance. Yet some aspects of balance improve almost daily. By the end of the month most toddlers can stand briefly on one leg.

At this age there is increasing precision in grasp, and toddlers are fairly proficient in using cups, spoons, and crayons. They usually hold a spoon with a full palm overhand grasp, they easily build a tower of two or three small blocks, and they turn pages of picture books and magazines.

Perception

At 10 months babies seem to recognize some of the similarities among groups of animals, that is, they can distinguish drawings of two somewhat dissimilar birds from the drawing of another animal. The toddler's ability to categorize improves significantly at around 15 months.

Laboratory studies show that, when toddlers of this age are given six toy milk bottles that differ slightly from one another and six toy dogs that also differ slightly, they sequentially touch the objects that go together. The 15-month-old discerns that a plastic toy Dalmatian dog and a wooden toy dachshund have fundamental similarities. Researchers call this process of recognizing similarities chunking information. In this instance, the toddler is chunking common qualities of dogness perhaps even before he has a word for dog. In his everyday world, the young toddler chunks information about many things: shoes, tables, chairs, and so on. Stated another way, he is engaging in a more complex form of perceptual classification. The value of classification is that it frees the toddler from having to devote cognitive energy to reanalyzing dogness every time he sees a dog; he now recognizes that a dog is a dog is a dog!

Language

Comprehension. At 15 months children understand many more words than they did three months ago. Exact numbers are difficult to come by because it is very painstaking to evaluate comprehension at this age, but systematically collected mothers' reports suggest that comprehended words may run into the hundreds. Toddlers of 15 months demonstrate that they understand names for a wide range of toys, household objects, and clothing, verbs used in everyday social interactions (*come, go, kiss*), and names of people and pets.

A toddler in one of my studies demonstrated how hard it can be to judge comprehension. The child's mother asked her to pick up her toys. The toddler continued to play. Did she understand the request? The answer to this question became crystal clear when her mother tried another tactic. After a few minutes of fruitless pleading, she asked, "Do you want your dinner? If you do, then pick up your toys and you can eat." At this, the 15-month-old determinedly set about picking up the toys.

Production. This month is another period when the pace of language development is uneven. Toddlers usually understand far more than they can talk about, and they often have difficulty making their needs and wants known. Not surprisingly, this disparity in cognitive and verbal ability is frustrating and no doubt a cause of the documented increase in the amount of crying from 13 to 15 months.

The 15-month-old is not totally at a loss in communicating. On the contrary, he has a set of gestures that often serve him well—pointing, tugging, and pulling, facial expressions of delight and displeasure—and he has a small vocabulary of words to convey some specific meanings plus a number of recognizable grunts and sounds that he uses regularly as stand-ins for words. Of the ten, fifteen, or forty words he may have, many are for labeling everyday objects and people.

However, there are times when the 15-month-old wants to talk about himself clearly and directly—I am tired; I am hungry; I want to go outside; I want you to change my shirt—but most of these words, particularly the word *I*, are not yet in his vocabulary. Moreover, the 15-month-old is not yet able to use sentences of more than one word. It is difficult to convey a feeling or a desire with just one word. Compounding these difficulties is the fact that language skills at this age degrade when the toddler is fatigued, hungry, or upset, the times he most wants to talk.

Toddlers use their limited vocabularies ingeniously. One 16-month-old had an eight-word spoken vocabulary. One of his favorite words was *dirtee* which he used to refer to soil, pebbles, and dirt on his clothes. For a while *dirtee* was the most frequent word he said, and he seemed uninterested in saying other words. This kind of word use is another example of classification.

Toddlers who have larger vocabularies also tend to use words that show their recognition of similarities among certain things. One child used *moon* as a classifying word for the moon in the sky, oranges, and a ball. Another used *po-po* to indicate red berries, red earrings, and a red toy truck. A noted researcher described how a $14\frac{1}{2}$-month-old used the word *ah* to tell an adult that he wanted a particular toy. He used *ah* several ways and several times (along with pointing and eye contact) to indicate that the toys the adult picked out of a toy box were not the ones he wanted. When the adult finally picked up the right toy, the child opened his hand to receive it.

Cognition

Researchers often use play activities to demonstrate cognitive growth at this age. The behaviors of Tim and Noah described in the Snapshot represent play that is a form of trial-and-error learning. What happens if I do this or that? Trial-and-error learning is especially easy to observe with playthings such as blocks, sticks, and playdough. Carefully and methodically, a 15-month-old takes a toy rake and uses it to tap a rectangular shaped block. She then pushes the rake, stands it on the prong end, and brings it back to the rectangular block again. She takes the rake to the playdough, indents the dough slightly, and peers at the change in the shape. This kind of learning has several benefits: the toddler increases her knowledge of what she can do; she learns that a hard object can have an effect on something soft; she learns that the shape of a hard object means that it can stand alone or can be stacked. As with Tim and Noah, trial-and-error activities may not have a well-defined goal, and even if it does include a goal, the toddler doesn't need to reach the goal to have a productive learning experience.

Play also reflects the 15-month-old's increasing awareness of the function of objects. Functional play is the term researchers use for children's attempt to use a toy brush to comb their own hair or use a rag to wipe a piece of furniture. Functional play can come about only when the child identifies a real object and associates the object with an action.

> *Hint*
>
> Assorted blocks, playdough, and different-size small balls promote play and learning.

An advanced form of functional play is occasionally seen in the 15-month-old's play with dolls. Here the toddler takes small-scale versions of real objects and applies them to a doll. She feeds the doll with a toy bottle or puts it to bed in a toy crib. In this kind of play, toddlers also transfer to the doll the kinds of care they have received. In effect they see the doll as a stand-in for themselves and themselves as a stand-in for a parent. When the toddler engages in a parent role using a doll as a child, she is engaging in an early form of role reversal that increases her understanding of the activities of parents as opposed to the activities of young children.

One final comment about functional play: it is a transitional form of play. It is more advanced than the play of the 12-month-old who is just beginning to combine two objects with or without regard to the objects' characteristics, but it is less advanced than the pretend play that is often observed at about 18 months. In pretend play, the child makes believe: she combs her hair with an imaginary comb. She does not need to have the real object in her hand; an image of the object in her mind is enough.

This month the toddler's play often shows an increase in learning about cause and effect. One of the most favored toys in my laboratory is a jack-in-the-box. With a great deal of assistance from his mother, 15-month-old Michael turns the handle so that jack pops up. Michael laughs merrily, and shrugging away his mother's assistance, he begins pounding on the box in an attempt to close it. He then bangs the box on the floor and tries turning the handle. He hasn't yet figured out that he has to push the jack into the box, but for the very first time he is indicating that he knows the jack has to go back into the box before he pops up again. Michael sees a cause-and-effect relation.

Michael's play shows not only causal awareness but the beginnings of a systematic plan to operate the jack-in-the-box on his own. What he lacks is knowledge of the final piece of the causal sequence. Michael's mother (or father or big brother) can play a vital role here by showing him how the jack goes into the box in the context of a joint play activity.

Social

The 15-month-old is especially interested in including others in his experiences. One toddler who saw a bird in a cage pulled his mother to the cage, pointed at the bird, and then pointed upwards as if telling his mother that birds fly in the sky. Another pointed to the family dog and said, "Grrr."

As mentioned in the Snapshot, a social behavior that develops around this age is comforting, sharing, and helping others. Researchers call these prosocial behaviors. Being able to respond prosocially involves a link between the child's developing cognitions, his ability to feel and interpet emotions, and his socialization experiences in which he has been cared for by others. Knowing when and how to comfort and help requires that the toddler distinguish among facial expressions, have had some exposure to other individuals' different responses to his own and another's distress, recognize that the distress one feels occurs because someone else is feeling distress, and sense how to respond.

The toddler months are the first age at which children have developed enough cognitive, social, and emotional prerequisites for prosocial acts. Children younger than 15 or 16 months are not unaffected by someone else's hurt, but their cognitive immaturity makes them uncertain about the source of their own distress and how to respond to another person's distress. Precursor behaviors are observed in babies, particularly toward the end of the first year. For example, one developmental scientist described how a 12-month-old handled his own distress by sucking his thumb and pulling on his ear. Upon seeing his father's sad face, he looked sad, sucked his thumb and pulled on his father's ear. A 13-month-old responded to an adult look of distress by offering his doll.

> *Hint*
>
> ---
>
> Make a point of praising your child's actions when he shows caring behaviors.

There is some disagreement about the origins of prosocial acts. Some developmental researchers suggest that caring is a part of being human, and therefore the toddler's caring is simply a function of a maturing biological predisposition. Others disagree, proposing instead that prosocial behaviors are learned from close and affectionate relationships with others. I tend to agree. Children learn from parents who are themselves openly caring and who offer explanations about hurts experienced by others.

Toddlers' prosocial behaviors are not directed indiscriminately. Those who have siblings may be less inclined to share and to offer comfort to them than they are to a parent. (In fact, one researcher has documented numerous instances of teasing and fighting among toddlers and siblings.) The point is that a child's history of experiences (including emotional experiences) with siblings and peers are brought to bear on prosocial acts. Thus, the seemingly simple act of showing caring rests on intricate social interactions.

Emotions

In my own studies, we found rapid mood swings at this age; the 15-month-old can be gleeful one minute, fretting the next, and laughing a minute or two later. Toddlers are often delighted with themselves, but they do have a low tolerance for some frustrations. If they are involved with peers, disagreements may arise about possessions. Some toddlers might get upset while waiting to get dressed when they're anxious to go outside. Although crying is fairly common, there are few instances of real tantrums. From a parent's perspective, the 15-month-old's emotional upsets are annoying.

This month the toddler's love of physical activity causes her to demonstrate attachments in several new ways. Ann will move over and sit close to another toddler, even though she doesn't actually play with her peer. When she is across the room from her brother, she periodically establishes eye contact to maintain her feelings of inclusion. While she is more inclined to wander about, Ann regularly looks back to see that a favorite person is still somewhere in sight. Mothers in one of my studies reported that toddlers engaged in more clinging at this age.

Sense of Self

Many of the behaviors that characterize this age illustrate the toddler's evolving sense of self. Trial-and-error activities and particularly persistent repetitions of behaviors demonstrate interest in mastery (competence). Preoccupation and annoyance with having dirty hands or being particular about what she wears indicate an increasing awareness of the appearance of the physical self. Frequent displays of clinging and empathic behaviors suggest that the sense of belonging is becoming a more conscious element of self. The rise in imitative actions of parents and siblings answers the toddler's awakening sense of the self within the context of the family.

❧ Developmental Close-up

Socializing Children to Everyday Standards of Behavior

Most of my research focuses on when parents begin to communicate do's and don'ts to their young children and how children respond to these requests and commands. Why do rules matter? Simply stated, families and societies endure and grow by socializing the young to accept values, conventions, and norms. I do not mean that socialization should consist of harsh directives on the part of parents or slavish obedience on the part of children. Rather, parents should try to impart some of the values that are important to them. Research shows that many children in our culture who have behavioral difficulties, such as acting out against others or being overly aggressive, did not receive or did not learn early socialization lessons.

The first concerted efforts in socialization occur early in the second year as children begin to walk and talk. Parents implicitly reason that an unconstrained walking child is a potential menace and assume that a talking child is able to reason. Parents' earliest attempts at socialization involve making the toddler aware of acceptable and unacceptable actions in relation to just a few issues. "No, you cannot climb on the table. You could fall off and be hurt." "Please take your shoes off when you sit on the couch so that it doesn't get dirty and worn."

During the past fourteen years, my colleagues and I have seen hundreds of children between the ages of one and seven years. We now have a good idea of what middle-class, educated parents ask for in the way of everyday rules, how their young children respond, what children understand about rules, and some of the factors that enable children to improve at going along with rules. It is clear that the road to socialization to standards has bumps and potholes for almost all parents and children.

One of the ways we learned about parents' do's and don'ts was to ask them. Specifically we asked about the behaviors they tried to prohibit and the behaviors they tried to encourage. At 15 months, most of the prohibitions were directed at safety: no climbing without supervision, no running in the street, no touching a light socket, or no playing near a hot stove. Although safety prohibitions continue to be a high priority for parents well into the preschool years, the content of the prohibitions changes. Older children are asked to hold an adult's hand while on an escalator or in a parking lot, not to go outdoors and ride a tricycle alone, and not to talk to strangers.

Increasingly, as children grow older, parents' prohibitions become more customized, that is, they reflect a family's unique routines and values. At 24 months, some specific ones are not pulling the dog's tail, not banging toys on baby brother's head, not putting small things in the mouth, not using a pacifier during the day. At 42 months, prohibitions include not drawing on the living room walls, not removing clothes when company is visiting, not trying to hang up the phone when someone is using it, and not fighting with children in school. And at 48 months, numerous prohibitions are directed toward making the child a citizen of the community: not screaming in public, not playing with guns, not going to the neighbor's house too early in morning, not using bathroom words, and not fighting with others.

Parents in our studies were as concerned about encouraging behaviors as they were about issuing prohibitions. This concern was generally quite modest when children were 13 to 21 months old. By 24 to 30 months, mothers reported their interest in fostering independence. They encouraged their children to play on their own, try new foods, pick up after themselves after toy play, cooperate in dressing, and walk instead of being carried. At age four or so, as with prohibitions, the theme of being a good citizen appeared. Children were encouraged to play nicely, develop table manners, dress themselves, observe family religious practices, read on their own, learn physical skills such as swimming, engage in family routines such as clearing the table and taking out the garbage, and be polite to tradespeople.

Although parents introduced prohibitions and restrictions relatively early, the children's compliance evolved slowly. Parents' reports were corroborated by the child behaviors we observed in homes and in the laboratory. Overall, children learned safety rules, prohibitions about others' possessions, and rules about being nice to others earlier and more successfully than other rules. Children had the hardest time learning to wait: to wait until a parent got off the phone, to wait for mealtimes, and to wait to open birthday presents.

It was particularly intriguing to observe the ways young children found to resist their parents' wishes. Early in the second year, they ignored and teased, even on safety issues. Beth, at 14 months, decided to take her teddy bear outside to the driveway. Her parents watched surreptitiously while she walked over to a berry bush that they had repeatedly warned her not to touch. Beth picked a berry and showed it to her bear, all the while saying "No!" Turning suddenly, she spied her parents. Beth flung the bear aside, put the berry in her mouth, and ran. Yes, her behavior was illogical from an adult perspective, but it was obvious that she was issuing a questioning dare to her parents: What will you do to me for breaking a rule? Her parents responded with an unmistakable scolding and later reported that they never saw her approach the berry bush again.

Throughout the second year, crying was also a relatively common way of resisting a parent's request; at about 30 months or so, crying was observed less often. Outright refusals (lots of forthright "No!"s) began to appear at around two years. In addition, early in the third year children began to engage in a primitive form of negotiation with their parents. We used the term negotiation to describe the child's willingness to continue a dialog with her parents even while denying a request. Sometimes the negotiation was an attempt to delay or avoid a response. "I have to go potty." "Read me a story first." "I'm hungry." As children got older, they negotiated in ways that indicated that they would obey but on their own terms. One child who was asked to pick up the toys he was playing with said he would first pick up all of the trucks. Another asked which fast food place he and his mother would go to when he finished putting his toys away.

I think negotiation is a wonderful behavior. It allows children to gain a sense of competency and importance in their own right. It also shows them that talking is a way to work out disagreements. And learning to negotiate with parents probably helps later on as children learn to reconcile their disputes with their peers.

Eighteen Months

thinks using ideas

pays attention longer

larger but still constraining vocabulary

seeks others' help

occasionally restless, irritable, and stubborn

Average Boy: Height is 32.5 inches, with most between 31 and 34 inches.
Weight is 25+ pounds, with most between 22 and 28.5 pounds.
Average Girl: Height is 32 inches, with most between 30.5 and 33.5 inches.
Weight is 23.5+ pounds, with most between 20.5+ and 27 pounds.

❧ Snapshot

The 18-month-old, a picture of conflicting behavioral maturity and immaturity, straddles a developmental fence. Sometimes she acts "grownup," playing contentedly with her toys, holding "conversations" with her parents, dolls, and herself, and more or less following her parents' requests. She is delightful to be with because her play is imaginative and she pays attention for longer periods of time. She clearly loves to be with others, showing great pleasure with children or adults. Other times, though, she reverts to babylike behaviors. She is fretful and clinging, unable or unwilling to play, listless with her food, and whiny when asked to do just about anything. *No* is a frequent word whether she means it or not. Restlessness is also an issue, and public excursions (restaurants, church/synagogue) can be nightmares for parents. What is happening?

Let's look first at behavioral maturity. The famous psychologist Jean Piaget viewed this age as one that ushers in six months of momentous cognitive growth. He contended that play between 18 and 24 months shows new modes of thinking. Piaget described toddlers as starting to form ideas (or concepts) that can be recalled and used as needed. Prior to this month, knowledge has been based primarily on sensory perceptions or motor skills; that is, on things the young child can currently see, hear, or touch. In the 18-to-24 month period, the child gradually learns to deal with events and objects that are not present in the here and now. By 24 months the toddler's ability to think in terms of ideas has improved considerably; now she can conjure up ideas about past events ("Yesterday we . . .") and the future ("Go when daddy home?"). Ideas open up a whole new world for the toddler; there is more to life than this moment's experience!

The toddler's emerging ability to think with ideas is observable in the way she plays, particularly pretend play in which she playfully reenacts her own experiences. Ann is not tired, but she plays out a little scene in which she pretends she is going to sleep: she gets her teddy bear and lies down on a piece of cloth. Her play shows that she has an idea about sleep and the props that go with it. Pretending may involve applying a familiar experience to a doll. Ann is outside in the play area of her preschool where she has just gathered a toy cup and plate and placed them in front of her rag doll. Her face serious, she pauses for a minute and looks around the yard. Her eyes land on a small pile of fallen pine needles. Ann walks over to the pile, picks up a handful of the needles, and puts them on the toy plate. She pretends to feed her doll the pine needles. Ann has ideas about food and where it is served. She knows that pine needles are not food but that they can serve as pretend food for her doll.

A great deal of research has documented the various forms of pretend play that emerge over the next 12 to 18 months. Moreover, a substantial amount of research supports Piaget's assertion that a major reorganization of capabilities occurs during the last half of the second year. Studies show a spurt in language production at about 18 months. There is strong evidence that the 18-month-old is beginning to consolidate her sense of self, her distinctiveness and identity. In the social domain, research shows that toddlers now recognize that some problems and situations are too difficult for them and intentionally turn to another for assistance. Overall, then, in the second half of the second year there is dynamic growth—cognitively, socially, linguistically, and personally—in behavioral maturity.

What about behavioral immaturity? Arnold Gesell, pediatrician and child psychologist, described this age as a time rich in behavioral transformations. Gesell focused on the challenges confronting the 18-month-old in coordinating and integrating new behaviors. While studying how 18-month-olds grapple with these challenges, one of Gesell's colleagues remarked that children of this age walk a one-way street in the direction opposite to that desired by others and with headstrong single-mindedness. Why? Learning how to put these skills in order and knowing when and how to use them demands a great deal of energy and self-absorption.

It is no wonder, then, that 18-month-olds are overwhelmed from time to time and have difficulty dealing with the world outside their own sphere. In this context, it is understandable why seemingly trivial events and requests such as "Let me wipe your face," "Don't walk with the bottle," and "Please sit over here" sometimes lead to fretfulness and volcanic bursts of emotions. Of the ages described thus far, this is the one most apt to test a parent's patience. Flexibility and humor help.

Yet even at stressful times, the 18-month-old can be both loving and contrite. Ryan and his mother came to class one morning. As Ryan's mother described him to my students, she mentioned the previous evening's crisis. She seemed a little sad as she spoke. Ryan had forgotten a family rule and had run in the living room. He bumped into a small table that fell over, and a valuable lamp broke. Everybody was upset. Ryan listened intently while his mother talked, then turning to her, he tugged at her skirt and urgently said, "Up, up." As his mother held him, he buried his face in her shoulder. The whole experience must have flashed before his eyes.

Ryan's actions in the classroom revealed prosocial (caring) behaviors, a sense of self and the wrong he had committed, and self-reproach for his actions. He also demonstrated some cognitive maturity: he clearly remembered the incident without requiring a visual hint such as a photograph, he understood some of the words spoken by his mother, and he anticipated the conclusion of the tale, responding to his mother's sadness and seeking her help to relieve his own distress. Ryan's behavior was direct and appropriate, a signal of developmental maturity.

Will Ryan consistently act so mature at this age? Probably not. His ability to remember the event was aided by the fact that he and his mother had experienced a very emotional interaction in which both cared intensely about what specifically happened and how each other felt about the incident. The classroom reenactment provided them with another opportunity to play out their feelings. His mother's emotion-charged re-creation of the event reactivated Ryan's prosocial behaviors. Most of the time, of course, the 18-month-old doesn't dramatically reexperience events in this way. Ryan's cognitive skills and self-awareness are still fairly rudimentary, and his recollection of all the details of this complex event would be difficult for him to reconstruct without cues.

❧ Images of Development

Motor

Occasionally, in certain circumstances, the 18-month-old blissfully walks, runs, and climbs, all within a minute or two, but in general he does not spend as much time in goal-directed gross motor activities as younger toddlers. This month the biggest changes in gross motor skills are improvements in balance. The 18-month-old strolls effortlessly on smooth surfaces, nimbly climbs on furniture, and can simultaneously wander about and pull a toy without losing his balance. A very noticeable change this month is that he is able to walk up stairs while holding on to a rail.

The toddler's fine motor skills continue to improve. He picks up small pieces (a quarter inch or less) of bread or cracker smoothly without extraneous finger movements. He turns pages of books, tries to use a crayon to imitate lines on a sketchpad, and builds block towers that are three or four blocks high. He uses spoons for eating, although he often reverts to finger feeding since he is still much more successful with this technique.

Perception

Form perception now includes differentiation of round puzzle pieces from square ones, and the 18-month-old appropriately places some block forms in a puzzle board. He recognizes one or two colors by name.

Language

🌺 *Comprehension.* The 18-month-old is beginning to understand word meanings as opposed to simple word associations. During a three-month period that begins at around 18 months, toddlers usually learn the meanings of the names of familiar persons, the labels given to everyday objects, action verbs such as *go, come,* and *bring,* and brief commands or statements such as "Put the book on the shelf," provided both the book and the shelf are within view.

The 18-month-old also realizes that certain responses are required for specific phrases such as "What's that?" or "What do you say?" She recognizes a single word in a sentence and uses the word to infer the meaning of the entire sentence. Despite impressive growth in understanding, the 18-month-old makes incorrect guesses about a word's meaning. One morning, Ann's mother, father, and aunt are talking about her father going to work as he prepares to leave. Ann is asked where her father is going. "Work," she replies. That afternoon she is told her aunt has to leave. "Where is your aunt going?" she is asked. Solemnly Ann says, "Work." Still later her mother realizes that the dog is not in the room and asks where the dog is. Ann answers, "Work." Is Ann's understanding of work tied to something or someone being present or absent? We just don't know.

🌺 *Production.* Word production at around 18 months is highly variable, but for most children this is an age where production increases rapidly, often by five or six new words a week. In one study the range of vocabulary of 20-month-old children was 1 to over 400 words and the average was more than 140 words, approximately a threefold increase in production during the time since the child celebrated his first birthday.

In one of my studies, we were curious about 18-month-olds' ability to produce sentences. Of thirty children, six routinely combined two or three

> ### Hint
>
> Sometimes reading a story can help clear up a child's confusion about a word. For example, a book that has stories about people going to work might help her understanding of the meaning of the word work.

words into a sentence, four produced no intelligible words, and the rest used only one word at a time. When an 18-month-old does produce a two- or three-word sentence, the sentence usually includes a noun (or pronoun) and a verb and is delivered with an intonation that replicates the sentences of older children and adults. Two-word speech is often used descriptively about current actions ("Car go"), possession ("Mommy shoe"), location ("Doll gone"), disappearance and reappearance of an object or person ("Where ball?"), negation ("No sleep"), and emotional states ("Daddy mad"). The words in these short sentences are often slurred together, for example, "Poppatruck" or "Seeya." Slurring also condenses words that have two or three syllables: *nana* for banana or *ple* for apple.

Overall, the most common words in the 18-month-old's vocabulary continue to be those used most in everyday interactions with people, objects, and events. Therefore, depending on their life experiences, two toddlers may produce the same number of words but substantially different words. Regardless of their specific rearing experiences, most 18-month-olds can identify and name one or two colors. They are also able to name a few pictures in their favorite books.

Several other interesting features of vocabulary growth may begin to occur at around 18 months. First, studies show that toddlers often repeatedly use a word involved in a concept they are in the process of learning. If a child is learning about the concept of disappearance, he may say "Gone" when a toy disappears, when food is eaten, or when someone leaves the room.

Second, word imitation is also common as children become more facile with words. As with comprehension, children may give the impression that they know the meaning of a word when they are simply enchanted by producing this particular sound. For example, Andrew heard someone say *gorilla*. He then said "rilla," he sang "rilla," and he demanded that his truck "rilla." However, when shown a picture of a gorilla, he was surprised when it was called a gorilla.

Third, children sometimes truly struggle to find words. New words do not necessarily come easily. For months Andrew had called his mother Mommy, his father Da, and his grandfather Poppa. One night when he was about 18 months old, Andrew turned to give me a hug. Looking at me he said, "Mommy." His face registered surprise. He looked at me again and said, "Poppa." His body stiffened; that wasn't right either. His mother and I simultaneously called out "Grandma." But it wasn't until weeks later that he said "Gama" on his own.

Not unrelated to these language developments is the 18-month-old's fascination with the word *No*. He says this word over and over again. This makes sense in the context of a concept he is learning as well as a word he often hears: his own mischief provides ample opportunity to receive prompts to imitate this word. True to form, it is often the case that the 18-month-old does not know what *no* means, even though he may use it in an appropriate context.

Other aspects of language growth are more subtle. At 19 months Ann is sometimes able to use a word in different contexts. This achievement is referred to as decoupling. Ann's first decoupled word was *side*, which was her term for outside. On different occasions she used *side* to inform her mother of the whereabouts of the family pet ("Puppy side") and the family car ("Car side"). She also used it to announce her desire to go for a ride in the car when her mother had just told her it was naptime. She said, "Car side," ran from the room, and headed for the front door.

At this age overgeneralization—use of one word to label related objects—is still common. One toddler used the word *jues* to indicate juice, water in his bottle, a small pond, and water that trickled from the garden hose. The word *puppy* covered the dinosaurs he saw on his socks, pictures of goats and lambs, and of course the neighbor's dogs. However, he was so amazed one day at seeing a huge heifer that he was speechless; no amount of encouragement could get him to say "puppy," much less "cow."

An aspect of speech that eludes the toddler is word flexibility, that is, locating the right word to say or substituting one word for another. Thus the 18-month-old may find himself speechless in times of stress. Unrelated words may tumble out of his mouth as he struggles to find the right words to communicate his feelings.

Hint

Don't hesitate to help your child find words when he is stuck.

Cognition

The toddler is able to devise new and complex forms of planning behavior when he begins to think in terms of ideas. For one thing, ideas allow him to envision potential consequences. Ideas also promote the complex behaviors toddlers need to come up with to carry out adaptive solutions. Michael discovers that a spring-loaded screen door slams shut unless he holds it open. His goal is to retrieve a toy that is just inside the door. He holds the door open with one hand and with the other reaches inside the room. Toy in hand, he lets go of the door.

Improvement in recall memory is appreciable this month and can be observed in object permanence tasks in which a toy is hidden under one of several felt pads. Most 18-month-olds have no difficulty solving the task that involves a complex series of toy moves. I show the child a toy, close my fist over it, and then randomly move my hand under three felt pads. I leave the toy under a pad and show the child my empty hand. Ignoring my hand, the 18-month-old typically goes for the right pad and finds the toy.

Recognition memory is also more efficient. Michael watched his mother make a pie crust. First she used a pastry blender to mix the dough, then she patted the dough into a pie pan, and then she set the pan in the oven. She said "Hot" while opening the oven door. A week later, on seeing the pastry blender in a kitchen drawer, Michael said, "Hot." This example of recognition memory shows an ability to use a cue to remember a complex sequence of events.

> ## Hint
> ---
> Children of this age love to be included in simple cooking activities. Just keep them safe.

The 18-month-old recognizes and remembers that others have possessions. Michael's father wears a necktie to work. When Michael observes his grandfather with a shirt and necktie, he climbs on his grandfather's lap, says "Dada," and thrusts his finger into his grandfather's chest. On another day, Michael greets his grandfather's arrival shrieking "Pop-pop!", goes to the living window looking for his grandfather's truck, sees it, and says "Pop-pop."

At this age improved memory skills often combine with the ability to think in terms of ideas to produce some complex play behaviors. When Tracy visited my class, I provided her with a small basket filled with wooden blocks of various shapes, dolls, a few wind-up toys, and toy plates. Inadvertently, I had neglected to include trucks and cars, and Tracy's passion was cars. She rummaged in the basket for a few minutes and then took out a long wooden block. It became a car. "Vroom, vroooom," she said, as she moved the block-car from one end of the room to the other. Tracy's improvisation showed that she remembered the shape of cars and so could choose an appropriate stand-in for a car.

Another benefit of the toddler's new cognitive skills is that she doesn't have to spend as much time in trial-and-error learning to figure out cause-and-effect relationships. Tracy is given a new pull toy, a bear on a platform with wheels. Attached to the platform is a colored string that can be used to pull the bear from place to place. For the past few months one of Tracy's favorite pastimes has been pulling a long-handled musical rolling toy. Now she looks at the bear, studies the string, and then grabs it to pull the bear around the living room. She has recognized that the long handle and the string share the common property of enabling a toy to be pulled.

Improved mental capabilities help the toddler learn about standards of "correctness" with respect to the world of objects. Tracy has a rudimentary idea about the way everyday objects ought to look. Her father keeps small treats for the family dog in a covered plastic jar. She discovers one day that the jar is lidless, and she pulls her father over to see the jar, jabbering to express her concern. Recognizing how physical things "should be" will lead later to dealing with how things should be in the social world.

Social

Toddlers of 18 months are often delightfully caring with parents, siblings, and other familiar relatives and friends, freely dispensing hugs, kisses, and gentle pats. They often react with prosocial responses when others show signs of hurt or distress. At the same time, toddlers increasingly seek out others' assistance, in contrast to the more passive looking behaviors (social referencing) observed at 10 months. Ann struggles with a puzzle, frets a bit, and then takes the puzzle to her mother. Help is received, and she trots off happily to continue her play.

Toddlers often seek parents' help when they encounter a new situation, such as a first visit to the zoo or an introduction to unfamiliar agemates. The toddler may briefly cling, fret, and avoid looking at the new surroundings or a strange child. Gradually she sneaks a few glances, furtively assesses the scene, acclimates to the situation, and eventually feels safe enough to venture forth. Knowing she can turn back to a caregiver gives her confidence.

The mobility of the 18-month-old means that parents increase their rules for safety, respect for possessions, and being nice. My research shows that by 18 months or so most children do comply with a few rules; at this age parents generally report compliance to a very specific rule, such as not going near a hot stove. If parents emphasize *please* and *thank-you*, some toddlers imitate the intonation, if not the words, in a few appropriate situations.

Children of this age often show rudimentary peer social skills by briefly maintaining play interactions with children of similar age in a meaningful sequence of behaviors. Two toddlers select a doll to play with. If one engages in feeding the doll, the other follows along. The children smile to each other and make eye contact. Verbalizations are infrequent.

Emotions

The 18-month-old is ordinarily a happy child who laughs easily and shows delight in running and jumping, playing with his toy trucks and trains, and going to the playground with his parents. But his tolerance for frustration is low. If he can't move his train tracks into position he frets, and he frets when someone has spilled sand all over the slide at the playground. The frets are signs of displeasure and pleas for help, and usually they last only a few seconds.

Sometimes frets indicate a general state of restlessness in which the toddler cannot settle down and cannot get across what he wants or needs. Michael indicates that he wants to go swimming, so his grandfather takes him to a nearby pool. But Michael frets repeatedly, and his grandfather finally takes him home. Thirty minutes later Michael is fretting again, tugging at his grandfather's hand and saying, "Pool, pool."

There are days when crying bouts are long and intense. Perhaps they are related to fatigue or being especially hungry or some unknown event. A child in one of my studies wanted a pen belonging to a family friend. His mother said "No" and offered him a familiar toy. The toddler lay on the floor and kicked his legs, his face became flushed, and he wailed loudly. The tantrum lasted six long minutes.

On some occasions it is easy to identify the source of fretfulness but a solution is not readily forthcoming. When Michael was 18 months old, his mother was in the hospital for two days after the birth of a new baby. During her absence Michael stayed with his grandparents. He had visited them many times and loved to be with them, and they doted on him. The first day of his mother's absence went well, with a normal number of brief upsets, but the next morning Michael woke up crying and whining, "Mommy, Mommy, Mommy." He was inconsolable for most of the morning. He cried when held by his grandmother and called out for Paulie, his favorite aunt, and Pah, his grandfather. When Paulie held him, he cried for Mah, his grandmother. When his grandmother took him again, he whined, "Mommy." Finally, despite miserable weather, Michael's grandmother dressed him warmly and took him for a walk in his stroller. Eventually he fell asleep, and when he awoke his fretfulness had disappeared. But he was subdued for the rest of the day.

This is the age at which 60 percent of toddlers turn to what scientists call a transitional object as a means of securing comfort. Linus's blanket in the Peanuts comic strip is an example of a transitional object, most often a soft and cuddly blanket or fluffy stuffed animal.

Adherents of psychoanalytic thinking suggest that a transitional object is a replacement for an unavailable mother. However, children become upset even when their mothers are present, and many a toddler chews on his favorite blanket while being held in his mother's arms. It may be more useful to think of transitional objects simply as all-purpose soothers that effectively reduce tensions or emotional distress.

> ## Hint
>
> The only problem with transitional objects is that they get dirty. Try to wash them now and then.

Sense of Self

Of all the developmental changes that occur at around 18 months, none seems as wondrous as the child's burgeoning sense of selfhood. Self-recognition, self-consciousness, shyness, and a behavior that looks like shame all appear in a matter of weeks. The behaviors are so pervasive and come into view so suddenly that it seems as if a button labeled selfhood was pushed. Of course, there is no magic developmental button. The 18-month-old's awareness of her own personhood and identity is a logical derivative of cognitive advances, specifically those related to thinking and remembering. The 18-month-old cares about her clothes, peers at her body parts, gladly accepts a chore such as putting napkins on the table. She raises her arms to help when her mother puts on her sweatshirt. She stuffs her mouth with cookies, then opens her mouth to show her father what she has done.

Recognition and labeling of body parts increases, and toddlers often describe themselves in terms of physical characteristics: "Big girl," "Little boy." At times a child may point to herself and say, "Baad." There is visual recognition as they regard themselves in a mirror. In a classic study, a researcher placed an 18-month-old in front of a mirror and let the child look at herself. Then he surreptitiously placed a bit of rouge on the child's nose and again placed her in front of the mirror. The toddler reacted negatively to her image with the spot. This study has been replicated many times, always with the same results. At 18 months, but not before, toddlers react with concern when their mirror image contains a violation of what they have come to expect.

I have observed behaviors that seem as if a toddler is somehow protecting his persona, another good indication of a developing self. Andrew woke up terribly irritable one morning and did not want breakfast. He took a cracker while standing near the kitchen table and whined and fretted. He cried when encouraged to sit at the table with his grandfather. Andrew then went behind a wooden chair, as if to hide from the others. The back of the chair had slats, so of course we could see him and he could see us. Yet, although he still fretted softly, it seemed as if he wanted to be alone. After a while he stopped fretting on his own and went to play with his train set.

The implications of self developments are profound: awareness of one's own needs, wishes, and feelings have long-term influences. The way a child comes to think about her "self" affects her motivation to achieve, her feelings of worth, and the success of relationships with peers.

> ## Hint
>
> Children of this age love to be told that they're good, cute, and big. Give them a lot of praise.

❧ Developmental Close-up

Joint Attention

One developmental theme of the first 18 months is the way behaviors are first displayed in an immature form, gradually become more coordinated, and finally become so routine that they require minimal mental energy and attention. Over time one behavior combines with another behavior that is developing concurrently, and together they result in a new level of developmental competency. Visual exploration is an example; so is grasping. In each case, the initial acts are occasional, awkward, and unsustained. As each matures, they work together: visual exploration of a toy happens at the same time the baby grasps a toy. Still later, the baby uses looking and finger movements to explore the working parts of a toy.

At about a year and a half, a linking process that has been developing for a long time shows a dramatic spurt. The behavior is called joint attention and involves a toddler's ability to systematically coordinate the attention he directs to people and to objects. The effective control of joint attention is fundamental to learning increasingly complex cognitive and social tasks. Some developmental theorists suggest that joint attention also is the reason for the surge in language production that occurs at around 18 months. Others speculate that it is the foundation for later conversations that involve ideas rather than objects. The point is that, when attention is under control, the child can concentrate on other challenges.

During previous months, the baby and then the toddler struggled to control attention in any number of situations. The very young baby tried to stay awake long enough to look around, the 5-month-old intently reaching for a toy was easily distracted by noises or other intrusive events, and the 14-month-old's delight in walking made it difficult to settle down and engage in play with small toys. Now, the 18-month-old's ability to coordinate attention to social interactions with attention to the object world provides an advantage for learning. He can, for example, recognize that he needs help doing a puzzle and smoothly moves his attention between the puzzle and the person helping.

Roger Bakeman and Lauren Adamson speculated about age trends in the growth of coordinated attention to people and to toys and did a study that supported their premises. Their research program provides a good illustration of how scientists go about investigating developmental issues. First they proposed a developmental summary, which goes like this. In the early months of life, almost all of the baby's attention during a social interaction, such as smiling to a person, is directed to the person and to the interaction. At around 6 months, babies' often direct attention to playing with objects; the face-to-face social interactions that were common in earlier months are now less frequent. Also at 6 months, a baby can switch his gaze from toy to person. By a year of age, a child can gesture to another about a toy or take a toy to another person.

Bakeman and Adamson argued that these examples of very specific kinds of attention did not necessarily mean that babies could readily display coordinated and active joint attention in unstructured play (that is,

> ### Hint
>
> Parents can help their babies and toddlers improve joint attention. Talking softly and animatedly while the young baby studies your face helps maintain attention. Talking about a toy while showing it to a toddler helps direct the child's attention to two points—the toy and you.

play that does not have a "formal" agenda or specific goal) with their mothers close by. The data obtained in their study supported their premise. They observed that an early form of coordinated joint attention was present at 6 months of age, but it was very brief (seven seconds in length) and represented only about 2 percent of all behaviors. Joint attention was a rare occurrence. At 13 months, the corresponding percentage of joint attention was 3.5 percent, and by 15 months it accounted for slightly more than 11 percent of play. However, three months later, at 18 months, coordinated joint attention represented more than 26 percent of behaviors, and the average length was about half a minute. Although 30 seconds is a relatively brief time span, the fact that toddlers spend a quarter of their unstructured play in joint attention means that they have numerous opportunities for learning to effectively coordinate their attention.

Some psychologists, and I am one, believe that effective attention control is very important to young children as they move into nursery school settings and peer social interactions. There are obvious reasons for the importance of attention control in school, but its role in play is often overlooked. Consider, for example, the play of four-year-olds. They play dress-up, take on adult roles, and otherwise engage in fanciful activities. Emotional displays are common, and children talk and play simultaneously. In order to be an effective play partner, a child has to monitor his peer's face, listen to his words, and also monitor his own play so that it is coordinated with his partner's play. Problems in monitoring can lead to problems in coming to terms with the play partner's goals, and consistently imperfect coordination makes it hard for a child to fit in with peers.

Twenty-One Months

applies ideas

runs, squats, and throws

understands me, my, mine, and I

replicates complex behavior sequences

can be exacting and resistant

Average Boy: *Height is 33.5 inches, with most between 32 and 36+ inches.*
Weight is 26.5 pounds, with most between 23 and 30+ pounds.
Average Girl: *Height is 33 inches, with most between 31.5 and 34.5 inches.*
Weight is 25 pounds, with most between 21.5 and 28 pounds.

❧ Snapshot

This month, behavioral changes tend to be evolutionary rather than revolutionary. It's a pleasant period of relatively smooth growth in which both child and parents can collect themselves.

Steady growth is especially apparent in the size of the toddler's vocabulary and his use of short sentences, and it demonstrates the toddler's increased cognitive maturity. He understands a state of possession (*mine*), classes of objects (different kinds of shirts), how to greet (*hi*) or protest (*no*), and how to describe an action (*train go bye*).

Another subtle change is a modest decline in irritability and fretfulness, although it's too early for parents to breathe a sigh of relief. The 21-month-old may cry less, but he is exacting, sometimes to the point of compulsiveness, in his wants and requests. At this age Michael wants his breakfast waffles served whole; if they are cut, he won't eat them. His peas and carrots must not touch the piece of chicken on his plate; if they do, he perceives the food as contaminated and will not eat. He will wear this shirt and not that one. His hands and his face must be washed right after he eats or he frets, "Dirty, dirty." "I hold milk," he insists, even though the cup of milk is likely to spill.

This need for control reflects a growing sense of self and mastery. To exercise control, Michael sometimes plans a course of action in terms of cause and effect. Michael's mother has repeatedly told him he is not to pull at her glasses. But Michael seems to have figured out that he can reach the forbidden eyeglasses if he is held. So he frets until his mother picks him up, and as soon as he is in her arms, he reaches out and snatches the glasses from her face. He laughs when she sets him back on the floor. Clever little guy, she smiles to herself. To Michael she sternly says, "That's a no-no!"

Michael also knows that if he plays with his mother's handbag, she will disapprove if she finds him out. No problem, he reasons; if she can't see me, she won't get mad. He hides behind the sofa and merrily explores the contents of her bag. The 21-month-old's efforts to control a situation can be exasperating for parents. But at this age the toddler isn't purposely being contrary, he's just being clever.

There is a side benefit to efforts to exert control: they demand close attention to other people and their actions. Michael watches intently the things that happen in his miniworld, and his precise imitation of others' actions even days after the action has occurred shows that he can store and retrieve memories of events that are important to him. One morning not long after his dad has gone off to work, Michael is playing quietly in a corner of the kitchen. He picks a small block from his toy basket and begins to rub it along each of his cheeks. Then he walks over to the sink and starts to wash his face. He clearly remembers what his father does when he shaves and needs no cue to imitate this sequence of events. Along with attention and memory, this kind of imitation is important because it means that the child has worked out an understanding that a sequence of events has a beginning and an end.

At this age it is rare to see elaborate forms of imitation carried over to play with peers. Small groups of 21-month-olds tend to play in brief episodes that involve physical activity: into the sandbox to fill buckets and dump them, over to the tunnel to explore, then inside to examine the new carpet for the play area. In their physical play they grunt, gesture to each other, and laugh. If imitation occurs, it is immediate, one little parrot imitating another. Every so often a dispute breaks out over toys and crying results.

Children of 21 months also enjoy quiet times and spend short periods stacking blocks and knocking them down, putting objects into containers and taking them out, and stacking rings on a spindle. When in a small group, they periodically make gestural bids to each other, such as holding out a toy, but most of the time they just sit next to one other, looking at each other but playing alone. Verbal exchanges, if they occur at all, are brief. At this age producing extended conversations still demands so much energy and attention that it is difficult to play with a peer and simultaneously hold a conversation with him, especially when he too is not conversationally adept. Talk is out and gestures are in!

Overall, this month many toddlers slow down motorically, though they can hardly be described as quiet and prim. They still love to run and climb, but they are also content to sit quietly and play with toys. Restlessness is not as big a problem as it was three months ago. On the other hand, they are continuing to develop a vision of how things "should be" and become upset when they're not. The mother who responds to the toddler's cry for help by sitting at his left side may be surprised to find that he becomes more distressed until she sits by his right side.

❧ *Images of Development*

Motor

Balance is even better this month, and the toddler now routinely squats while playing. Now she sometimes walks down steps holding on with one hand. She is more comfortable this month walking up stairs by herself, although she still holds on to the rail. She runs faster because her toddler gait is less pronounced. Her feet tend to point straight or even inward a bit as opposed to the outward foot stance that characterizes the young toddler.

Although she can kick a large ball after watching her big brother kick strongly and forcefully, her kick is largely uncoordinated and somewhat unbalanced. The toddler is also better able to throw things this month. She seems to realize now that the whole arm, not just the wrist, is needed to throw. This ability is not without its drawbacks for parents. The 21-month old is not selective about what she throws, and food and sand from the sandbox rank right up there with balls as objects to hurl.

The 21-month-old's hand control is increasingly precise. Ann clenches a crayon in her palm; and when presented with a piece of paper, she uses the crayon to scribble. Unfortunately, she may color on just about anything, including walls, tables, and her favorite book. Ann's fine motor skills also lead to some explorations that increase safety risks. For instance, she is intrigued by electrical outlets and putting things like paper clips into them. Parents have to step up safety vigilance this month.

Many toddlers enjoy showing how well they do in everyday dressing activities. They wriggle out of clothes when it is time to undress—and sometimes when it is not time to undress. They successfully pull off socks and shoes and might work an arm out of a sweater or jacket. Some children of this age can partially zip up large zippers and unbutton large buttons. Much depends on how adept their fingers are; like adults, some toddlers are more deft than others.

Hint

Buy or make little books that have zippers, buttons, and snaps so that the toddler can practice these skills. Tennis shoes with velcro fasteners allow the toddler to remove her shoes on her own. This gives her a feeling of independence.

Perception

Visual form perception again shows improvement. The 21-month-old not only recognizes the difference in shape of circular, square, and triangular puzzle pieces, she can also place them with assistance in a simple puzzle.

Most toddlers enjoy the feel of different textures and are fond of play that involves getting their hands into water, sand, cookie dough, and shaving cream. Mud is a different story. Many a 21-month-old pleasurably wiggles her toes in mud but wouldn't dream of making mud pies: "Dirty!"

Language

Production shows growth in the number of new words the 21-month-old has in her vocabulary and in her ability to construct two-word sentences. She also is better able to come up with the correct word label for an object or person. Sentences usually consist of a noun and a verb and do not include conjunctions such as *and*. Adjectives and adverbs are rarely used, however, sometimes babies use them to describe emotional states.

The way words are used expands considerably. Toddlers now use words used to refer to themselves. At 18 months the most common personal referents are *me* and *mine*; this month a small percentage of children also use *my* and *I*, as well as their own names. Being able to refer to themselves in a variety of ways marks a profound change in the effectiveness of the toddler's communication with others. There is no mistaking the message in the statement "Me go" or "Mine doll," but there could have been a misinterpretation of the single-word sentences "Go" or "Doll" or "Mine."

In addition to labeling themselves and their possessions, toddlers of this age also use words to label their body parts. Nose, eye, hair, ears, and mouth are body parts that are most easily identified. Many little boys also use the label *penis*. It seems to be easier for boys to learn the label for their genitalia because the body part is so obvious. Little girls have a harder time with a term such as *vagina* because the body part is not visible to the child and the word is hard to pronounce.

Equally as important as being able to talk about possessions and wants is being able to talk about feelings. By 21 months, many toddlers can describe in a shorthand way their emotions and their internal states. It's not unusual to hear "Me mad," "Head owie" (head hurt), "Me tired." Overall,

> *Hint*
>
> Most children of this age love to play in water. If this doesn't pose a problem, let your child play in a shallow wading pool.

toddlers of this age have so many more spoken words that the gap between comprehension and production is less of a problem for them.

For all the growth in speech skills at this age, toddlers have a difficult time with pronunciation of some letters and words. (Fully mastering pronunciation will take several more years.) Researchers who study language development suggest that young children need to simplify their language production in order to get their ideas across. It's as if their energy has to go into the communicative intent of their message rather than into correct pronunciation. At this age the toddler's vocal apparatus is developed enough to say full words and to use the right consonants, yet they don't. If a group of consonants appears in a word, one of the consonants tends to be dropped. *Street* becomes *treet*. Sometimes final consonants are dropped: *bring* becomes *brin*. The first consonant and vowel of some words are repeated to make up the word: *water* becomes *wawa*. In general, *g* and *k* sounds are difficult for toddlers.

Fortunately, parents become expert at deciphering toddler language. More often than not, they get the right message from their toddler's fractured word or sentence.

Hint

Make a game out of teaching your child numbers. Break up bits of cracker and drop three pieces into a plastic jar, counting as you drop. Then let your child drop the crackers into the jar while you count for her.

Cognition

The toddler's grasp of ideas continues to evolve. Notions of past, present, and future are now part of his mental repertoire and are obvious in the toddler's word comprehension and speech. The 21-month-old understands ideas in which words are a stand-in for events that will happen at a later time. Michael's father says, "We are going to grandma's house" or "We have to buy some more soap," and Michael understands what his father means even though the words are about a distant event.

At 21 months, toddlers display ideas about the concepts of time and quantity. Ann to her mother: "Wan cookie now"; Michael, at the beach, to his sister carrying a pail of sand: "Hurry!"; Ann looking at two animal crackers: "Two"; looking down at her shoes while her mother dresses her: "Two."

Some words represent categories of things: colors, chairs, stories, dresses, shirts. At this age, toddlers know that color is a category that stands for red, orange, blue, and so forth. (This is another example of classification.) When Michael's mother asks Michael to find a shirt in the laundry basket, he knows the meaning of shirt and goes to the clothes basket to select one of his favorites.

In addition to ideas that are represented in the meaning of words, ideas can also be organized in terms of scripts. Developmental scientists define scripts as skeletal frameworks of everyday events. A script is not necessarily remembered in terms of words but rather in terms of a sequence of episodes that make up an event. A fine example was described by a long-time colleague of Piaget. She observed a 22-month-old boy at play accurately replicate a scene of his mother feeding the baby. His mother was not present; the only participants in the drama were the boy and his doll. Among the things he did was to carefully position the doll in the crook of his arm, hold the doll's bottle to visually inspect it, pull on the nipple to unclog it, and shake the bottle as if to enhance the flow of milk. This sequence of actions is considered a script. The boy reproduced the skeletal framework of a real feeding in correct temporal sequence.

What does this example reveal about cognitive development? The boy's memory of the sequence of feeding events indicated some understanding of the temporal aspects of an event: A happens first, B is next, and then C occurs. His careful positioning of himself and his doll showed understanding of spatial dimensions of an event: two people have to be positioned in a certain way in order for certain kinds of interaction to occur. The boy also showed awareness of cause and effect: milk will not flow through a nipple that is clogged.

Children of this age often have scripts for events that occur repeatedly. When Andrew was around this age, he began to show a script for his early morning greetings. It started during the course of overnight visits with us when we began to let him sleep in a bed rather than a crib. The first time he slept in the bed, he awoke in the morning, got out of bed, wriggled out of his wet diapers, found one of his books, came into our bedroom, and climbed into our bed. The script was and still is the same for every overnight stay, except that now Andrew wears pajamas. Andrew's script probably evolved from the days when I would take him out of his crib, change his diapers, and bring him to our bed. Andrew added the book to the script on his own.

Social

This month many toddlers show an increasing interest in social exchanges with their agemates. One group of researchers who observed children of this age found all kinds of social exchanges: individual toddlers would attempt to join in another's play, they laughed and talked (at least briefly) to each other, they imitated each other, and they showed, offered, and gave toys. They also protested when a peer did something not to their liking. At least a third of the time the toddlers actively tried to engage another child in play.

Toddlers of this age are not always willing or able to engage in social play with peers. They are relatively inexperienced in dealing with their equals, even though they are skilled in social interactions with their parents and to some extent with their siblings. Peer interactions have a different set of requirements and a different set of rules. Young children at play have to learn that a peer's bid to play requires a response and that the response needs to be directly related to the bid. A peer is unlike a parent; parents know what toddlers mean, and—unasked—they often fill in the rest of incompleted sentences or help a toddler complete a task. About a third of the time, toddlers of this age do not understand each others' bids in play. Overall, then, peer play episodes at this age tend to be short because of difficulties in comprehension, speech production, and reciprocal turn taking.

Both boys and girls of this age enjoy dress-up play: dad's cap and mom's purse are good props. But gender separation is occurring in the toys they select for play. Girls tend to play with dolls and small toys, while boys opt for trucks and large toys, even though parents might have given their toddler girl an opportunity to play with trucks or their toddler boy an opportunity to play with dolls. In general, differences in toy preferences are stronger at this age than are differences in the sizes of boys' and girls' play groups or in the types of motor activity they engage in. Girl toddlers are as likely to run and chase in a group of three children as are boys.

> ### Hint
>
> If your child shows strong preferences in gender-related toys, it's probably not worth getting upset about.

Emotions

Toddlers of 21 months become upset when angered, when afraid, and when their wishes are not met. Their cries are often relatively short. The frequency of tantrums varies considerably, but overall, fewer tantrums occur this month than at 18 months.

At this age the toddler attempts to control her own negative emotions. Ann is fearful of cats. One day when visiting an older cousin, she sees the cousin's cat and immediately runs from the room. When her cousin encourages Ann to come back, Ann calls out, "Da, da," and looks worried. She looks around, and then cautiously walks back into the room. She says, "Kitty," and looks at the cat. When the cat goes out of the room, Ann follows but keeps her distance.

Sense of Self

Autonomy and self-recognition continue to evolve. Sometimes Ann uses descriptive evaluations when she refers to herself: "Bad girl, sticky hands." Once in a while she lowers her eyes in a nascent form of shame. In the morning she may greet her mother with "No cereal," as she starts the day off exerting her selfhood. One toddler unexpectedly found a visiting baby in her crib. She immediately indicated her displeasure about the intrusion in her space. All in all, this month we see more specific evidence of the person the toddler is gradually becoming.

❧ Developmental Close-up

Toilet Training

Parenting practices differ a great deal among families. Differences arise in the particular ways parents nurture, feed, and otherwise care for their babies. Some parents hold their babies to a fairly strict feeding schedule and others feed their babies without regard to the clock. Amazingly, most babies adapt just fine to variations in parenting, provided, of course, that the parenting is supportive, not harsh.

One of the most striking differences in parenting practices, I have found over the years, is in methods of toilet training toddlers. Some parents let it happen as a matter of course when the toddler indicates that he wants to sit on the potty. Other parents want to get the chore over with—the sooner the better. In a conversation I had with Dr. Benjamin Spock a number of years ago, he revealed that he later changed some of the advice on toilet training he had given in the first edition of *Baby and Child Care*. In the first edition he suggested that mothers put off toilet training until children were close to three years old. Mothers complained bitterly to him:

no, toilet training shouild start earlier; enough of diapers! And so Dr. Spock modified his advice.

Freud and other psychoanalysts said that toilet training that was too severe led to the "anal" personality, a personality that is excessively compulsive. Alternatively, a child might rebel against rigid training by turning out to be excessively messy. Erik Erikson, a more modern interpreter of psychoanalysis, suggested that harsh toilet training could lead to feelings of shame and doubt among toddlers.

Following up on this theme, a number of years ago a husband and wife research team conducted a major study of child rearing in six different cultures around the world. These researchers were somewhat influenced by Freud's writings, so they thought important child-rearing issues for parents (would) include weaning babies from the breast, toilet training of toddlers, and gender training to teach young children appropriate sex roles. Years later, when all the observations and interviews had been analyzed, the researchers found that weaning was relatively unimportant, toilet training was rarely mentioned as a problem, and sex role training actually took place during later childhood and adolescence.

What were parents concerned about? Aggressive acts (for example, fighting and hitting) and developing independence (for example, walking). These two common concerns were approached differently by parents. Some parents were more permissive and others were stricter about when training began and how regularly they enforced training.

What about today's parents? Is toilet training of great concern? Some of my own research findings shed some light on the question. We asked parents, primarily mothers, to respond to several child-rearing questions when their children were 13, 15, 18, 21, 24, 30, 36, 42, and 48 months of age. Particularly interesting to us were the answers to two questions: What do you prohibit your child from doing? What do you encourage your child to do on his/her own? As might be expected safety issues (for example, touching electrical outlets), touching valuable household things, and hitting and biting were high on the prohibition list. As to encouraged independent behaviors, self-feeding, putting toys away, brushing teeth, and self-dressing were mentioned often. Only a few out of the hundreds of answers mothers gave to these questions mentioned toilet training! One mother of a 30-month-old said that she admonished her daughter for "peeing on the floor when her diaper was off," another stated she had started potty training "but the results haven't been great," and still another said, "He's old enough and we'll be more insistent." Three mothers, one of a 42-month-old and two of 48-month-olds, said they encouraged their children to use the toilet on their own. That was it.

This doesn't mean that toilet training doesn't matter to parents. There were two times that toilet training was an important issue for me. We lived in the East when our daughter was little. We bundled up and ventured out in all kinds of cold weather, but I was ill at ease knowing she was toddling around in the cold with wet diapers. When we moved west to the warmth of Southern California, toilet training became an issue for another reason. Our second child was ready for a few hours of preschool, but the director said he could be enrolled only if he was toilet trained. So we devoted ourselves to the task. By the time our third child was ready for preschool, that rule had been abolished. Toilet training just evolved naturally.

My suggestion is to do what feels comfortable for you, your schedule, and your child. Whenever you start toilet training, do it without threats and punishments. Some children are afraid of regular-sized toilets, so use a little potty. In general, parents who don't make a big issue of it often find toilet training is easier than teaching their child to put his toys away.

Twenty-Four Months

often wants to assert self

fantasy play; problem solving; creativity

uses 2-, 3-, or 4-word sentences

knows name, gender, some family roles

likes consistency in family routines

enjoys play with agemates

has a sense of humor

Average Boy: Height is 34.5 inches, with most between 32.5+ and 36+ inches.
Weight is 27.5 pounds, with most between 24 and 31.5 pounds.
Average Girl: Height is 34 inches, with most between 32.5 and 35.5+ inches.
Weight is 26+ pounds, with most between 22.5 and 30 pounds.

❧ *Snapshot*

The two-year-old is a child in transition. She is miles beyond babyhood but still has a way to go to childhood. Yet when compared to the one-year-old, she is practically a grown-up. Following are some of her grown-up behaviors:

- thinks using ideas
- understands concepts such as *broken, pretend*
- speaks in short sentences
- moves about with assurance
- remembers everyday routines
- acts independently
- responds to others' moods

The two-year-old uses words and sentences in all kinds of conversations: "Grandma get up," "Doll go up," "Mommy go work," "Toy go there." Her sentences grow in length, and she sometimes includes prepositions: "Put shoes on and go." She proudly shows that she knows the correct words for a cup, mug, and a bowl. Just a short time ago, she called all of these *cup*.

New forms of behavior are emerging. One in particular is the desire for autonomy and independence. Sometimes stubborn and exacting in earlier months, independence now at times makes the two-year-old downright contrary. There are days when she doesn't comply with rules that are really important: she won't sit in her car seat without a protest; she looks at her mother and then hits her baby brother; she walks across the sidewalk to the curb, looks back at her father, and then dangles her foot over the edge of the curb. As trying as these kinds of behaviors can be, often the two-year-old is simply attempting to understand more fully who she is, what she is capable of doing, and which kinds of behaviors others will accept and not accept from her. And despite these contrary kinds of behaviors, overall the two-year-old is easier to get along with and to deal with than a month or so ago when she was stubborn and exacting.

There are many occasions, like the following scene enacted in my research laboratory, when we have to marvel at the two-year-old's cleverness. Claire had been asked by her mother to put the lab toys away on the toy shelves. Claire responded to the request by neatly arranging a few toys on the top shelf. She then sat down in a chair near the shelves. Although her mother encouraged her to put more toys away, Claire sat unmoving. Her mother continued, "There are more shelves to be filled." Claire eyed the shelves and then moved the toys she had placed on the top shelf to the second shelf. Returning to the chair, she swung her feet and grinned. Her mother continued her prompting, at which point Claire responded, "Too tired I watch you. Need to talk to you." As I watched this interchange unfold, I wanted to applaud. Claire brought some of her key skills—language, planning and problem solving, sense of humor, and emotion control—to this situation that she did not like and coordinated them in the service of resisting a simple request! I was also impressed with Claire's mother; she never lost her cool in the face of her daughter's clever resistance.

Although children of this age are mostly good-natured, their anger and frustrations go out of control now and then. The resultant emotional storms can be tornado-size. Esther, her twin brother, her mother, and her baby brother are walking outside on an uncomfortably hot day and all are tired. Esther says, "Birdie." Her mother doesn't understand, and besides the baby needs attention. Fatigue, heat, and being ignored are just too much for Esther. She throws herself on the sidewalk and has a gigantic tantrum. Later that day she tells her mother that she just wanted her to look at the birdie on a mailbox.

Then there is David, who is about to celebrate his second birthday with a mid-afternoon party for his playmates. At noontime his mother takes him to a favorite ice cream store to buy the cake. David is beside himself with glee as he peers at the display case. After paying for the cake, David's mother starts to leave, but David pulls and tugs at her, grunting and pointing to the case. "Cone!" he yells. "Cone!" Clearly, she must have forgotten why they are here! His mother tries to explain that the cake is an ice cream cake and will be eaten later in the day. "No," David screams, "ice creeeeem!" No ice cream now, says his mother. A dazzling temper tantrum follows. In hindsight, David's mother realized that he expected an ice cream cone because she had always bought him a come when in the ice cream store. Besides, David does not know that birthday cakes can be made of ice cream.

To sum up, the two-year-old is a study in contrasts. He is an independent child who can be helpful, attentive, and cooperative. He uses language effectively, and he has a sense of humor. Sometimes his reasoning is good; sometimes he just does not understand. On these occasions he can become so distraught that he literally decomposes and loses his language skills. Fortunately, these emotional outbursts are short-lived. As children approach their third birthday, the incidence of tantrums diminishes markedly, because they think better and have better control of their speech even when they are upset.

✿ Images of Development

Motor

At 24 months, the toddler stance has almost disappeared. Besides walking adeptly, two-year-olds run, go up and down stairs, and squat for minutes at a time. They squat when they wish to play at floor level; for some reason they don't seem to want to be on their hands and knees. They generally exhibit better body control in maneuvers (leaning over, squatting) where flexibility is needed. Two-year-olds also easily climb into chairs and seat themselves. They balance themselves on tiptoe.

Overall, most toddlers of this age love physical activity, and well they should. Not many months ago they struggled to get around. Now they seem to glide. And even if they fall, they now know to break the impact with their arms.

Although the two-year-old fumbles when playing with very small toys, hand coordination is generally good at this age. Turning pages, building a tower with blocks, and inserting rods into holes are easily accomplished. Fingers and thumb work well together when grasping an implement such as a spoon; mishaps occasionally happen because navigating a filled spoon from bowl to mouth is difficult. Many children of this age demonstrate preferential handedness.

The one disconcerting aspect of toddlers' motor agility is the hazards they create for themselves. They start to move and don't know how to stop. Andrew was bouncing up and down on the curb while his grandfather retrieved his jacket from the back of the red truck. Uncontrollably, Andrew bounced from the curb to the forbidden street. A frightened grandfather reacted with a spanking, followed by tears and hugs. Then there is the story of the nephew of a colleague, who started to run and couldn't stop. He ended up against a wall with a broken leg, even though he had seen the wall.

> ## Hint
>
> Stringing large wooden beads and stringing cards are great coordination activities for two-year-olds.

Perception

At this age the toddler goes beyond recognition of two-dimensional illustrations. He now tries to copy a line. He tries to draw a vertical line by imitating one that has been drawn for him. He also tries to draw a circle. The significance of copying is twofold. First, the child is adopting a tool (pencil, crayon) that others use to write and to draw. Second, he adds to his concept of his own competence when he sees that he can use the tool and that he is capable of reproducing another's mark.

The two-year-old is occasionally fooled by his preconceptions, his expectations of the appearance of things. Andrew was sitting in a restaurant with his grandfather and heard him ask for a glass of cola. The waiter brought the glass of soda. Andrew asked for some, so his grandfather poured a small amount into an empty coffee cup. Andrew refused the cup, saying that it contained coffee, and no amount of persuasion could convince him otherwise.

> ## Hint
>
> Extra vigilance is needed at this age because children are more coordinated and move more quickly than younger aged toddlers.

Language

🌿 *Comprehension.* There is a steady increase in the number of classes of objects the toddler identifies and her knowledge of the specific items in the group. She understands that *rooms* are parts of the house and goes off to the room called *kitchen* when her mother tells her that's where she has left her toy. She knows the word *animal* and correctly points to pictures of different animals in her book.

Another development is improved association of a word with a whole sequence of behaviors (an event). For example, last month the toddler could imitate his father's shaving routine; now he knows the word that is associated with the routine. In fact, he runs to the bathroom to watch when his mother tells him that his father is shaving.

Occasionally, two-year-olds indicate that they recognize the different roles of family members in routines. When Ann's mother says that they are going to eat, even though she is hungry she ignores her mother's pleas to come to the kitchen. When she asks Ann what is wrong, she says, "Karen

Hint

Read aloud picture-story books that include simple descriptions of families and family members' everyday activities.

not home." Sister Karen sets the table, so how can they eat when Karen is not home?

❧ *Production.* A two-year-old largely discards one-word sentences in favor of two-, three-, and four-word sentences. One child's vocabulary during an afternoon in an infant care program included sentences such as "Finished juice already"; "Oh, oh, dropped cracker"; "I can't turn around"; "It's glued up"; "It's ringing, it stopped"; "I want tape"; "Don't choke" (to a child who was eating a cob of corn); "Billy took play-dough from Jill." Bear in mind, though, that there is considerable variability in children's language skills at this age; a few children still produce only single words.

When a two-year-old speaks in sentences, the words are in the right grammatical order: "Doll go there," "Daddy go work," "Boy fell down." Most toddler sentences refer to immediate experiences and personal activities. The two-year-old correctly uses *I, me,* and *you,* although use of other pronouns is infrequent. His sentences rarely contain *the,* but they do sometimes include *and, so,* or *'cause.* These words demonstrate his command of cause-and-effect relations: "Open door so daddy come."

Despite the impressive growth in language, the two-year-old's speech is not always clear. It has been estimated that spoken words are incomprehensible one third of the time. Sometimes toddlers are aware that they are not understood. Ann was talking to her father while he was driving. When she said something that was incomprehensible to him, he did not reply. Ann repeated herself as if she knew that her father did not understand her words. "Ann, I still don't understand," he said. She accepted his comment and went on to talk about something else.

Studies show that 24-month-old girls tend to be slightly more advanced in language production than boys, perhaps because they tend to be talked to more than boys. Toddlers with older siblings tend to talk earlier than only children. Children reared in families in which two or more languages are spoken tend to produce speech later than children reared in families in which one language is spoken; it seems as if they have to take time to sort out the words that go with each language. Occasionally, the two-year-old from a bilingual family mixes words from both languages. Most of the time this kind of variability has no discernible long-term consequences, and in fact many developmental scientists believe that bilingualism has long-term cognitive benefits for children.

For many children of this age, language is becoming a tool that they can use to their advantage. Words help them express needs, communicate intentions in social play, and control negative emotions.

Cognition

One of the most notable cognitive achievements of this age is the development of insightful problem solving. In prior months toddlers figured out some cause-and-effect relations with objects and developed ideas about the functional use of objects. Now for the first time they are able to derive solutions for problems that involve nonconventional uses of an object. They are thinking both intelligently and creatively. Why is this an accomplishment? Well, even the most mundane chores of our everyday lives sometimes require intelligence and creativity. Who hasn't had to put together dinner at the last minute from a refrigerator that is almost bare?

We studied insightful problem solving by adapting an idea from Piaget. We used a prop that consisted of an opaque tube about six inches long containing a cookie enclosed in a wad of tissue. Sitting at a table, the toddler is given the tube and a short toy rake. The toddler is told there is a cookie in the tube. In order to retrieve the cookie, she has to use the rake's handle to push the cookie out of the tube; she has to figure out how to use the rake in a way that she is not accustomed to. This is a pretty difficult problem. Children younger than two years of age find it inordinately difficult, even after the solution is shown to them. But at around two, a few come up with the solution on their own. And even if they don't solve the problem, they do reproduce the solution once it is demonstrated to them.

Also at this age toddlers are better able to integrate multiple sources of information. Ann knows that her cousin lives with his mother, father, and the grandfather of both children. When her cousin comes to her house, she yells "Poppy" for her grandfather, then runs to a table to pick up her grandfather's photograph, points to it, and says, "Poppy." Ann understands the relationship of a photo to a real person, she knows how to produce names for family members, and she knows some elements of her family's structure.

Another important cognitive activity at this age involves the elaboration of pretend play. A few months ago pretend play took the form of

You can make a story game with photographs of people your child knows. Together you can talk about who the person is, what he/she is wearing, and what the person is doing. Hang a small corkboard in your child's room for favorite photos.

Hint

Fill a basket with an assortment of pretend play and dress-up props and leave it in a corner of your child's room. Change the contents every so often.

reproducing an everyday behavior. Now children may use objects and toys in ways that are not conventional, and they take on roles of people outside the family. One child dragged a bench before a bush and used two of its branches to create a control wheel for an airplane cockpit. Of course, this type of play means that the child steps out of his real world to create a make-believe one, and sometimes he becomes so absorbed in it that he has to ask, "This is pretend, right?"

Still another cognitive activity that emerges at around 24 months is a new form of planned behavior that the child uses to control other behaviors when asked to do so. In one of our studies, we showed 18-, 24-, and 30-month-old children a bright red old-fashioned telephone and asked them not to touch the phone for a couple of minutes. We left the telephone on a table in front of the children and then disappeared behind a screen. The children's mothers sat nearby but were looking at magazines. By two years of age, but not before, more than half of the children did not touch the phone. Almost as soon as we made the request, some two-year-olds turned to their mothers and talked (one little girl talked about her nails needing nail polish), some sat on their hands, and some squirmed around in their chairs so as not to look at the telephone. Very impressive! These children figured out a way to distract themselves so that they could comply with a request. Isn't this what we all do when we want something but can't have it yet? Isn't this another example of intelligent behavior?

Two-year-old children are quick to realize when they are unable to do certain things, such as work a complicated puzzle, and without the least sign of frustration, they seek out assistance. They give help or solace faster, as if they process information about another person's distress more quickly. When her mother cuts her finger, the two-year-old immediately runs to find a bandage.

Social

The two-year-old is generally good company. He may do simple errands and is often interested in helping with routine tasks. He is getting better at complying with family rules, particularly those that have to do with safety and touching prohibited objects. He tends to have trouble with not interrupting, not yelling in the house, and putting toys away. He's also not quite ready to think about applying rules from one situation to another. Why should his mother's warning "Don't run" in the grocery store have anything to do with how he is to act in a clothing store?

Often children of this age do not understand why certain rules are imposed, and many think that the best way to get clarification is to check out a parent's reaction. In spite of having been admonished to put his shoes in the closet after taking them off, my son Paul used to stand in front of the toilet bowl with a shoe in hand looking at me. Did he really think little brown shoes belonged in the toilet bowl? Of course not. One researcher found that, on the average, children of this age commit five rule infractions an hour!

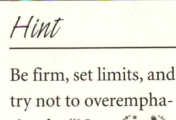

Hint

Be firm, set limits, and try not to overemphasize the "No, you must . . ."

Two-year-olds increase their play with other children and at times show genuine cooperation for several minutes. This is impressive because they're not highly skilled in planning a play script with each other. As at younger ages, nonverbal imitation is still a popular play activity (he runs, she runs), but children also coordinate their behaviors with each other. They sometimes take turns and occasionally talk to each other while they play. Because of their language skills, they are more likely to talk and less likely to show physical aggression to each other. Also, two-year-olds tend not to interfere and break up other children's play. Their fights primarily involve heated disputes over possessions, which can lead to pushing, hitting, or grabbing toys.

A two-year-old tends to be very accepting of other children who differ in some way, such as skin color, garbled speech, or a physical handicap. Mostly the difference just doesn't matter.

Sometimes two-year-olds are content to sit next to each other and play alone. It's a way for them to rest from social challenges and to replenish their energy. Sometimes very shy children of this age just want to watch. They'll join in when they feel ready for social play.

Emotions

There is no mistaking the emotional intensity of the two-year-old in displays of pleasure (exuberance or elation) as well as dismay. "Wow! Wow!" Andrew exclaimed each time he visited us and saw his train set. Contrarily, one afternoon he stood in front of the refrigerator and whined and whined. "Milk, apple juice, orange juice? What, Andrew?" I asked. He stood there and kicked at the refrigerator door, tears running down his face. I picked him up, and we went for a walk.

The well-known reasons for crying are fatigue, hunger, parents' departure for an evening, and loss of a possession (a toy) to a peer. Children of this age also get upset if major changes are made in their lives and routines. Thus, when a major change occurs, such as moving to a new house, the birth of a sibling, or even a new daytime babysitter, the two-year-old perceives a violation of his sense of control and a disruption of the consistency in his life.

Emotional distress also comes from dreams. This interesting dream episode was described by the mother of a two-year-old girl. One Sunday the mother and her husband entertained relatives who had two preschool-age boys. The boys were rough and appropriated the little girl's toys. She watched and was unusually quiet. The family left. That night the two-year-old woke up screaming and crying. Between heaving sobs, she told her mother that the boys were still in the house and were taking her toys. She was frantic and would not believe the boys were gone until her mother carried her from room to room to show her that they were empty.

In addition to the negative emotions that result from fear, hurt, and anger, the two-year-old shows emotions that are precursors to shame and embarrassment. When caught in the act, they cry, hang their heads, and bite their lips. Clearly they don't understand the meaning of shame, but they do realize that they have behaved in a way a parent does not like. Children do not show shame until they have a mature sense of self and how that self is supposed to act; this sense evolves with cognitive growth.

Sense of Self

The two-year-old refers to herself by name. She talks about herself using such verbs as *can, can't, hurt, know, like, want,* and *need.* When she uses words such as these, she indicates that she understands the everyday definition of the words; she is able to apply the definition of a particular word to her own self ("I hurt"; "I want the cookie"); she realizes that we also know the definition of the word and therefore can respond to her wishes/dislikes/abilities in the "right" way.

No wonder she tries to assert herself: she now has the cognitive skills to understand in her own way her own identity. However, she does have a hard time recognizing her limits. She declares, "I do it," even when it is impossible. "Mine," she says, when clearly it is not. Sometimes she uses the word *mine* when she actually wants to say *yours!* These assertions help her learn to distinguish *mine, yours,* and *others'*.

Not surprising, then, that the two-year-old also has the cognitive ability to understand that she's a girl and has the attributes girls (and mothers) have. She's learned about girlness through observation, play with other children, and stories. She is certain that some tasks go with mothers and some with fathers: she is more likely to play "mom cooks dinner" than "dad cooks dinner," even though in her real life her father cooks dinner now and then.

❧ *Developmental Close-up*

Parenting

Each time I teach a course in infant development, I organize it in the same way. The first few sessions cover the meaning of development, two or three classes discuss prenatal life, and the rest of the classes are devoted to infant and toddler development. I invite my students to ask friends and relatives who have babies and toddlers to join us in class for about half an hour. Fortunately, there is always a good supply of mothers and fathers who are willing, and we can usually arrange their visits to coincide with the age group we are studying. I encourage the visiting parents to talk about themselves as parents and to describe life with their babies. I want my students to understand that babies do not grow up in a social vacuum and that parents get this message across effectively.

Not too long ago, two mothers visited class during the week we were talking about prenatal development. Each came on a separate day. These two mothers were remarkable; even I, who have seen hundreds and hundreds of parents over the years, was awed by their special qualities. Both women were mothering young children who placed extraordinary strains and demands on them, yet they accepted their responsibilities with a grace and commitment that was compelling. Each also unhesitatingly mentioned her own frailties and mistakes.

One mother, I'll call her Maddy, loves children, and she and her husband plan to have as many as they can. She came to class with her fourth baby, who was about a year old. Maddy told the class about her pregnancy, which had not gone well, the week before the baby's birth when she came down with a serious case of the flu, and the unexpected Caesarean section she had to undergo while she still had the flu. A baby girl was born prematurely who was very, very sick, and Maddy knew she might not survive. Spellbound, we listened as Maddy told us about her inability to cope with the baby's birth because of her own illness; although she felt guilty, her own pain and misery were overpowering. Fortunately, Maddy told us, she soon began to feel better. Somewhat more slowly the baby improved and was well enough to go home at three weeks. However, for six months the baby was constantly attached to a special respiratory monitor because she could stop breathing at any time. Either Maddy or her husband kept watch, but it was mostly Maddy's responsibility because her husband had a business to run. Maddy hardly slept for six months, but as she matter-of-factly told my class, "You do what you have to do." And she did. And the baby was doing fine.

The second mother, we'll call her Deanne, came to class with her little boy, who was three years old and had spina bifida, a condition that has its origins early in the prenatal period. At birth, the baby's spinal tissue was exposed right above the buttocks. In medical terms, there was risk of paralysis below the lesion; the boy might not have use of his legs and might not have control of his bladder and bowel. The physicians told the parents that the baby would be severely impaired.

Deanne brought us pictures of the baby at the time of his birth, after his surgery, and while he was an infant, and she brought articles and books about spina bifida for my students to read. Almost from birth, Deanne arranged for her baby to routinely receive special therapy. She also worked with him at home, and he began to thrive. Later on, he even began to walk on his misshapen feet. In time, Deanne found a toddler class for him and eventually a preschool. The boy dazzled us with his play and language, the affection he had for his mother, and the affection he had for a friend of the family who had come along. Deanne told us she still did not know if her son would have bladder and bowel control, but she would face that in time. For now her concerns were to provide a good developmental start for her son. Clearly, she was doing just that.

Not all parents must deal with the strains of an early birth or severe physical impairment. Nevertheless, sleeplessness, crying, sickness, and so on are stresses every parent faces. Weathering these storms requires unlimited commitment. In fact, good parenting requires sensitivity and responsibility equal to Maddy's and Deanne's.

Because infants and very young children are captive audiences for their parents and substitute caregivers, they are particularly susceptible to good or bad rearing influences. Because babies are naturally attracted to people, it stands to reason that very early on parents begin to exert influences on a child's development. These influences become easier to recognize as the baby begins to identify familiar caregivers, and they attain progressively greater import as the young child learns to distinguish emotions, comprehend words, and imitate behaviors. In times of distress, the baby looks to familiar people for affection, play, and solace.

One of the most important research findings that has come out of studies of parents and children is that parents' unrealistic expectations about development can lead to harsh punishment and abuse. Young babies cry, sometimes for reasons that we do not understand. But their cries are not merely a ploy to annoy us. They cry because something is bothering them. It is up to us to make them feel better. Similarly, the exploring toddler is not wilfully disobedient; he is seeking to know his world. It is a fact that some explorations are bothersome for us or unsafe for him. That he needs to be monitored is a certainty; that he should not be assaulted is also a certainty.

Research has also repeatedly found that parent knowledge and education are invariably linked to children's developmental outcomes. Many factors are involved here. As one example, educated parents in our country generally have larger and more complex vocabularies than parents whose education ceased at high school or earlier. Not surprisingly, educated parents tend to talk a lot to their children. They explain and reason with their children, play games that involve words and songs, and read books to them. These young children grow up surrounded by a verbal environment. They enter school more verbally adept than children whose early years were spent in relatively impoverished verbal settings. So often in our society, language skills are linked to educational and social competencies.

It is also true that the more educated the parent, the more likely it is that he or she tries to obtain information about developmental trends and attempts to learn what children of one or another age can or cannot do. Parent education also plays an important role in ensuring that babies and young children get good starts in their intellectual growth. Parents who realize that cognition is important for a child's academic success, social skill development, emotion control, and self-concept will facilitate child learning with age-appropriate playthings, books, excursions, and informal lessons.

Researchers have studied the influence of parents on child development in a variety of contexts. Among the research questions that have immediate application for helping parents become more competent are: How do parents respond to their babies' irritability? What are parents' beliefs about good and *not-so-good* babies? How do parents feel about *punishment* for young children? For older children? What characteristics make some parents truly *effective*? I have touched upon a few of these themes. For example, in the 7-month Close-up regarding day care, the effect of separation from parents on a child's attachment and the influence of attachment on social adjustment were discussed. The influence of a parent's facial expression was discussed in the 10-month Close-up. The impact of differences in parenting patterns—the degree of routine in babies' lives, the amount of time parents read to their young child, the extent to which parents participate in social games—have been emphasized throughout this book.

One research team described various kinds of parent influences. There is an influence that provides emotional security for children, and another that involves providing good role models as, for example, in being kind to others (prosocial behaviors). Other influences come from the way parents give rewards for good behavior and discipline for unacceptable behaviors. Discipline that is restrained (for example, time-outs) as opposed to discipline that is harsh (for example, repeated spankings) leads to fewer childhood fights and less aggression. Still other influences derive from the ways parents provide opportunities for learning, such as trips to zoos, local supermarkets, and the like. Trips provide new inputs for learning.

The point is that a child's social motivation and social behavior skills are affected by all these parental acts. At a practical level, this means that children do better when their parents set good behavior examples, praise children when they do well and reprimand them when they err, take time to explain what is expected, and make their children feel they have someone to turn to if things go awry. That's a pretty tall order for parents. The goal for parents is not to reach a state of perfection, which is all but impossible, but rather to approach parenting with sensitivity, knowledge, patience, humor, and commitment.

DEVELOPMENTAL OVERVIEW:
THE SECOND YEAR

Developmental Highlights

	15 Months	18 Months
Motor	Loves to climb; fairly proficient with crayons, spoons, and cups; builds two- or three-block towers; turns pages of picture books; walks with wide-spread gait	Comfortably walks, runs, and jumps; climbs more easily; coordinated fine motor skills; walks up stairs with assistance; balance is generally better; tries to make lines with crayon
Perception	Sequentially touches objects that go together—makes groupings	Differentiates round puzzle pieces from square ones
Vocalization and Language	Tries to make self understood; understands words for toys, pets, people, and actions; comprehends much more than she can say; uses gestures well; continues to overgeneralize, one word for moon and sun; sentences are one word; production varies greatly	Imitates words; increase in comprehension of word meanings; understands brief commands if requested item is in view; learns five to six words a week; may use a few two-word sentences; repeatedly uses a word he is learning; recognizes labels for two colors

HOW TO BE HELPFUL

Give your child enough structure: have a defined play space, try to establish regular sleep routines, try to be consistent in setting rules.

Be flexible, patient, low key. Be willing to concede sometimes.

Childproof your home. Safety is a real issue with young toddlers.

Read as often as possible to your child.

	15 Months	18 Months
Cognition	Systematic trial-and-error learning continues; more aware of functions of objects; uses dolls in play; recognizes and uses more cause-and-effect relationships; some repetitive play sequences	Thinks in terms of ideas; recall memory is better; has primitive idea of "should be"—puts lids on jars; pays attention better; recognizes that others have possessions
Social	Sympathetic—prosocial; teases parents and siblings; plays independently but checks to see that familiar person in view; may comply with one or two rules; increasingly tries to include others in play	Acclimates slowly to new situations; at times seeks others' advice; has brief peer interactions but contact is visual rather than verbal; compliance improves
Emotion and Self	More mood swings; is more caring to agemates; strongly prefers certain clothes; gets annoyed by dirty hands; may fret or cry often but usually briefly	Can be restless and stubborn; may sometimes have tantrums; uses transitional objects to soothe self; uses adjectives to refer to self; sometimes shy; shows shame

	21 Months	24 Months
Motor	Routinely squats; runs faster; better hand control; walks down stairs holding another's hand	Definite preference for one hand; walks up and down stairs alone; tries to put rods into holes; builds block towers that are five or more blocks high
Perception	Differentiates round, square, and triangular puzzle pieces and puts them in puzzle with assistance	Occasionally fooled by perceptions; tries to copy lines on paper
Vocalization and Language	Uses two-word sentences; labels own body parts; uses *me* and *mine*; Uses words to describe own feeling states: *sad, tired*; still mispronounces many words	Uses two-, three-, and four- word sentences; recognizes labels for rooms; grammar is improving and *and* is now used; one third of speech is not clear; girls usually speak more words than boys; uses *I, me,* and *you*; uses language as a tool

	21 Months	24 Months
Cognition	To some degree understands past, present, and future; consistently uses scripts to organize activities into episodes; Some understanding of the idea of categories, e.g., colors	Fantasy play—elaborate play sequences; recognizes that family members have specific roles; creative problem solving; begins to use strategy-like (planned) behaviors
Social	Shows more interest in agemates; gender toy preferences emerge; may engage in numerous short interactions with peers	Better at complying with safety rules and being nice; cooperates better with peers but toy disputes are frequent; takes interest in family routines; adapts to change, but separation is still a difficult experience
Emotion and Self	Some attempts to control negative emotions; irritability and restlessness continue; increases efforts to control situations; begins to understand parent values; appropriately refers to self as *good* or *bad*	Can be contrary; refers to self by name; responds to others' moods; very intense; may be overwhelmed by changes; can be upset by dreams; identifies self by gender; talks about self by using I and a verb: *hurt, need*; keen to experience world on own terms

When to Seek Help (at the End of Eighteen Months)

Not interested in parents or toys

Cannot stand without assistance

Does not remember any routines

Understands no words

Cannot distinguish circle from square

Does not combine toys in play

Does not comply with any household rules

No maternal attachment

When to Seek Help (at the End of Twenty-Four Months)

Does not walk

Does not group perceptually

Does not show planning behavior

No imitative learning

Never shows functional play

Does not use jargon

Does not show pleasure at accomplishments

Afterimages

looking back

looking forward

is my child okay?

❧ Looking Back

Our knowledge of early child development is constantly evolving. Research studies continue to reconfigure our understanding of how growth comes about. The behaviors discussed in this book represent normative development as it is currently known to the developmental research community. What follows is a summary of development during the first two years.

In the first few months, development primarily involves improvements in physiological functioning, inhibition of reflexes, and increase in muscle strength. As body functions stabilize, the baby's sleep patterns become more like adults', and the amount of crying subsides. At around three months, the first verifiable cognitive skills (memory), forms of distinctive vocal expression (coos), and sustained interest in social interactions (the social smile, coos) emerge.

In the next four months, the baby develops better control over gross body movements, including reach and grasp. Gross motor control gives rise to rudimentary locomotion skills (pivoting and crawling). The baby also begins to develop expectations about events, to recognize familiar people, and to form attachments. The baby is doing, thinking, and feeling!

At 8 and 9 months, the pace of change accelerates and rapid growth continues to the end of the first year. Social skills (playing games, making bids, and referencing) come on line in rapid succession. Cognitive growth is impressive: problem-solving skills improve; understanding of cause and effect becomes more mature; imitative learning and trial-and-error exploration increase the baby's store of information; recall memory emerges.

Meanwhile, individual variability is increasingly evident as individual temperament qualities are becoming increasingly apparent. On top of all these advances, the young child develops limited skill in the two behaviors that distinguish humans from all other species, upright locomotion and language. She walks! She talks!

In the second year, the toddler's selfhood exerts a strong influence on behaviors. A major developmental challenge this year is reconciling sense of self with socialization requirements, that is, learning how to recognize and comply with parents' requests. Cognitive developments include the onset of the ability to think in terms of ideas, understanding the functional uses of objects, better memory skills, and improved attention control.

Throughout this period motor skills consolidate, and by the end of the second year running, squatting, and standing on one leg are all easily accomplished. Language development moves along as well. For most children, comprehension skills increase faster than do language production abilities. Yet by 24 months, many children have vocabularies that consist of hundreds of words and speak sentences that consist of two, three, and even four words.

Overall, during the first two years, the dependent baby is transformed into an autonomous child who is grappling with an increasingly social world and ever-rising demands. Selfhood is a powerful motivator now, and efforts to demonstrate individuality can produce some behaviors in the service of autonomy and independence. What may seem as contrariness for the sake of contrariness is often an attempt to answer the questions "Who am I?" and "What are my social boundaries?"

One of my colleagues used to say, "Everyone grows up similarly, everyone grows up differently." In describing the similarity part of growing up in this book, I have qualified generalizations with the differences, emphasizing that familial genetic material and environmental influences produce variability in development. How much variability can there be in a child's behaviors to still regard them as "normal?" That's the question I examine in the section of this chapter entitled Is My Child Okay?

❧ *Looking Forward*

Toddlerhood is characterized by the emergence of self and the young child's fledgling efforts to self-regulate his behaviors. In the third year, the preschool child's personality becomes more integrated, and he is better acclimated to socialization requirements. The young child is really starting to "put it all together." Following are some things to look for in the next twelve months.

BEHAVIORS AT AROUND 30 MONTHS

Language
- Begins to use the word *think* in terms of having a belief and the word *know* to indicate an understanding.
- Consistently uses words such as *yesterday* and *tomorrow* to refer to past and future but may not fully understand their meanings.
- Realizes when a sentence is incorrect grammatically and makes some attempt to repair the errors; may or may not be successful.
- Correctly identifies pictures and drawings of common objects and events.
- Experiments with different ways of saying the same thing: "I'll, I'm gonna, I hafta . . . ."

Cognition

- Recognizes when it is appropriate to try to negotiate a change in a parent request.
- Knows that people have specific names.
- Shows knowledge of sequences of events that occur outside the home.
- Understands the principle of numbers: 2, 3.

Emotions

- Verbally attempts to control own emotions: "Don't make me feel bad."
- Uses words to convey emotion, such as *happy, funny, love, proud, good, feel good, sad, scary, mad, angry, yucky, bad, feel bad.*
- Talks about reasons for her own and others' emotions: "I fall down, and I cry."
- Cries less often.

BEHAVIORS AT AROUND 36 MONTHS

Cognitive

- Knows when he is pretending and when he is dealing with reality.
- Understands that a model represents something real.
- Still does not always appreciate the difference between appearance (what the eyes and ears tell us) and reality (what is really true): the child may insist that a sponge that looks like a rock is a rock.
- Has difficulty recognizing that what he finds desirable may differ from another person's notion of desirability.
- Engages in deceptions but does not really understand the point behind a deception.

Social

- Sometimes settles disputes with peers without adult intervention.
- Engages in planning behavior (figures out how to gain entry into a game without disrupting the game) in peer social situations in order to satisfy her own needs.

Emotions

- Shows self-evaluative/self-conscious emotions of pride and shame.
- Attempts to control emotions of fear: moves away from a large, frightening dog.

Sense of Self
- Recognizes that some activities and possessions are more often associated with one sex.
- Easily sorts pictures of men and women into male and female categories.
- Sometimes is very egocentric: when asked why a child might have a bandage on, he begins to talk about his own hurt at some previous time.

❧ *Is My Child Okay?*

It's the rare parent who hasn't wondered in private, "Is my baby okay?" Maybe the baby didn't roll over on schedule, or for a while she was slow in focusing her eyes on toys, or he didn't say words when all the other toddlers his age were talking. Most of the time, parents' worries dissolve because, given a little time, the baby is fine. Andrew, our grandson, had to be hospitalized a few days after birth because of severe jaundice. Months of concern later, it was apparent that there were no lasting effects.

There are, however, situations when month after month parents feel that the baby's behaviors show consistent differences when compared to his agemates' behaviors. Perhaps the parents were alerted that this might happen: the mother had a serious infection during pregnancy; the baby was born very early; the newborn was very ill. Sometimes there is no clue at all. What should parents do? Where should they seek help? What are the implications of development that does not seem right?

Infancy and toddlerhood are the time when important foundations —motor, perceptual–cognitive, social–emotional, language, sense of self— are set in place. As an example, the basic forms of attention and memory emerge in infancy and gradually get better and better. These behaviors are important because they are fundamental tools for young children's learning. I would be concerned if a baby showed consistent difficulty paying attention to his surroundings: his learning and development could be jeopardized. The effects could be profound and last long after the infancy years have come to a close. The point is: what happens in infancy is important.

If parents have a sense that something is not right with the baby or toddler, the first person to talk to is the child's pediatrician. This is the professional most familiar with the baby's health and developmental history. The pediatrician might handle detailed developmental assessments on her own or she might offer a referral to an infancy developmental specialist. This could be another pediatrican who has had specialized training in child development, a developmental psychologist, or some other individual who is trained in early development.

The purpose of a careful evaluation of the baby's developmental status is not simply to obtain a test score. The evaluation should include an analysis of the baby's behavioral strengths (for example, he is very social), possible problem areas (for example, he is 8 months old and hasn't yet rolled from back to tummy), and the developmental implications of these behaviors. If problem areas are consistently found, then the next step involves consultations with professionals who provide ideas for helping the baby move forward developmentally.

I wish I could assure parents that evaluating a baby or toddler's developmental status is an exact science. In the absence of gross physical impairments or major signs of developmental deviation, making a judgment about developmental problems can sometimes be difficult. To begin with, there is a good deal of variability in normal development. Infants naturally differ from one another in their rates of growth and their behavioral styles. Remember the little girl who said 500 words when she was a year old? Well, she did not walk on her own until she was close to 17 months old, an age approaching the far side of the curve for the normal onset of walking.

Second, some key features of development relate not only to the presence of a specific behavior but also to the quality of the behavior. I once evaluated a sturdy 9-month-old whose overall developmental test capabilities were clearly within the normal ranges. If I had paid attention only to his test profile, I could have concluded that he was fine. But there was something about the quality of his behaviors that was clearly inappropriate. The baby's smile was inconsistent and wan, he made sounds but rarely and took no delight in this accomplishment, and he just didn't seem to care whether people were around or not. These are developmental signs that are worrisome. It turned out that he was the last baby in a very large family and was not receiving much attention or being talked to enough. I was impressed with the baby's ability to sustain his development as well as he had, but his relative isolation and his lack of interest in other people did not bode well for his long-term language or social development.

Professionals differ in how they evaluate babies' development. I'll explain the way I go about doing an evaluation, but bear in mind that other approaches work just as well. My developmental evaluations usually have four components: a parent interview, my informal observations of the child, administration of one or more standardized development tests, and my clinical judgment.

I try to answer several basic questions. For this age, what constitutes the developmental norm for each domain of behavior? What do I consider a developmental deviation for this age? Are some of the baby's behaviors okay? Which are not? Why do I think a behavior is questionable? If I observe deviations from developmental norms, are they major or minor deviations? Do the baby's behaviors reflect organization or disorganization? What are the implications of developmental deviations for the baby's overall ability to play, to be social, to learn? Are there detectable ramifications for long-term competencies? I try not to draw firm conclusions until I've had a chance to see the baby and his parents on two or three separate occasions. At that point I might feel confident about stating that a baby is developmentally normal, has developmental delays, or shows signs of development that are troubling.

While my multistep process of evaluation is comprehensive, I know that there are no precise rules for determining when a baby's behaviors signify developmental delay. Good clinical judgment is essential. I also tend to be cautious about making definitive statements of either delayed or suspect development early in infancy. For one thing, labeling a young baby as having a developmental problem can be a risky proposition: labels can lead to social interaction patterns that reinforce deficiencies at just the time a more supportive environment might put the baby's development back on course. Second, there are strong self-corrective mechanisms in development, and although a baby may seem delayed early on, he may be fine six or eight months later. Third, our standardized infant development tests are not precise tools. Thus the information obtained from them has to be used cautiously.

Many parents are familiar with intelligence and achievement tests. However, evaluations of infants and toddlers are very different. They do not consist of straightforward, programmed question-and-answer sessions. Young babies do not talk, and older babies do not talk well. Younger and older babies have limited comprehension. Also, babies are blithely unconcerned about the goals of adults; they have their own agendas. A developmental evaluation has to be done by a sensitive clinician. A famous psychologist once commented that the perfect test takes place when the ever-moving, squalling baby becomes relatively quiet, attentive, and responsive. Obviously, perfection is not easy to achieve.

Let me describe two recent evaluations to show how these general principles work in practice. Not long ago I was asked to consult about the development of two toddlers. One was a little less than two years old; he spoke a few words that were often unintelligible. The other boy was close to two and a half years old, and he was not talking at all. The parents of both children were worried about their language development.

The first boy, let's call him Sandy, was attentive and affectionate with his parents. They reported that his overall development seemed fine, except for his speech. Although wary of me, Sandy accepted the toys I offered him and even gestured briefly to me. His motor skills were good, his play was age-appropriate, and he was quite interested in the toys. He periodically went from toy to parent and back again to toys. Sandy clearly understood what his parents said to him and pleasantly jabbered to each parent with correct conversational intonation. He was generally a happy child who was quick to laugh when he found something amusing. Although I did not complete a formal developmental test, I could see that Sandy's behaviors were developmentally appropriate in all but one domain—language. Also, Sandy's behaviors were nicely interrelated: his play reflected the coordination of his motor, cognitive, and social skills.

After observing Sandy and talking with his parents, I felt fairly certain that Sandy was developing normally. His language was just moving along at a slightly slower pace than his other abilities. I thought he would be talking in a few months—which he did. At the time, his parents and I agreed on a number of consultative contingencies if Sandy did not develop speech within the year.

As for the other boy, I'll call him Eddie, I began to feel that something was wrong within a short time after he first came into the consulting room with his parents. In the first few minutes, Eddie showed some affection to his parents by cuddling with them. But he rarely looked at them, never smiled, and in general showed very little emotion. When he moved away from his parents, he repeatedly climbed on chairs and the back of the couch. Despite his parents' and my attempts to entice Eddie to play with toys, he acted as if he did not hear. I asked if Eddie's hearing had been checked. It had been and was fine. Eddie's parents told me that the behaviors I observed were like the ones he showed at home. I was genuinely concerned about Eddie's development: there were too many signs of dysfunction across too many domains of development.

In dealing with a child like Eddie, it is essential to learn about the child's developmental history. The goal is to determine how long parents have seen potentially problem behaviors. I learned that Eddie's infancy had seemed normal in all respects. He had said three or four recognizable words when he was about 14 months of age. Then when he was 18 months old, he no longer said any words. At this age he also began to lose interest in toys. Although Eddie had been receiving speech therapy for several months, there had been no improvement. His parents had received conflicting advice and diagnoses, and they were confused about what help would now be best for Eddie.

Eddie's behaviors were somewhat consistent with those seen in the developmental disorder called autism: developmental regression in speech and play, no eye contact with parents, disregard for toys, aimless climbing, and unresponsiveness to parents' requests. However, there were other diagnostic possibilities that needed to be checked out. I recommended a series of genetic tests; the tests were all negative. When I saw Eddie a few months later it was clear that he was autistic. His parents, educated and caring, had suspected autism for a while. Still, it was a shock for them to hear confirmation of their own diagnosis from myself and from a specialist on autism to whom I referred them. Later on the specialist designed an intensive program of assistance for Eddie and his parents. It is too early to say how Eddie's developmental future will turn out.

When to seek help is one of the hardest things to prescribe. At the end of each age group (3 months, 7 months, 12 months, and 18 and 24 months in the second year) in this book I list key negative behaviors that indicate seeking professional advice. But the behaviors do not include every one that indicates developmental delay or a developmental problem. Fortunately, parents have a sixth sense about their child's wellness. If a parent has a gut feeling that the baby or toddler is missing too many developmental deadlines, then it is time to seek advice. Infancy is an important time, and it is better to err on the side of caution when it comes to seeking help.

Charting the First Two Years

maturation of grasp

visual perception

speech acquisition

brain growth and development

sociability

emotions

developing self-concepts

❧ Maturation Of Grasp

Some Developments in Grasp

Age	Examples of Behavior
Early weeks	Palmar reflex grasp
1 month	Hands usually closed into fists because of reflexes
2 months	Fingers open as baby touches rattle
3 months	Begins to reach for objects and to lightly touch toys; amuses self by playing with fingers
4 months	Excitedly reaches for objects—vision guides efforts; briefly holds small toy and drops it at slightest distraction; brings toys to eyes or mouth for inspection
5 months	Approaches toys with a push-pull scraping motion; fingers still move uncontrollably sometimes; cannot yet hold a toy in each hand
6 months	Adjusts hand to fit shape of toy; transfers a toy from one hand to the other and can hold two small toys at once
7 months	Picks up toy with thumb and side of forefinger; enthusiastically practices reaching for and picking up toys
8 months	Examines objects by turning them over and over while peering at them intently
9 months	More easily picks up objects with thumb and forefinger; begins to release a toy by extending fingers rather than flinging it
10 months	May begin to show right- or left-hand preference; begins to use (albeit clumsily) some household implements
11 months	Uses thumb-forefinger grasp to feed self finger food; can now move fingers to set things down without dropping them—voluntary release
12 months	Grasp and release more coordinated—can stack two blocks; may try to insert a peg in a pegboard
15 months	Fairly proficient with crayons, spoons, and cups
18 months	Tries to make fine lines with crayons
21–24 months	Definite preference for left or right hand; tries to put rods into holes; builds block towers that are five or more blocks high

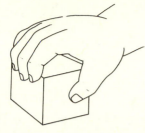

4–5 months: Tentative grasp. The baby's initial attempts to grasp a toy are tentative, sporadic, and brief. The baby barely touches the toy: he can't close his hand around a toy and doesn't have much control over his hands.

4½– 6 months: Palmar grasp. The baby holds a toy in his palm with his fingers curled around the toy so it doesn't drop. With the palmar grasp the baby can pick up fairly large objects (rattle, one-inch blocks) but not small ones (small crackers). The palmar grasp never disappears. Children and adults often use a palmar grasp when they want to hold onto an object securely.

8–9 months: Scissors grasp. With the scissors grasp, the baby can pick up a bit of bread that is as small as ¼ inch.

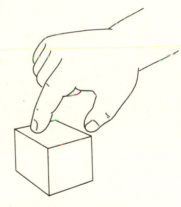

9–10 months: Index finger point. The index finger point indicates the beginning of independent use of the fingers. Independent fingers offer more flexibility.

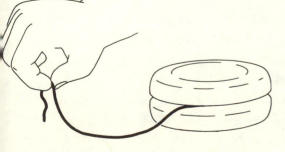

10–12 months: Coordinated thumb-and-fingertip grasp. This is the most precise grasp of all and one that is uniquely human. With this grasp we can pick up a pinhead-sized object.

❧ Visual Perception

Perception

The ability to discriminate (distinguish) information from the senses. The senses are also referred to as sensory receptors.

1. Smell, taste, and touch are referred to as near sensory receptors, while the distance receptors are vision and hearing. Near receptors are more functionally developed at birth than hearing and vision.
2. Research with very young babies shows that they have relatively poor vision but even so make perceptual discriminations. A classic study showed that even newborns recognize the difference between a picture of a checkerboard and a picture of a bullseye enclosed in a square, even though the image they see is very blurry.

Some Developments in Vision and Visual Perception

Age	Examples of Behavior
Early weeks	Saccadic (short, jerky) eye movements
1 month	Scans and likes to look at faces
2 months	Tracks objects from side to side
3 months	Sees objects more clearly
4 months	Distinguishes colors, shapes, and sizes
5 months	Attends to smaller, less obvious objects; depth perception improves; recognizes a face as a face even if it is upside down
6 months	Recognizes familiar people easily, acuity approximates adult vision (20/100)
7 months	Distinguishes male and female faces; recognizes features of faces
8 months	More interested in distant objects
9 months	Aware of tiny objects (a small piece of paper)
10 months	Begins to group similar objects; discriminates an object within an object (cookie in a jar)
12 months	Groups toys with like characteristics (shape or color)
13–24 months	Perception gets more and more refined; aware of more details; distinguishes greater range of colors and shapes

Visual cliff. This is a classic experiment in psychology. Richard Held and Eleanor Gibson wanted to find out when babies showed depth perception and devised the visual cliff box. The top of the box is heavy glass (or plexiglass). Half of the bottom is painted with large checks, the other half with small checks. A baby with depth perception has the illusion of a drop-off (a cliff) as he moves across the glass from large checks to small ones. He stops crawling when he sees the small checks below him.

❧ Speech Acquisition

Some Developments in Speech Acquisition

Age	Examples of Behavior
Early weeks	Makes distress cries
1 month	Makes soft sounds
2 months	Imitates a short string of vowel sounds; makes "conversation" by alternating making sounds with another person
3 months	Coos; cries to "express" boredom
4 months	Vocalizes some consonants (*m, b, k, g,* and *p*); laughs and gurgles
5 months	Makes more consonant sounds and "says" consonants more often; makes fretful cries; intonations move toward speech patterns most often heard
6 months	Babbles strings of vowels and consonants (canonical babbling); sounds bear resemblance to speech; whines
7 months	Babbles a lot in familiar settings but often quiet in unfamiliar places; may invent own sound for "happy" and one for "sad"
8 months	Produces a sound for a familiar toy or object; experiments a lot with sounds
9 months	Sentencelike quality to babbles; may "say" a word—*bah* for bottle or *mama* for mother
10 months	Experiments with new words: *cuh* for cookie
11 months	May say *No* but doesn't always mean no
12 months	Says two or three words (a few children say more); overgeneralizes: uses same word for a group of items, e.g., *wah* for water and milk; cries when displeased
15 months	Sentences are usually one word; tries hard to make self understood; continues to overgeneralize; number of words spoken varies greatly
18 months	Imitates words and may repeatedly use a new word; may use a few two-word sentences; may uses adjective to refer to self (good boy)

| 21 months | Labels own body parts; uses *me, my, mine* to refer to self; still many errors in pronunciation; uses words to describe feeling states—*hungry* or *tired*; two-word sentences are more common |
| 24 months | Uses two, three and four-word sentences; grammar is improving—uses *and, I,* and *me*; one third of speech is unintelligible; identifies self by gender; girls usually speak more words than boys |

✤ Brain Growth and Development

At 24 months, a child's brain is approximately 75 percent of the size it will be in adulthood! Infancy is a critical stage in cerebral growth, and brain growth underlies many of the behavioral developments of the first two years. Much of the brain development in the first 24 months involves improved functioning of various areas of the part of the brain called the cortex.

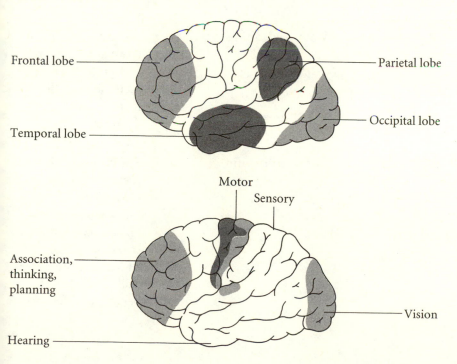

How Some Behaviors Change as the Brain Develops

Age	Motor	Cognitive
Birth–1 month	Reflexive movements	Habituates to sensory stimuli
1–4 months	Initiates some movements (reach)	Anticipates a few events; begins to remember if cued
4–8 months	Moves body from point *a* to point *b*	Increased anticipation—adjusts reach and grasp; associates better—reacts differently to familiar and unfamiliar
8–12 months	Erects self to a standing position	Uses props to achieve goals; begins to remember without cues; coordinates attention better
12–18 months	Walks and climbs	Imitative learning is more apparent; trial-and-error learning increases; recall memory and attention control improve
18–24 months	Runs, jumps, and squats	Thinks using ideas; pretend play shows recognition of functional uses of objects; is aware of social roles; can coordinate motor skills into playful behavior with others

Some Features of Early Brain Development

Age	Brain (cortex) functioning	Examples of associated behavior
Birth–1 month	Primary motor and sensory areas	Attention
1–4 months	Motor and sensory area	Anticipation, recognition, memory
4–8 months	Sensory and sensory association areas	Responds more quickly to changes; develops expectations
8–12 months	Additional association areas	Problem solving; beginning of recall memory; beginning of comprehension
12–18 months	All cortical areas functioning; functioning of association area still premature	Trial-and-error learning; improved spatial awareness; speech
18–24 months	Cortical areas functioning and maturing; connections between cortical areas incomplete	Thinks in terms of ideas; remembers without cues; begins to think in terms of cause and effect

❧ Sociability

The Evolution of Sociability

Age	Examples of Behavior
Early weeks	Is not sociable
1 month	Alert when talked to
2 months	Makes eye contact; smiles faintly
3 months	Smiles to others broadly and often
4 months	Directs smile to familiar people; initiates social bid: coo, smile; has nascent expectancy about others' social/emotional responses; associative learning regarding others' activities
5 months	Becomes quiet in unfamiliar settings
6 months	Makes social bids with tentative gestures; recognizes general configuration of familiar people
7 months	Greets others with babbling; makes pick-me-up gesture; attentive to simple social games
8 months	Affectionate to specific people; makes more social bids; may be wary of unfamiliar people
9 months	Makes specific affectionate displays; tries to "be like" by eating same food as parents and/or siblings
10 months	Looks to others for cues in ambiguous situations
11 months	Affectionate to a greater number of people; more interested in agemates; better participation in social games
12 months	Shows toys to others; imitates simple behaviors; loves to practice "taking turns"; relies on one or more individuals to provide solace when upset and to provide security for exploration
14 months	Teases others
15 months	Empathetic to others' distress; increasingly tries to include parents in activities; explores on own, but checks back that parent is nearby; imitates household actions
18 months	Has brief visual interactions with peers; recognizes a few do's and don'ts; communicates *No* to others; aware of others' approval of actions, clothing, etc.; discovers inanimate sources of comfort

21 months   May engage in verbal or physical exchanges with agemates; turns for help when recognizes difficult situation; empathic and also offers aid

24 months   Takes interest in family routines; tries to help; imitative play with peers; aware of others' everyday roles; makes excuses to others; may try to deceive others

At 12 months the baby knows he can get someone to visually follow his directions (his point). What a boost to his budding awareness of self!

❧ Emotions

Emergence of Emotional States

Age	Examples of Behavior
1 month	Generalized distress
2 months	Pleasure
3 months	Excitement and boredom; smiles
4 months	Laughter
5 months	Glee and frustration
6 months	Mirth matches emotions to others
7 months	Fear and anger
8 months	More individuality in emotional expression
9 months	Frowns; negative emotions when restrained; seeks comfort when fatigued
10 months	Intense positive and negative emotions; occasionally testy
11 months	Temperament more evident
12 months	Some signs of jealousy; aroused when others are distressed; cries when displeased
15 months	More mood swings; more caring—empathetic; attempts to control negative emotions
18 months	Can be irritable and stubborn; sometimes shy; shows nascent form of shame
21 months	Likes to exert control; can be finicky and exacting
24 months	Can be contrary but also appropriately contrite; very intense; responsive to others' moods

❧ *Developing Self-concepts*

The development of self has several dimensions. Initially, the young child acquires an understanding of his physical separateness and of the dimensions of his physical self. Other components are developing a social self and a self-consciousness.

Some Examples of Behaviors Related to Early Development of Self

Physical Self	Rubs head on mattress; puts toes in mouth; "swims" on tummy; rubs back of legs and arms; stands; cruises and walks; jumps and squats
Social Self	Smiles at others; makes social bids; interested in social games; invites others to participate; imitates others; takes others' roles in play; shares with others
Self-consciousness	Shows embarrassment around strangers; may be coy (shy) when someone says "Aren't you cute!"; feels sense of pleasure at own success; sometimes contrite (ashamed) after

The Birthday Party

❧

*M*any developmentalists focus on comparing development at different ages. In fact there is a whole literature on
normative development. Looking at development this way
gives us a perspective about behaviors at any stage of growth.
A simple model for comparison of behaviors at 12, 24, and 36
months is a child's birthday party. The examples mentioned
don't take into consideration family traditions and religious
and ethnic backgrounds.

	Year 1	Year 2	Year 3
Who decides who will come	Parents	Parents; child	Child makes 1 or 2 suggestions
Who comes	Family	Family and one or two peer "friend(s)"	Peers
Location	Home	Park	Child-oriented restaurant
Food served	Cake	Cake and ice cream	Menu: Sandwiches, hot dogs, dessert
Activities	Parents talk; children play by themselves or with parents	Child may play with peer(s)	Organized games
Presents	Child doesn't know they exist	Likes all presents	Shows preference for some presents

Keeping Your Baby Safe

Some General Hints
- Cover all electrical outlets; plastic covers are available in many hardware stores.
- Remove all dangling electrical cords.
- Tie up cords from window blinds so that baby can't reach them.

Cribs
- Crib rails should be close enough so that baby's head cannot get between two rails.
- Do not give baby any toy smaller than his fist.
- Do not give baby toys that have cords or laces.
- As soon as baby begins to sit/crawl, remove toys/mobiles that hang between crib rails.

Changing Table
- Make sure it is sturdy enough to withstand baby using a leg to pull himself up.

Swings, Infant Seats, Strollers
- Check for stability; they should not tip over.
- Each should have a seat belt, so that baby can be strapped in.

Stairs
- Protect with gate.
- Use plastic panels on landings if there is open area that baby could slip through.

Bathroom

- Make a habit of placing lid on toilet.
- Place all electrical appliances in closets.
- Secure all closet/cupboard doors with safety locks.
- Use a safety lock on medicine cabinet.
- All medication containers should have childproof lids.

Kitchen and Laundry Area

- Remove all cleaning and caustic agents from low kitchen cabinets.
- Put safety latches on all low cupboards/closets.
- Remove stove knobs if they are low enough for baby/toddler to reach.
- If baby/toddler tries to climb in kitchen, remove him immediately, and tell him "No."
- If you allow baby to have access to pot cupboard (babies love to play with pots and lids), remove all glass cookware and cookware with sharp edges.
- Keep knives, forks, and sharp kitchen tools inaccessible to prying hands.

Workshop

- Keep baby out of this room.

Living Room, Family Room

- Remove all objects from low tables.
- Prohibit climbing on tables.
- Make sure lamp tables are sturdy, and not easily tipped over.
- For floor plants, cover dirt with plastic cover.
- Cover front of fireplace with sturdy screen; keep matches in covered container, off of the floor.

Further Reading

Abt, I.A. (1944). *Baby doctor.* New York: Delacorte. A charming personal and professional account of the life of a pediatrician in the early days of the 20th century.

Brazelton, T.B. (1971). *Infants and mothers.* New York: Delacorte. An introduction to how babies and mothers interact and how they learn to adapt to each other.

Brazelton, T.B. (1992). *Touchpoints.* Reading, MA: Addison-Wesley. A sensitive discussion of social and emotional difficulties that may arise in the early years.

Chess, S., and Thomas, A. (1987). *Know your child.* New York: Basic Books. The pioneers in the study of temperament discuss how a young child's temperament influences overall development.

Fraiberg, S. (1959). *The magic years.* New York: Scribner. The classic book for parents, teachers, and professionals on young children's emotional and social lives.

Spock, B., and Rothenberg, M.B. (1985 rev.). *Dr. Spock's baby and child care.* New York: Pocket Books. *The* source for information about physical ailments and general health concerns.

Winnicott, D.W. (1987 rev.). *The child, the family, and the outside world.* Reading, MA: Addison-Wesley. A British pediatrician with a psychoanalytic orientation discusses the intertwined lives of infants and their families.

References

DEVELOPMENTAL THEMES

Bayley, N. (1969). *Bayley scales of infant development.* New York: The Psychological Corporation.

Belsky, J. (1984). The determinants of parenting. A process model. *Child Development, 55,* 83-96.

Brazelton, T.B. (1984). *Neonatal behavioral assessment scale.* Philadelphia: Lippincott.

Bowlby, J. (1967). *Maternal care and mental health.* New York: Schocken.

Bowlby, J. (1969). *Attachment and loss: Vol.1. Attachment.* New York: Basic Books.

Bridges, K.M.B. (1931). *The social and emotional development of the pre-school child.* London: Kegan Paul, Trench, Trubner.

Bronfenbrenner, U. (1979). *The ecology of human development.* Cambridge, MA: Harvard University Press.

Bühler, C. (1935). *From birth to maturity.* London: Lund Humphries.

Church, J. (1966). *Three babies.* New York: Random House.

Colombo, J., & Fagen, J.W. (1990). *Individual differences in infancy: Reliability, stability, and prediction.* Hillsdale, NJ: Erlbaum.

Darwin, C. (1877). A biographical sketch of an infant. *Mind: Quarterly Review of Psychology and Philosophy, 2,* 285-294.

Escalona, S.K. (1963). Patterns of infantile experience and the developmental process. *Psychoanalytic Study of the Child, 18,* 197-244.

Escalona, S.K. (1963). *The roots of individuality.* Chicago: Aldine.

Frank, L.K. (1967). *On the importance of infancy.* New York: Random House.

Freud, S. (1963). Introductory lectures in psychoanalysis. In *The complete psychological works of Sigmund Freud* (Vol. 15). London: Hogarth, 1963. (Orginally published 1915).

Gesell, A. (1928). *Infancy and human growth.* New York: Macmillan.

Gesell, A., & Amatruda, C. (1941). *Developmental diagnosis.* New York: Hoeber.

Gesell, A., & Thompson, H. (1938). *The psychology of early growth.* New York: Macmillan.

Harris, D.B. (Ed.) (1957). *The concept of development.* Minneapolis: University of Minnesota Press.

Hinde, R.A. (1974). *Biological bases of human social behavior.* New York: McGraw-Hill.

Horowitz, F.D. (1987). *Exploring developmental theories: Toward a structural/behavioral model of development.* Hillsdale, NJ: Erlbaum.

Kagan, J. (1984). *The nature of the child.* New York: Basic Books.

Kaye, K. (1982). *The mental and social life of babies.* Chicago: University of Chicago Press.

Kessen, W., Haith, M. & Salapatek, P. (1978). Human infancy: a bibliography and guide. In P.H. Mussen (Ed.), *Carmichael's manual of child psychology* (3rd ed.). New York: Wiley.

Kopp, C.B., & Krakow, J.B. (Eds.) (1982). *The child: Development in a social context.* Reading, MA: Addison-Wesley.

Kopp, C.B. (1993). Infant assessment. In C. Fischer & R.M. Lerner (Eds.), *Applied developmental psychology.* New York: McGraw-Hill.

Krasnegor, N.A., Blass, E.M., Hofer, M.A., & Smotherman, W.P. (Eds.). (1987). *Perinatal development.* Orlando, FL: Academic Press.

Krasnegor, N.A., Rumbaugh, D.M., Schiefelbusch, R.L., & Studdert-Kennedy, M. (Eds.). (1991). *Biological and behavioral determinants of language development.* Hillsdale, NJ: Erlbaum.

Lerner, R.M., Spanier, G.B., & Belsky, J. (1982). The child in the family. In C.B. Kopp & J.B. Krakow (Eds.), *The Child: Development in a social context.* Reading, MA: Addison-Wesley.

Lerner, R.M. (1986). *Concepts and theories of human development* (2nd ed.).New York: Random House.

Maccoby, E.E., Kahn, A.J., & Everett, B.A. (1983). The role of psychological research in the formation of policies affecting children. *American Psychologist, 38,* 80-84.

Mahler, M.S., Pine, F., & Bergman, A. (1975). *The psychological birth of the human infant.* New York: Basic Books.

Osofsky, J.D. (Ed.). (1979). *Handbook of infant development.* New York: Wiley.

Parmelee, A.H., Kopp, C.B., & Sigman, M. (1976). Selection of developmental assessment techniques for infants at risk. *Merrill-Palmer Quarterly, 22,* 178-199.

Peiper, A. (1963). *Cerebral functioning in infancy and childhood.* New York: Consultants Bureau.

Piaget, J. (1952). *The origins of intelligence in children.* New York: International Universities Press.

Piaget, J. (1954). *The construction of reality in the child.* New York: Basic Books.

Plomin, R. (1989). Environment and genes: Determinants of behavior. *American Psychologist, 44,* 105-111.

Ribble, M.A. (1943). *The rights of infants.* New York: Columbia University Press.

Rovee-Collier, C., & Lipsitt, L.P. (Eds.) (1990). *Advances in infancy research* (Vol. 7). Norwood, NJ: Ablex.

Rutter, M. (1970). Psychosocial development: Predictions from infancy. *Journal of Child Psychology and Psychiatry, 11,* 49-62.

Sameroff, A.J. (1983). Developmental systems: Contexts and evolution. In W. Kessen (Ed.), *Handbook of child psychology: Vol. 1. History, theory, and methods.* New York: Wiley.

Sameroff, A.J., & Emde, R.N. (Eds.) (1989). *Relationship disturbances in early childhood.* New York: Basic Books.

Scarr-Salapatek, S. (1976). An evolutionary perspective on infant intelligence: Species patterns and individual variations. In M. Lewis (Ed.), *Origins of intelligence.* New York: Plenum Press.

Scarr, S., & McCartney, K. (1983). How people make their own environments: A theory of genotype–environment effects. *Child Development, 54,* 424-435.

Spitz, R.A. (1965). *The first year of life.* New York: International Universities Press.

Stone, L.J., & Church, J. (1979). *Childhood and adolescence: A psychology of the growing person* (4th ed.). New York: Random House.

Thompson, R.A. (Ed.) (1990). Socioemotional development. *Nebraska Symposium on Motivation* (Vol. 36). Lincoln: University of Nebraska Press.

Thomas, A., Chess, S., & Birch, H. (1963). *Behavioral individuality in early childhood.* New York: New York University Press.

Vygotsky, L.S. (1962). *Thought and language.* Cambridge, MA: MIT Press.

Wachs, T., & Gruen, G. (1982). *Early experience and human development.* New York: Plenum Press.

Werner, H. (1957). The concept of development from a comparative organismic view. In D. Harris (Ed.), *The concept of development.* Minneapolis: University of Minnesota Press.

Whiting, J.W.M. (1977). A model for psychocultural research. In P.H. Leiderman, S.R. Tulkin, & A. Rosenfeld (Eds.), *Culture and infancy: Variations in the human experience.* New York: Academic Press.

Winnicott, D.W. (1964). *The child, the family, and the outside world.* London: Penguin Books.

Wohlwill, J.F. (1973). *The study of behavioral development.* New York: Academic Press

MOTOR DEVELOPMENT

Bertenthal, B.I., & Campos, J.M. (1990). A systems approach to the organizing effects of self-produced locomotion during infancy. In C. Rovee-Collier & L.P. Lipsitt (Eds.), *Advances in infancy research* (Vol. 6.) Norwood, NJ: Ablex.

Bruner, J.S. (1970). The growth and structure of skill. In K.J. Connolly (Ed.), *Mechanisms of motor skill development.* New York: Academic Press.

Campos, J.J., & Bertenthal, B. (1989). Locomotion and psychological development. In F. Morrison, K. Lord, & D. Keating (Eds.), *Applied developmental psychology* (Vol 3). New York: Academic Press.

Hindley, C.B., Filliozat, A.M., Klackenberg, G., Nicolet-Meister, D., & Sand, E. A. (1966). Differences in age of walking in five European longitudinal samples. *Human Biology, 38,* 364-379.

Kopp, C.B. (1979). Perspectives on infant motor system development. In M. Bornstein &

W. Kessen (Eds.), *Psychological development from infancy.* Hillsdale, NJ: Erlbaum.

Kopp, C.K. (1974). Fine motor abilities of infants. *Developmental Medicine and Child Neurology, 16,* 629-636.

Lipton, E.L., Steinschneider, A., & Richmond, J. (1960). Autonomic function in the neonate: Physiologic effects of motor restraint. *Psychosomatic Medicine, 22,* 57-65.

McGraw, M.B. (1943). *The neuromuscular maturation of the human infant.* New York: Columbia University Press.

Mittlemann, E. (1954). Motility in infants and adults: Patterning and psycho-dynamics. *Psychoanalytic Study of the Child, 9,* 142-177.

Paine, R.S., Brazelton, T.B., Donovan, D.E., Drorbaugh, J.E., Hubbell, J.P., Jr., & Sears, E.M. (1964). Evolution of postural reflexes in normal infants and in the presence of chronic brain syndromes. *Neurology, 14,* 1036-1048.

Ruff, H.A., Saltarelli, L.M., Capozzoli, M., & Dubiner, K. (1992). The differentiation of activity in infants' exploration of objects. *Developmental Psychology, 28,* 851-861.

Rushworth, G. (1961). On postural and righting reflexes. *Cerebral Palsy Bulletin (Developmental Medicine and Child Neurology), 3,* 535-554.

Thelen, E. (1982). Rhythmical behavior in infancy: An ethological perspective. *Developmental Psychology, 17,* 237-257.

Thelen, E., & Ulrich, B.D. (1991). Hidden skills: A dynamic systems analysis of treadmill stepping during the first year. *Monographs of the Society for Research in Child Development, 51* (1, Serial No. 223).

von Hofsten, C. (1990). A perception-action perspective on the development of manual movements. In M. Jeannerod (Ed.), *Attention and performance XIII.* Hillsdale, NJ: Erlbaum.

SENSATION AND PERCEPTUAL DEVELOPMENT

Aslin, R.N. (1987). Visual and auditory development in infancy. In J.D. Osofsky (Ed.), *Handbook of infant development* (Vol. 2.) New York: Wiley.

Banks, M.S., & Ginsburg, A.P. (1985). Early visual preferences: A review and new theoretical treatment. In H.W. Reese (Ed.), *Advances in child development and behavior* (Vol.19). New York: Academic Press.

Bornstein, M. (1981). Psychological studies of color perception in human infants. In L.P. Lipsitt (Ed.), *Advances in infancy research* (Vol. 1). Norwood, NJ: Ablex.

Cohen, L.B., & Salapatek, P. (1975). *Infant perception: From sensation to cognition* (Vols. 1 and 2). New York: Academic Press.

Collis, G.M., & Schaffer, H.R. (1975). Synchronization of visual attention in mother-infant pairs. *Journal of Child Psychology and Psychiatry, 16,* 315-320.

Colombo, J. (1986). Recent studies in early auditory development. *Annals of Child Development, 3,* 53-98.

Colombo, J., McCollam, K., Coldren, J.T., et al. (1990). Form categorization in 10-month-olds. *Journal of Experimental Child Psychology, 49,* 173-188.

Crook, C.K. (1978). Taste perception in the newborn infant. *Infant Behavior and Development, 1,* 52-69.

Crook, C.K. (1979). The organization and control of infant sucking. In H.W. Reese & L.P. Lipsitt (Eds.), *Advances in child behavior and development* (Vol. 14). New York: Academic Press.

DeCasper, A.J., & Fifer, W.P. (1980). Of human bonding: Newborns prefer their mothers' voices. *Science, 208,* 1174-1176.

Fagan, J.F. (1976). Infant's recognition of invariant features of faces. *Child Development, 47,* 627-638.

Fernald, A., & Kuhl, P. (1987). Acoustic determinants of infant preference for motherese speech. *Infant Behavior and Development, 10,* 279-293.

Frank, L.K. (1957). Tactile communication. *Genetic Psychology Monographs, 56,* 209-255.

Gibson, E.J. (1970). The development of perception as an adaptive process. *American Scientist, 58,* 98-107.

Gibson, E.J., & Spelke, E.S. (1983). The development of perception. In J.H. Flavell & E.M. Markman (Eds.), *Handbook of child psychology, Vol 3. Cognitive development* (4th ed.). New York: Wiley.

Gottfried, A.W., Rose, S.A., & Bridger, W.H. (1978). Effects of visual, haptic, and manipulatory experiences of infants' visual recognition memory of objects. *Developmental Psychology, 14,* 305-312.

Haith, M.M. (1980). *Rules that babies look by: The organization of newborn visual activity.* Hillsdale, NJ: Erlbaum.

Lipsitt. L.P. (1977). The study of sensory and learning processes of the newborn. Symposium on Neonatal Neurology. *Clinics in Perinatology, 4,* 163-186.

Maurer, D. (1985). Infants' perception of facedness. In T.M. Field & N.A. Fox (Eds.), *Social perception in infants.* Norwood, NJ: Ablex.

Salapatek, P. (1975). Infant pattern perception in early infancy. In L.B. Cohen & P. Salapatek (Eds.), *Infant perception: From sensation to cognition.* New York: Academic Press.

Sigman, M., Kopp, C.B., Parmelee, A.H., & Jeffrey, W.E. (1973). Visual attention and neurological organization in neonates. *Child Development, 44,* 461-466.

Spelke, E.S. (1987). The development of intermodal perception. In P. Salapatek (Ed.), *Handbook of infant perception* (Vol.2), Orlando, FL: Academic Press.

Spelke, E.S. (1988). Where perceiving ends and thinking begins: The apprehension of objects in infancy. In A. Yonas (Ed.), *The Minnesota Symposia on Child Psychology* (Vol. 20.) Hillsdale, NJ: Erlbaum.

Tennes, K., Emde, R., Kisley, A., & Metcalf, R. (1972). The stimulus barrier in early infancy. In R.R. Holt and E. Peterfreund (Eds.), *Psychoanalysis and contemporary society: An annal of integrative and inter-disciplinary studies.* New York: MacMillan.

Walters, R.H., & Parke, R.D. (1965). The role of distant receptors in the development of social responsiveness. In L. Lipsitt & C. Spiker (Eds.), *Advances in child development and behavior* (Vol. 2.) New York: Academic Press.

Watson, J.S. (1973). Smiling, cooing, and "the game." *Merrill-Palmer Quarterly, 18,* 323-339.

Yonas, A., & Granrud, C. E. (1985). Development of visual space perception in young infants. In J. Mehler & R. Fox (Eds.), *Neonate cognition: Beyond the blooming, buzzing confusion.* Hillsdale, NJ: Erlbaum

Vocalizations and Language Development

Bates, E., Bretherton, I., & Snyder, L. (1988). *From first words to grammar.* Cambridge: Cambridge University Press.

Birns, B., Blank, M., & Bridger, W.H. (1966). The effectiveness of various soothing techniques on human neonates. *Psychosomatic Medicine, 28,* 216-221.

Bloom, L. (1970). *Language development: Form and function in emerging grammars.* Cambridge, MA: MIT Press.

Bloom, L. (1991). *Language development from two to three years.* New York: Cambridge University Press.

Brazelton, T.B. (1962). Observations on the neonate. *Journal of the American Academy of Child Psychiatry, 1,* 38-58.

Brazelton, T.B. (1962). Crying in infancy. *Pediatrics, 4,* 579-588.

Chomsky, N. (1957). *Syntactic structures.* The Hague: Mouton.

Kuhl, P.K., & Meltzoff, A.N. (1988). Speech as an intermodal object of perception. In A. Yonas (Ed.), *The Minnesota symposia on child psychology* (Vol. 20), Hillsdale, NJ: Erlbaum.

Lester, B. M., & Zeskind, P.S. (1982). A biobehavioral perspective on crying in early infancy. In H. Fitzgerald, B. Lester, & M. Yogman (Eds.), *Theory and research in behavioral pediatrics.* New York: Plenum Press.

Luria, A.R. (1960). Verbal regulation of behavior. In M.A.B. Brazier (Ed.), *Conference on central nervous system and behavior.* New York: Josiah Macy Foundation.

Nelson, K. (1979). The role of language in infant development. In M. Bornstein & W. Kessen (Eds.), *Psychological development from infancy: Image to intention.* Hillsdale, NJ: Erlbaum.

Nelson, K. (1989). *Narratives from the crib.* Cambridge, MA: Harvard University Press.

Papousek, M., & Papousek, H. (1990). Excessive infant crying and intuitive parental care: Buffering support and its failures in parent-infant interaction. In R. Evans (Ed.), *Early Child Development and Care, 65,* 117-126.

Piaget, J. (1926). *The language and thought of the child.* New York: Harcourt, Brace & World.

Ratner, N., & Bruner, J. (1978). Games, social exchange and the acquisition of language. *Journal of Child Language, 5,* 391-401.

Schaffer, H.R. (1979). Acquiring the concept of the dialogue. In M.H. Bornstein & W. Kessen (Eds.), *Psychological development from infancy: Image to intention.* Hillsdale, NJ: Erlbaum.

Schaffer, H.R., Hepburn, A., & Collis, G.M. (1983). Verbal and nonverbal aspects of mothers' directives. *Journal of Child Language, 10,* 337-355.

Tamis-LeMonda, C.S., & Bornstein, M.H. (1990). Language, play, and attention at one year. *Infant Behavior and Development, 13,* 85-98.

Wolff, P.H. (1969). The natural history of crying and other vocalizations in early infancy. In B.M. Foss (Ed.), *Determinants of infant behavior IV.* London: Methuen.

COGNITIVE DEVELOPMENT

Bauer, P.J., & Mandler, J.M. (1989). One thing follows another: Effects of temporal structure on 1- to 2-year olds' recall of events. *Developmental Psychology, 25,* 197-206.

Bretherton, I. (Ed.). (1984). *Symbolic play.* Orlando, FL: Academic Press.

Bretherton, I., & Beeghly, M. (1989). Pretense. In J.J. Lockman & N.L. Hazen (Eds.), *Action in social context.* New York: Plenum Press.

Brown, A.L. (1975). The development of memory: Knowing, knowing about knowing, knowing how to know. In W.H. Reese (Ed.), *Advances in child development and behavior* (Vol.10). New York: Academic Press.

Butterworth, G., & Grover, L. (1990). Joint visual attention, manual pointing, and preverbal communication in human infancy. In M. Jeannerod (Ed.), *Attention and performance XIII.* Hillsdale, NJ: Erlbaum.

Caron, R.F., & Caron, A.J. (1978). Effects of ecologically relevant manipulations on infant discrimination learning. *Infant Behavior and Development, 1,* 291-307.

Case, R. (1978). Intellectual development from birth to adulthood: A neo-Piagetian interpretaton. In R.S. Siegler (Ed.), *Children's thinking: What develops?* Hillsdale, NJ: Erlbaum.

Charlesworth, W. (1969). The role of surprise in cognitive development. In D. Elkind & J. Flavell (Eds.), *Darwin and facial expression.* London: Oxford University Press.

DeLoache, J.S. (1990). Young children's understanding of models. In R. Fivush & J. Hudson (Eds.), *What children remember and why.* New York: Cambridge University Press.

Diamond, A. (1990). Differences between adult and infant cognition: Is the crucial variable presence or absence of language? In L. Weis-

krantz (Ed.), *Thought without language.* Oxford: Clarendon Press.

Fischer, K.W. (1980). A theory of cognitive development: The control and construction of hierarchies of skills. *Psychological Review, 87,* 477-531.

Fischer, K.W., & Bidell, T.R. (1991). Constraining nativist inferences about cognitive capacities. In S. Carey & R. Gelman (Eds.), *Constraints on knowledge in cognitive development.* Hillsdale, NJ: Erlbaum.

Fivush, R., & Hudson, L. (1990). *What children remember and why.* New York: Cambridge University Press.

Flavell, J. (1985). *Cognitive development* (2nd ed.). Englewood Cliffs, NJ: Prentice-Hall.

Gesell, A. (1925). *The mental growth of the preschool child.* New York: Macmillan.

Harris, P.L., & Kavanaugh, R.D. (1993). Young children's understanding of pretense. *Monographs of the Society for Research in Child Development, 58,* (1, Serial No. 231).

Kaler, S.R., & Kopp, C.B. (1990). Compliance and comprehension in very young toddlers. *Child Development, 61,* 1997-2003.

Lewis, M. (Ed.). (1976). *Origins of intelligence.* New York: Plenum Press.

Mandler, J.M. (1988). How to build a baby: On the development of an accessible representational system. *Cognitive Development, 3,* 113-136.

Mandler, J.M., & Bauer, P.J. (1988). The cradle of categorization: Is the basic level basic? *Cognitive Development, 3,* 247-264.

McCall, R.B., Eichorn, D.H., & Hogarty, P.S. (1977). Transitions in early mental development. *Monographs of the Society for Research in Child Development, 42,* (3, Serial No. 171).

Melzoff, A.N. (1988). Infant imitation and memory: Nine-month-olds in immediate and deferred tests. *Child Development, 56,* 62-72.

Nelson, K., & Gruendel, J. (1981). Generalized event representations: Basic building blocks of cognitive development. In M. Lamb & A. Brown (Eds.). *Advances in developmental psychology* (Vol. 1). Hillsdale, NJ: Erlbaum.

Nelson, K., & Ross, G. (1980). The generalities and specifics of long-term memory in infants and young children. In M. Perlmutter (Ed.), *Children's memory.* San Francisco: Jossey-Bass.

Roberts, K., & Cuff, M.D. (1989). Categorization studies of 9- to 15-month-old infants: Evidence for superordinate categorization? *Infant Behavior and Development, 12,* 265-288.

Rogoff, B. (1990). *Apprenticeship in thinking.* New York: Oxford University Press.

Rovee-Collier, C., & Hayne, H. (1987). Reactivation of infant memory: Implications for cognitive development. In H. Reese (Ed.), *Advances in child development and behavior* (Vol. 20). Orlando, FL: Academic Press.

Rovee-Collier, C. (1987). Learning and memory. In J.D. Osofsky (Ed.), *Handbook of infant development* (2nd ed.). New York: Wiley.

Sinclair, H., Stambak, M., Lezine, I., Rayna, S., Verba, M. (1989). *Infants and objects: The creativity of cognitive development.* San Diego: Academic Press.

Uzgiris, I.C. (1967). Ordinality in the development of schemes for relating objects. In J. Hellmuth (Ed.), *The exceptional infant: Vol.I. The normal infant.* Seattle, WA: Special Child Publications.

Wenar, C. (1976). Executive competence in toddlers: A prospective, observational study. *Genetic Psychology Monographs, 93,* 189-285.

Wentworth, N., & Haith, M.M. (1992). Event specific expectations of 2- and 3-month old infants. *Developmental Psychology, 28,* 842-850.

SOCIAL DEVELOPMENT

Ainsworth, M.D.S., & Wittig, B.A. (1969). Attachment and exploratory behavior of one-year-olds in a strange situation. In B.M. Foss (Ed.), *Determinants of infant behavior IV.* London: Methuen.

Ainsworth, M.D.S., Blehar, M.C., Waters, E., & Wall, S. (1978). *Patterns of Attachment.* Hillsdale, NJ: Erlbaum.

Als, J., Tronick, E., & Brazelton, T.B. (1979). Analysis of face-to-face interaction in infant–adult dyads. In M. Lamb, S. Suomi, & G.R. Stephenson (Eds.), *The study of interaction.* Madison: University of Wisconsin Press.

Bakeman, R., & Brownlee, J.R. (1980). The strategic use of play: A sequential analysis. *Child Development, 51,* 873-878.

Bakeman, R., & Adamson, L.B. (1984). Coordinating attention to people and objects in mother–infant and peer–infant interaction. *Child Development, 55,* 1278-1289.

Belsky, J., & Most, R.K. (1981). From exploration to play: A cross-sectional study of infant free play behavior. *Developmental Psychology, 17,* 630-639.

Bridges, K.M.B. (1933). A study of social development in early infancy. *Child Development, 4,* 36-49.

Brownell, C.A. (1986). Cognitive correlates of early social development. *Annals of Child Development, 3,* 1-51.

Brownell, C.A. (1988). Combinatorial skills: Converging developments over the second year. *Child Development, 59,* 675-685.

Bretherton, I., & Waters, E. (1985). Growing points of attachment theory and research. *Monographs of the Society for Research in Child Development, 50* (1–2, Serial No. 209).

Campos, J.J., & Stenberg, C.R. (1981). Perception, appraisal and emotion: The onset of social referencing. In M.E. Lamb & L.R. Sherrod (Eds.), *Infant social cognition: Empirical and theoretical considerations.* Hillsdale, NJ: Erlbaum.

Clarke-Stewart, K.A. (1989). Infant day care: Maligned or malignant? *American Psychologist, 44,* 266-273.

Clarke-Stewart, K.A., & Gruber, C.P. (1984). Day care forms and features. In R.C. Ainslie (Ed.), *The child and the day care setting.* New York: Praeger.

Dunn, J. (1987). The beginnings of moral understanding: Development in the second year. In J. Kagan & S. Lamb (Eds.), *The emergence of morality in young children.* Chicago: University of Chicago Press.

Eckerman, C.O., Davis, C.C., & Didow, S.M. (1989). Toddlers' emerging ways of achieving social coordinations with a peer. *Child Development, 60,* 440-453.

Egeland, B., & Farber, E. (1984). Infant-mother attachment: Factors related to its development and changes over time. *Child Development, 59,* 753-751.

Eisenberg, N. (1982). The development of reasoning regarding prosocial behavior. In N. Eisenberg (Ed.), *The development of prosocial behavior.* New York: Academic Press.

Emmerich, W. (1964). Continuity stability in early social development. *Child Development, 35,* 311-332.

Fagot, B.I. (1974). Sex differences in toddlers' behavior and parental reaction. *Developmental Psychology, 10,* 554-558.

Feinman, S. (1992). *Social referencing and the*

social construction of reality in infancy. New York: Plenum Press.

Goldsmith, H.H., & Rothbart, M.K. (1991). Contemporary instruments for assessing early temperament by questionnaire and in the laboratory. In J. Strelau & A. Angleitner (Eds.), *Explorations in temperament.* New York: Plenum Press.

Gralinski, J. H., & Kopp, C.B. (1993). Everyday rules for behavior: Mothers and young children. *Developmental Psychology, 29,* 573–584.

Gunnar, M., & Donahue, M. (1980). Sex differences in social responsiveness between six months and twelve months. *Child Development, 51,* 262-265.

Heinicke, C., & Westheimer, I. (1966). *Brief separations.* New York: International Universities Press.

Kagan, J., & Lamb, S. (Eds.). (1987). *The emergence of morality in young children.* Chicago: University of Chicago Press.

Kochanska, G., Kuczynski, L., & Radke-Yarrow, M. (1989). Correspondence between mothers' self-reported and observed child-rearing practices. *Child Development, 60,* 56-63.

Kopp, C.B. (1982). Antecedents of self-regulation: a developmental perspective. *Developmental Psychology, 18,* 199-214.

Kopp, C.B. (1987). The growth of self-regulation: Caregivers and children. In N. Eisenberg (Ed.), *Contemporary topics in developmental psychology.* New York: Wiley.

Kuczynski, L. (1984). Socialization goals and mother-child interaction: Strategies for long-term and short-term compliance. *Developmental Psychology, 20,* 1061-1073.

Lamb, M.E. (1976). Interaction between eight-month-old children and their fathers and mothers. In M.E. Lamb (Ed.), *The role of the father in child development.* New York: Wiley.

Lamb, M.E., & Sherrod, L.R. (Eds.). (1981). *Infant social cognition.* Hillsdale, NJ: Erlbaum.

Lamb, M.E., Thompson, R.A., Gardner, W., & Charnov, E.L. (Eds.). (1985). *Infant-mother attachment.* Hillsdale, NJ: Erlbaum.

Lewis, M., & Feinman, S. (Eds.). (1991). *Social influences and socialization in infancy.* New York: Plenum Press.

Lytton, H. (1980). *Parent-child interaction.* New York: Plenum Press.

Maccoby, E.E., & Martin, J.A. (1983). Socialization in the context of the family: Parent-child interaction. In E.M. Hetherington (Ed.), *Handbook of child psychology: Vol. 4. Socialization, personality, and social development* (4th ed.). New York: Wiley.

Main, M., Kaplan, N., & Cassidy, J. (1985). Security in infancy, childhood and adulthood: A move to the level of representation. In I. Bretherton & E. Waters (Eds.), Growing points of attachment theory and research. *Monographs of the Society for Research in Child Development, 50* (1-2, Serial No. 209).

Murphy, C.M., & Messer, D.J. (1977). Mothers, infants, and pointing: A study of gesture. In H.R. Schaffer (Ed.), *Studies in mother-infant interaction.* New York: Academic Press.

Parke, R.D., MacDonald, K.B., Beitel, A., & Bhavnagri, N. (1988). The role of the family in the development of peer relationships. In R. DeV. Peters & R.J. McMahan (Eds.), *Marriages and families: Behavioral treatment and processes.* New York: Brunner/Mazel.

Putallez, M. (1987). Maternal behavior and childrens' sociometric status. *Child Development, 58,* 324-340.

Rheingold, H., & Eckerman, C.O. (1973). Fear of the stranger: A critical examination. In H.W. Reese (Ed.), *Advances in child development and behavior* (Vol. 8). New York: Academic Press.

Radke-Yarrow, M., Zahn-Waxler, C., & Chapman, M. (1983). Children's prosocial dispositions and behavior. In E.M. Hetherington (Ed.), *Handbook of child psychology: Vol. 4. Socialization, personality, and social development.* New York: Wiley.

Ross, H.S., Lollis, S.P., & Elliott, C. (1982). Toddler-peer communication. In K.H. Rubin & H. Ross (Eds.), *Peer relations and social skills in childhood.* New York: Springer-Verlag.

Schaffer, H.R., & Crook, C.K. (1978). The role of the mother in early social development. In H. McGurk (Ed.), *Issues in childhood social development.* London: Methuen.

Stern, D. (1977). *The first relationship.* Cambridge, MA: Harvard University Press.

Stern, D. (1985). *The interpersonal world of the infant.* New York: Basic Books.

Vandell, D.L. (1980). Sociability with peer and mother during the first year. *Developmental Psychology, 16,* 355-361.

Vaughn, B.E., Kopp, C.B., & Krakow, J.B. (1984). The emergence and consolidation of self-control from eighteen to thirty months of age: Normative trends and individual differences. *Child Development, 55,* 990-1104.

Whiting, B.B. (Ed.). (1963). *Six cultures.* New York: Wiley.

Zahn-Waxler, C., Radke-Yarrow, M., & King, R.M. (1979). Child-rearing and children's prosocial initiations toward victims of distress. *Child Development, 50,* 319-330.

EMOTIONAL DEVELOPMENT

Bates, J.E. (1987). Temperament in infancy. In J.D. Osofsky (Ed.), *Handbook of infant development* (2nd ed.). New York: Wiley.

Bretherton, I., Fritz, J., Zahn-Waxler, C., & Ridgeway, D. (1986). Learning to talk about emotions: A functionalist perspective. *Child Development, 57,* 529-548.

Bridges, K.M.B. (1932). Emotional development in early infancy. *Child Development, 3,* 324-341.

Campos, J.J., Campos, R.G., & Barrett, K.C. (1989). Emergent themes in the study of emotional development and emotion regulation. *Developmental Psychology, 25,* 394-402.

Demos, V. (1986). Crying in early infancy: An illustration of the motivational function of affect. In B.T. Brazelton & M.W. Yogman (Eds.), *Affective development in infancy.* Norwood, NJ: Ablex.

Dunn, J., Bretherton, L., & Munn, P. (1987). Conversations about feeling states between mothers and their young children. *Developmental Psychology, 23,* 132-139.

Emde, R.N., Gaensbauer, T.J., & Harmon, R.J. (1976). Emotional expression in infancy. A behavioral study. *Psychological Issues, 10* (1, Whole No. 37).

Field, T., & Fogel, A. (1982). *Emotion and early interaction.* Hillsdale, NJ: Erlbaum.

Fogel, A. (1982). Affect dynamics in early infancy: Affective tolerance. In T. Field & A. Fogel (Eds.), *Emotion and early interactions.* Hillsdale, NJ: Earlbaum.

Gallup, G.G. (1982). Self-awareness and the emergence of mind in primates. *American Journal of Primatology, 2,* 237-248.

Kohnstamm, G.A., Bates, J.E., & Rothbart, M.K. (Eds.). (1989). *Temperament in childhood.* Chichester: Wiley.

Kopp, C.B. (1989). Regulation of distress and negative emotions. *Developmental Psychology, 25,* 343-354.

Kopp, C. B. (1992). Emotion distress and control in young children. In N. Eisenberg (Ed.), *New directions for child development: Emotions, motivation, and self-regulation.* San Francisco: Jossey-Bass.

Lewis, M., & Brooks, J. (1978). Self-knowledge and emotional development. In M. Lewis & L. Rosenblum (Eds.), *The development of affect.* New York: Plenum Press.

Lewis, M., & Michaelson, L. (1982). The socialization of emotions. In T. Field & A. Fogel (Eds.), *Emotion and early interaction.* Hillsdale, NJ: Erlbaum.

Malatesta, C.Z., Culver, C., Tesman, J.R., & Shepard, B. (1989). The development of emotion expression during the first two years of life. *Monographs of the Society for Research in Child Development, 54* (1-2, Serial No. 219).

Matheny, A.P., Jr., Wilson, R.S., & Nuss, S.M. (1984). Toddler temperament: Stability across settings and over ages. *Child Development, 55,* 1200-1211.

Murphy, L.B. (1956). *Personality in young children* (Vols. 1 and 2). New York: Basic Books.

Murray, L., & Trevarthen, C. (1985). Emotional regulation of interactions between two-month-olds and their mothers. In T.M. Field & N.A. Fox (Eds.), *Social perception in infants.* Norwood, NJ: Ablex.

Rothbart, M., & Derryberry, D. (1984). Emotion, attention, and temperament. In C. Izard, J. Kagan, & R. Zajonc (Eds.), *Emotion, cognition and behavior.* New York: Cambridge University Press.

Saarni, C. (1989). Children's understanding of strategic control of emotional expression in social transactions. In C. Saarni & P.L. Harris (Eds.), *Children's understanding of emotion.* New York: Cambridge University Press.

Sroufe, L.A. (1979). Emotional development. In J. Osofsky (Ed.), *Handbook of infant development.* New York: Wiley.

Stipek, D.J. (1983). A developmental analysis of pride and shame. *Human Development, 26,* 42-54.

Thomas, A., & Chess, S. (1977). *Temperament and development.* New York: New York University Press.

SELF DEVELOPMENT

Amsterdam, B., & Greenberg, L.M. (1977). Self-conscious behavior of infants: A videotape study. *Developmental Psychology, 10*, 11-16.

Anthony, E.J. (1968). The child's discovery of his body. *Physical Therapy, 48*, 1103-1114.

Berthenthal, B., & Fischer, K.W. (1978). Development of self-recognition in the infant. *Developmental Psychology,14*, 44-50.

Block, J.H., & Block, J. (1979). The role of ego-control and ego-resiliency in the organization of behavior. In W.A. Collins (Ed.), *Minnesota Symposium on Child Psychology* (Vol. 13). Hillsdale, NJ: Erlbaum.

Brownell, C.A., & Kopp, C.B. (1991). Common threads, diverse solutions: Concluding commentary. *Developmental Review, 11*, 208-303.

Bullock, M., & Lutkenhaus, P. (1988). The development of volitional behavior in the toddler years. *Child Development, 59*, 664-674.

Cicchetti, D., & Beeghly, M. (Eds.). (1990). *The self in transition.* Chicago: University of Chicago Press.

Emde, R.N. (1983). The prerepresentational self and its affective core. *The Psychoanalytic Study of the Child, 38*, 165-192.

Emde, R.N. (1988). Development terminable and interminable. *International Journal of Psycho-Analysis, 69*, 23-42.

Emde, R.N., Biringen, Z., Clyman, R.B., & Oppenheim, D. (1991). The moral self of infancy: Affective core and procedural knowledge. *Developmental Review, 11*, 251-270.

Fagot, B.I., & Leinbach, M.D. (1989). The young child's gender schema: Environmental input, internal organization. *Child Development, 60*, 663-672.

Neisser, U. (1988). Five kinds of self-knowledge. *Philosophical Psychology, 1*, 35-59.

Spitz, R.A. (1949). Autoerotism. *Psychoanalytic Study of the Child, 3-4*, 85-119.

Spock, B. (1963). The striving for autonomy and regressive object relations. *Psychoanalytic Study of the Child, 18*, 361-364.

Stipek, D.J., Gralinski, J.H., & Kopp, C.B. (1990). Self concept development in the toddler years. *Developmental Psychology, 26*, 972–977.

Index